LIBRARY
MANCHESTER COLLEGE
Y0-CLG-443

PRESIDENTS I'VE KNOWN

AND TWO NEAR PRESIDENTS

Presidents I've Known

and

Two Near Presidents

By

Charles Willis Thompson

The Bobbs-Merrill Company

Publishers Indianapolis

Printed in the United States of America

PRESS OF
BRAUNWORTH & CO., INC.
BOOK MANUFACTURERS
BROOKLYN, N. Y.

BY WAY OF EXPLANATION

This book is confined rigidly to matters within my own knowledge. In trying to avoid, as much as possible, the inevitable personal pronoun I often state things as facts without giving the source. The tolerant reader will please imagine, in such cases, that I am trying desperately to keep from saying, "Roosevelt told me," or, "as I once heard Bryan say." It can't always be done, more's the pity.

The aim is to set down the exact truth. The book is not intended for a book of character sketches or a book of anecdotes, though it contains both. Neither is its object. No anecdote is told unless it brings out more clearly a character or an occurrence. As for character portraiture, there is no attempt here to cover all the sides of any man's character. I sketch only the sides I saw. There were other sides, but if they were not known to me, only surmised, I do not touch on them.

The aim being the truth of history, I cover only those actions of a man which I myself saw and studied. Where I had no personal knowledge of any public action, even an important one,—for instance, Wilson's demand for war with Germany, or the proceedings leading up to the Versailles Peace Conference,—I do not refer to it at all. There is no attempt to tell the whole. All I assert is that the things I know about I have told truthfully; and that if I have not given the whole character of any man, I have given truthfully all of it that I learned.

In writing a book of this kind the temptation is always strong to round out a presentation, to fill in the details so as to make it cover everything, and to make use for this purpose of things which the author has heard, and believes to be true, but does not know of his own knowledge. If this book suffers from my failure to do this, and seems to lack completeness, the only compensation to be found for that lack is that there is nothing here which will mislead anybody or give a false impression; nothing I am not sure of, from my own knowledge.

The book aims to give such modest aid as it can to the understanding of the principal figures in American politics in the last three decades. For this purpose, I have selected from the public men of my time (nearly all of whom I knew) six Presidents, one man who overshadowed a President—Marcus A. Hanna—and one who stood constantly just out of reach of the Presidency, William J. Bryan. Except as they fit into the story, I have made no reference to any of the other public men of my acquaintance.

In a few cases, where it seemed best, I have made use of parts of some articles heretofore written by me and published in newspapers and magazines. For permission to make use of them my thanks are rendered to *The American Mercury, The Commonweal, The New York Times* and *The New York Herald-Tribune.* For the rest, I have depended on my diaries.

Many times I quote not only what a public man said, but a whole conversation, and describe the manner and tone in which he and the others spoke. Generally, when such quotations are made by writers, they are made from memory, subject to the corrosion of time. In this book, however, the reader can rely on them. They were written down at the time, in my diaries, and are transferred now from these diaries to *Presidents I've Known.*

CHARLES WILLIS THOMPSON

CONTENTS

CONTENTS—*Continued*

PRESIDENTS I'VE KNOWN

AND TWO NEAR PRESIDENTS

HANNA-McKINLEY

PRESIDENTS I'VE KNOWN

CHAPTER I

HANNA, THE STATESMAN (AND McKINLEY, A PRESIDENT)

ONE evening in 1893 I heard Robert G. Ingersoll say, "Washington is now only a steel engraving." And, despite the efforts of the currently fashionable biographical school to create a "new" Washington, a "true" Washington, despite the herculean attempts to portray him as a gay dog, profane, bibulous, girl-crazy, and therefore meet for election to our more enlightened twentieth-century society, he remains a steel engraving. "The glass through which we look at him," Ingersoll added, "is of such high magnifying power that the features are exceedingly indistinct." The "portrait" school of biography, I fear, will ultimately have to give Washington up as a bad job.

McKinley is now only a steel engraving—or rather, since steel engravings have gone out since 1893, he is only a rotogravure photograph. It might be better to say that he is preserved in amber. He does not speak to us audibly, as Jackson, Lincoln, Roosevelt, Wilson do and always will. They did their work and went their way, their way down the years, down the centuries. History will always be curious about them, and voracious, unsatisfied, eager to know more. McKinley, too, did his work, but he did not, like them, go his way; he stayed put. There is no curiosity about him. He will always have his honorable place, but the tourist through our national portrait gallery will always see the same McKinley.

Though I use the word "portrait" as a figure of speech, the same thing is literally true of McKinley's physical portraits. In his photographs he is always the same. There is a never-varying expression on his face; he looks at you from under heavy brows with the same luminous dark eyes, set in the same solemn visage, and always wears the same expression. It is curious but true that this was McKinley's own doing. He never would consent to be photographed in a negligent pose, and always took the most meticulous care about every detail of his appearance and his posture. He embalmed himself, so far as posterity is concerned. There is just one exception. Once he was in a hurry when he kept his appointment with a photographer, and did something he never did before or after in all his life; he dashed into his office in the White House without looking to see if he had assembled himself. He sat down at his desk, arranged his body and his features as usual, bent over some papers, poised a pen and awaited the consummation of the deed. The faithful photographer did his duty. In his haste McKinley had failed to make his hair stay down, and out from the back of his head stood mutinous locks. The picture shows the same inhuman correctness as all the rest; those rebellious locks are the only testimony on photographic record that McKinley's hair and the rest of his appearance were not painted on him at birth by the hand of God. Looking at that picture, a generation yet unborn may be stricken by a sudden suspicion that McKinley, after all, was human and not a statue.

He was, indeed. So was Washington, though all the "portrait biographers" in the world will never be able to make him speak. They say Washington could use profanity;

why, so could McKinley, and he did. There is nothing more beautiful than his long devotion to his invalid wife, whose invalidism was not of the body alone. The terrible illness which ruined her health permanently impaired her spirit, but this only made her man her knight; it made him more unselfishly devoted, more tender. All through those years he incessantly, morning, noon and night, covered her with the flowers of his love.

But this, perhaps, is not "the human touch"? You were looking, Messrs. Portrait-Biographers, for something more snappy, something more spicy? When you seek, gentlemen, to make some historic man "a human being," it is his vices or his frailties that illustrate him most. Yet other qualities are human, too. Other things go to the making of a man's character. The long devotion of this true knight to his stricken lady is as "human" a thing as Jackson's dueling pistols, Clay's deck of cards, Webster's debts, or Grant's whisky bottle.

If you ask why he should remain a steel engraving, my only answer is that some men are gaited that way, and there is nothing you can do about it. Even the men who knew him best have nothing much to tell about him. But he was far from being a colorless character. There was something charming about his personality. There was nothing cold about him, as there was about Benjamin Harrison. He did not try to charm you; he was no glad-hander; it was the unconscious effect of a nature created to be winning. Yet, somehow, he never impressed even his friends and contemporaries with any saliences. In spite of his enjoyable smile and hearty manner, the picture I retain of the man I saw so often in the White House is pretty nearly indistinguishable from those carefully posed photographs of his. There was no pretense, no humbug about it; he was no poseur; he acted out his own nature as truly as his rockbound predecessor, Cleveland, and his stormy successor, Roosevelt, acted theirs. Nothing more could be asked of any man than that he should be himself.

But, though McKinley is a steel engraving, Hanna is not. Though McKinley is preserved in amber, Hanna is not. The McKinley administration will come, more and more, to live, not as the McKinley period of American history, but as the Hanna period; and this though McKinley, contrary to a too-general belief, was the master and Hanna the faithful lieutenant. McKinley is fixed imperishably in one place and one attitude, but Hanna is buoyantly alive and growing. Already the words "in the days of Mark Hanna" are falling from the pens of ready writers, in ever-increasing repetition, to denote a specific time that was marked in the story of the United States. The interest in Mark Hanna does not down.

As significant a straw as I have seen is in a sentence in a book that arrives just as I finish writing these last words. It is *Drifting Sands of Party Politics,* a study of American political changes written by that profoundly able statesman, ex-Senator Oscar W. Underwood. In explaining why he emphasizes the last years of the nineteenth century in his study of our governmental evolution, that sagacious and far-sighted writer says that he does it "to mark the point where the era of Lincoln's elementary government of our country ended and the era of Mark Hanna with all its complications began." The era of Mark Hanna; not the era of McKinley; and he means an era which covered much more than the lifetime of Hanna himself, in its relation to the alteration in the American political system. I believe he is right, and that the time is coming when McKinley will be thought of as the man who was President in the era of Mark Hanna.

At present McKinley is not thought of at all, except as

James Knox Polk is thought of. The thing is not unprecedented. Tyler and Taylor were Presidents, but, though Taylor was an able and far-seeing President, there is neither a Taylor period nor a Tyler period in history; there is a Webster-Clay period. Pierce was President, but the man who is remembered from his administration is Stephen A. Douglas. Hayes, like Taylor, was a statesman, but it is not of the Hayes period that one speaks offhand; it is of 'the days of Blaine and Conkling."

When Mark Hanna came to Washington as a Senator from Ohio, after having engineered McKinley's nomination and election, he was, next to the new President, the most talked-of man in the country. For the moment not much was being said of Bryan. The curiosity about this new figure was universal, though most people had made up their minds about him. The Republicans had not much to say. The Democratic idea of him was that he was a moneymaker who had picked out a nominal President he could rule, and was now going to dominate the President, the Republican party and the nation. My old friend, Alfred Henry Lewis, who could always say a thing more trenchantly than any one else, looking forward to the destined election of McKinley, had said in 1896: "Hanna and his syndicate are breaking and buying and bullying a road for McKinley to the White House. And when he's there," continued Lewis, "Hanna and the others will shuffle him and deal him like a deck of cards."

The Republicans in Congress rather thought so too. It was the general impression. In 1897 Mark Hanna's name was a good stick to beat any dog with. "He's Mark Hanna's man" was an opprobrious epithet which was stretched to cover the most unlikely candidates—even Democrats. At that time Tom L. Johnson, the fighting Mayor of Cleveland, was managing Henry George's last campaign for Mayor of

New York. Johnson had been a striking figure on the Democratic side in the Congress of 1892 and in Grover Cleveland's second campaign for President, and was now leading the revolt of independent New York Democrats against Tammany, as crystallized in George's bolt. Apparently because he came from Cleveland, where Hanna lived, Tammany and the Republicans charged that he had been the political ally of Hanna there, and that Hanna was now trying to control New York through him. In campaign times no canard is too absurd to be believed. This one had so much effect that Johnson was obliged to meet it, and he did it by a stratagem. He appeared on the platform at a mass meeting in the Clermont Avenue rink, in Brooklyn, and made a speech for George. When he reached the end he said, "Now I'm ready to answer any questions anybody in the audience may see fit to ask." A man in the middle of the big rink rose and said, "I have a question that maybe you don't care to answer. It is charged that you are an ally of Mark Hanna, and that you and he——"

Before he could complete the sentence those in the audience who were for George began to yell, "Put him out!" and some of them started toward him. But Johnson stilled the uproar with a smile, waved his hand and shouted, "That's a fair question. Let him alone. I'll answer." When order was restored he went on, "I see in this audience the faces of several men whom I knew in Cleveland when I was in politics there, before I came to Brooklyn. I don't know where they stand politically, and I don't care. But I'll ask them to stand up and tell this man, and this great audience, if they know who it was that I fought most relentlessly and most unremittingly, both in politics and in business, when I was conducting my battles in Cleveland." Immediately half a dozen men sprang up in widely separated parts of the hall and called out, "Mark Hanna!" The applause was deafening. From that moment nothing more was heard of the Hanna roorback.

The little drama was a plant. I recognized the man who asked the question and some of those who replied to it with Johnson's vindication. They were New Yorkers, who had probably never been in Cleveland in their lives. I knew that the man who asked the question was one of the Henry George campaign workers, because I happened to be on the stump for George myself in that campaign. It was a typical Ohio political trick, and it worked with the unsophisticated New Yorkers. I tell the story simply because it illustrates rather tellingly what a black eye it gave in those days to any one, Republican or Democrat, to be tagged with Mark Hanna's name.

The full meaning of Hanna was not grasped in his own day, because he was too much in advance of his time. The country has been growing up to him ever since. He did make on us the impression of power, but his significance was missed. Yet, unlike most such men, he was not forgotten; the impression he made is still present, and, as the times unfold, the nature of that power becomes clearer.

Hanna was the first statesman to understand that public questions must be viewed from a new angle, and for a long time he was the only one. He viewed things from the standpoint that the world had become industrial and not political; that its problems must be grappled with in that spirit. Others were still politicians of the Blaine mental mold, of the Lincoln mold, of the Clay-Webster-Calhoun mold, even of the Jefferson-Hamilton mold. There had been no essential change since the Declaration of Independence; plentiful changes in ideas and attitudes, but none in standpoint. Nor was it conceived, except by Hanna, that any would ever be necessary. He saw that it was necessary right then and there.

This frame of mind was not understood at the time, but we all did see that Hanna was different.

Then the industrial situation was in a state that this present generation can scarcely realize. There was, on the one side, the old laissez-faire conception, which had once been radical and now was so conservative as to be reactionary. On the other side were those who believed that civilization was dividing into two cutthroat camps and doomed to fight bloodily for its life, perhaps to die, to give victory to one or the other. No possibility of agreement or compromise was seen; the idea of cooperation was politically unknown. Men were eagerly scanning the horizon for the imminent signs of anarchy and chaos, when the two armies should meet and fight to the death, with no quarter. Such signs were always being found. *The Saturday Review* of London found one in Bryan's first campaign and said:

"The Presidential campaign of 1896 was an event of profound historical significance from every point of view, political, social, ethical, international. There is no exaggeration in putting it among the great epoch-making occurrences, like the gathering of the States General in 1789."

But the Reign of Terror has not arrived; it is farther off, and Marat and Hebert are strangely slow in setting up the guillotine. Men began, even in those days, to think unconsciously the thoughts, not of Marat, but of Mark Hanna.

It was Mark Hanna, alone among statesmen, who realized that in a world become wholly industrial men could be induced to work in harmony, and that no irrepressible conflict existed; no conflict that must end in blood and flame, along with civilization itself. Mussolini said recently that as the nineteenth century had seen the rise of capitalism, so the twentieth would see its decline and fall, and its supersession by cooperation. Mark Hanna saw this a generation before Mussolini. His contemporaries did not see it, but he did. He worked for it. Nobody understood the workings of his mind, but they did see that there was force of some sort in him. I am not theorizing; I am reporting, as faithfully as possible, the talk and feeling of my day, a mental atmosphere that this generation can by no means visualize.

Therefore, Mark Hanna created the National Civic Federation, in which he intended that capital and labor should sit down together and work out a solution for every problem. During the short remainder of his life it was a power; and when he died the idea he had germinated bloomed in other fields. It is as a fruit of his idea that the American Federation of Labor steadily and increasingly insists, year after year, on the fostering of the cooperative principle. When men to-day speak of enmity between capital and labor, they do not mean it in the sense in which the word was used in the 1890's. In those days it meant, quite literally, an impending civil war like that in the Vendée in 1793. A great man, Henry George, writing in *Progress and Poverty* of the fall of civilization in the fifth century and its coming duplication, said:

"Gibbon thought that modern civilization could never be destroyed because there remained no barbarians to overrun it, and it is a common idea that the invention of printing by so multiplying books has prevented the possibility of knowledge ever again becoming lost. Whence shall come the new barbarians? Go through the squalid quarters of great cities, and you may see, even now, their gathering hordes! How shall learning perish? Men will cease to read, and books will kindle fires and be turned into cartridges!"

In the opposite camp from George the idea of an irrepressible conflict was differently expressed, but it was there.

In that same campaign of 1896, in which *The Saturday Review* saw the omen of the coming Reign of Terror, Theodore Roosevelt was sitting in a Pullman car talking with several men, and one of them, Willis J. Abbott, told him Governor John P. Altgeld, of Illinois, was on the train and asked if he would like to meet the Governor. Roosevelt declined; and, according to Abbott, he gave as his reason that he thought it better not to meet socially "a man whom some day I may have to meet at the head of my regiment." When Abbott published this occurrence Roosevelt was indignant; but his indignation, as I remember it, was that Abbott should have violated a confidence, not that he had quoted Roosevelt incorrectly. The point is that Altgeld was the Governor who had pardoned the so-called Chicago Anarchists and who had resisted President Cleveland's sending of Federal troops to break up the Debs railway strike.

It was not so much that Mark Hanna tried to avert an impending civil war. He simply did not believe there would be any. There would certainly be an evolution of industrialism out of immaturity into maturity, and it was his job to find what way evolution was going to travel and help it along. Nobody else in politics had that idea.

William McKinley could never have got such an idea in a million years. He would not have got it if it had been explained to him. It was not that he was stupid; it was that his mental direction was still that of Cleveland, Blaine, Lincoln, Clay, Webster, Calhoun, Jackson, Jefferson and Hamilton.

As opposed to these men who looked forward to a bloody struggle between the Haves and the Have-Nots there were those who believed God had created a permanent class of masters and slaves. It was the same idea the feudal lords had been obliged to part with at the guillotine; the same idea the Southern slave-holders had been forced to give up at Appomattox. The difference was that there had been a solid basis for the pretensions of the feudal lords and the slave-holders. God might be conceived as desiring that the wise and strong should govern, for the good of all, the ignorant and weak. God might even be imagined as desiring that the superior race should govern, for the good of both, the inferior. But that God should desire a man to govern another for the master's good because the master had dollars and the man had none, that was grotesque. As Carlyle said, of all the aristocracies which in turn had ruled the world, the basest was an aristocracy of mere money-bags—"infinitely baser; the basest yet known."

But in those days it was seriously believed in—not by Mark Hanna. It was stated with sincere conviction by George F. Baer, the President of what is now the Reading Railroad, when in discussing the conflict between capital and labor he spoke of himself and his fellow-capitalists as "the Christian men and women to whom God in His wisdom has given the care of the property interests of this country." Divinely appointed, you see. How Mark Hanna's heavy brows must have come down over his deep eyes when he read that innocent and honest credo of his capitalistic colleague.

They could not at all understand him; but then, none of us could in those days. It is remarkable that he was never laughed at, his ideas were so out of harmony with his time. It is equally remarkable that, so far as I remember now, his sincerity in all this was never impugned by anybody of any consequence. It is still more remarkable that the labor men so quickly overcame their distrust of him and entered into his spirit and forwarded his plans. For Hanna was no labor man and made no pretense of being one. He was not a philanthropist, was not actuated by any tender desire to uplift the "down trod." He was not a reformer; he was a man of vision. He was one who would march with the Zeitgeist. He aimed to find out where the Zeitgeist was going, and he found out; and no other statesman of his day had found it out, or even knew that there was a Zeitgeist.

In Hanna's day the alternative to capitalism was State socialism and nothing else. No one who tried to forecast the future saw any other conclusion, unless brute capitalism were the final form of civilization; and that, if not exactly stated, was taken for granted. Any reform had to be a panacea. The idea that evolution and not panaceas was to be looked for never occurred to any single-taxer, Anarchist, or other world doctor. Neither did it occur to any of the George F. Baers. Nor to any politician. Except to Mark Hanna. Certainly it could not have forced its way into the mind of McKinley.

The period from 1896 to 1901 is not the McKinley period. The period from 1896 to 1904 is, however, the Hanna period.

CHAPTER II

THE UNFOLDING OF MARK HANNA

When Hanna came to Washington we all thought we had his measure; there was no misgiving about it. He was just another of a type which had grown very familiar since the War of Secession. You do not see it in the Senate now. It was a product of the days when Senators were elected by the Legislatures and when American life had no spirituality and was dominated by dollars, because of the great rush of riches which had followed the post-war commercial expansion. Senators were common who came in because they had grown wealthy and wished to round out their lives with a title, just as their English counterparts like to end their careers of money-making by being called Lords. Outside of business they were dull men; they sat in the Senate as if it were a club, never speaking and taking no distinguishable part in the other Senatorial activities. Such a man was William A. Clark of Montana. Outside the ranks of the commercial or industrial Senators there were others who came to Washington for the same reason, the desire for a title to consummate their careers. These men, who were not so numerous, were party bosses who wanted a distinction to confer on their wives and children, and, being Americans, could not do it by entering a peerage. They therefore signified to the Legislatures they controlled that they desired a title, and the Legislatures obediently conferred that of Senator. They too sat in the "Millionaires' Club," as the

Senate was nicknamed in those days, cheek by jowl with the money kings; like them, silent, dull, wondering probably what Spooner and Hoar and Vest and the other old-fashioned Senators were so busy about. Such a Senator was Edward Murphy, Jr., of New York. These two types are seen no more. The Constitutional amendment providing for the election of Senators by popular vote abolished them. Popular election of Senators did not raise the character of the Senate; it lowered it. The Senate now is crowded with footless, ineffective men of narrow minds and small capacities; Vests and Hoars and Spooners are seldom elected. But the type has changed; the popular election amendment did that.

So, as I say, we all thought we had Hanna's measure, and gave ourselves no trouble about how he would silently sit out his dull and futile term. Our interest was solely in how the arrogant, ruthless, small-minded money-maker would "shuffle and deal," as Lewis said, the President he had made, for his own money profit.

Mark Hanna came trotting down one of the graveled walks leading from the White House one fine Spring night, just as I was walking up it. I had hoped to find Hanna there, but not to bump into him. The interview he had just had with President McKinley had not lasted as long as I expected. He regarded me with an air of smoldering ferocity. Hanna was a new Senator then, and had not got as well used to correspondents as he subsequently did. I proffered my modest request, which was that he should tell me what he had said to the President and what the President had said to him.

Hanna walked on, switching at the grass with a heavy stick he carried. "Damned if I do," he said in a voice husky with anger. "Your Eastern papers have been holding me up as a crook and a fathead both. They have cartooned me with dollar marks all over me. They have pictured me starving poor people to death to make more money. They have intimated and said that I haven't got brains enough to do anything but steal, and that I am so fond of stealing that I do it in my sleep. And now they have the nerve to ask me for information which they can't get unless I give it to them, just as if they had always given me a square deal and never called me a liar and an ass and a thief. Damned if I give it to them!"

"Did *The New York Times* ever call you those names?" I asked. "I know it's Democratic and it's Eastern, but hasn't it always given you a square deal?"

Hanna still strode on and still switched the grass. He didn't say anything for a minute or two, nor did I. Then he looked at me with a friendly twinkle and said abruptly, "You win. Walk along with me over to the Arlington and I'll tell you the whole story."

After that Hanna and I were the best of friends.

He did, at first, as we had expected. He sat silent in the Senate, as the other title-taking millionaires had sat, as the Sharons and Fairs had sat, as the Clarks and Murphys were sitting now. I shall never forget the electric shock that ran through the gallery one day in 1900 when Mark Hanna rose with fire in his eye and did something that was utterly apart from the rôles set down for the millionaire Senators. He loomed portentously over one of the men who had been treating him contemptuously and made a speech.

The man was a Senator, Richard Franklin Pettigrew, of South Dakota. Pettigrew was a malicious-minded man whose guiding star was hatred. His sole pleasure lay in hurting somebody. He was suspicious to an almost insane degree, and saw evil in every action of other men. He had an uncanny genius for tormenting people. He was so skilful in hurling his poisoned darts that men were afraid of him, and let him go unrebuked; though one day a Senator who was his direct antithesis in character, sturdy, jolly, open-hearted Ed Wolcott, of Colorado, who feared no man, woke the Senate echoes with a speech painting Pettigrew as one who "views the world with jaundiced vision," and who, "when the sun shines, sees only the shadows that it casts." Pettigrew listened with a white face that grew whiter, and when Wolcott ended he made a low-voiced bitter reply that sounded to me like the hiss of a rattlesnake.

He continued digging his stiletto into one after another of his fellow-Senators, who shivered silently and were thankful when he was done with them, until one day he suddenly fell tooth and nail upon Mark Hanna. The drift of his speech was that Hanna was a filthy money-grabber who had soiled the Senate by getting into it through bribery. I believe I have sufficiently indicated Hanna's sensitiveness to that sort of talk; but what I have not indicated is that Hanna had a positive reverence for the dignity of the Senate, and consequently for his position as a member of it. Not even Hoar of Massachusetts, the spiritual heir of Webster and Everett, held the Senate higher than Mark Hanna. And now the picture of "Dollar Mark" which hurt him so had been taken out of the hands of the cartoonists and unrolled by a Senator in the revered Senate itself.

Mark Hanna believed, in those days, as fully as anybody else that he was not a speech-making Senator and could not be one. Pettigrew's speech did not enlighten him suddenly. When he sprang up from his seat just behind Pettigrew it was the impulse of an insulted and wounded man, translated into action in the Senate Chamber as it would have been in any other place; nothing more. To his intense astonishment, he found himself talking with white-hot passion, his words coming in a torrent but with the ease of a professional orator, and—most surprising of all—the revered Senate listening with a startled respect equal to that it would have given to Hoar himself.

At the close of his maiden Senate speech he leaned over till he almost touched Pettigrew's back and threatened him with the coming of November; and he shouted down at Pettigrew's bent head:

"When it comes to personality, I will stand up against him and compare my character with his. I will let him tell what he knows; then," and Hanna made a long pause after each word, "I—will—tell—what—I—know—about—him."

It was a most unusual speech. Probably Pettigrew concerned himself little about Mark Hanna's threat. He had South Dakota comfortably sewed up and was sure of reelection. Besides, the prejudice against Hanna in South Dakota was so general and inveterate that if Hanna did try to injure him there it would only increase his majority. The early days of the campaign contained nothing to disturb Pettigrew's serenity; for it was the year of a Presidential election, Hanna was the Chairman of the National Committee, and he had his hands full at his desk, engineering the reelection of McKinley. In fact, if anybody at all remembered that scene in the Senate, it was only to suppose that the busy Chairman had cooled off and forgotten all about his vendetta.

But as soon as Hanna felt that the election of McKinley was sure, he dropped his work at campaign headquarters, went into South Dakota and for the rest of the campaign camped on the trail of Pettigrew. He toured the State, speaking and working with all his tremendous energy. Pettigrew's hold on South Dakota was so strong that all the political prophets, while giving its electoral vote to McKinley, conceded to him the Senatorship. Up to the very eve of election that was the chart. Mark Hanna changed all that; and when he came back to Washington in November he brought not only the State's electoral vote for McKinley, he brought the scalp of Pettigrew. When he came back to Washington he had become an orator and Pettigrew had become an ex-Senator.

It was rough on the Washington correspondents. We missed Pettigrew. He made copy. Washington was not so interesting as it had been before he made the fatal mistake of waking up Mark Hanna. Charles Reade says, "It is droll and sad, but true, that Christendom is full of men in a hurry to hate." Pettigrew was in a hurry to hate; and, in a Senator, that peculiarity is grist for the correspondents' mill.

With that slaughter of Pettigrew, Hanna had found himself. His inferiority complex in the presence of the Senate had fled. He stepped at once, easily, into a position of leadership. Having found that he could talk, he went on talking; and as he did so his style immediately improved. In time he became one of the most effective speakers in the Senate. He did not try to be eloquent, but there was a salty frankness about his manner that was captivating, and unlike that of any other Senator. He also became, at a bound, a leader in affairs of state. Hitherto he had been a business man grown into a party boss; now he ceased to be either and became instantly a statesman. He had only three years and a half to live, and in that time he made the enduring part of his fame. If he had died in 1900 he would have been remembered, if at all, only as a good political manager who had forced a second-rate man into the Presidency and successfully managed one campaign.

To give an idea of Hanna's manner of speaking after he found he could speak, and of its effect on his hearers, I can not do better than quote from a book I wrote in 1906 called *Party Leaders of the Time,* long out of print and forgotten. It will show the difference between Hanna's style and the conventional politician's style, between his mode of thought and the mode of thought then and now characteristic of the Senate; and incidentally it has something to say about another man who became Vice-President of the United States and who came much nearer than most people know to being President—a singular proof, like the narrow escape of the United States from having Champ Clark as President, of how God watches over this country. In this book I wrote of Hanna:

"There was a breezy directness about him, a blunt downrightness, that gave his speeches a charm all their own. The difference between him and some other Senatorial orators [what I should say now is the difference between him and Senatorial oratory in general, in 1928 as well as 1906] was illustrated once when he and Senator Fairbanks, now Vice-President, spoke on the Chinese exclusion bill, in 1902. He and Fairbanks were then the only Republicans generally talked of as Presidential candidates, Mr. Roosevelt being new in the White House and still on trial. [Another reason was that it was then an article of political faith that no Vice-President who had succeeded to the Presidency through his predecessor's death, as Roosevelt had, could ever be elected to succeed himself—because none ever had.] The appearance of the two Senators on the same afternoon attracted a crowd. Later on both Presidential booms fizzled out, but that joint debate illustrated luminously two kinds of Senatorial oratory, as it did two very different characters.

"First came Hanna, firm of face and square of chin, with an eye that seemed to bore its way into you. Then came Fairbanks, a bald-headed man without the courage of his baldness; with three long black locks plastered across the front of his pate where the beginning of the whole thatch was twenty years ago. These three hairs look as if they were painted on. Perhaps they are; the mystery of the Fairbanks hair has never been officially explained.

"Hanna was frankly opposed to the proposition before the Senate, which was strongly anti-Chinese and devised in the interest of labor. He swung his arms and hammered himself in like a nail. His talk was made in a sturdy, common-sense, businesslike manner that was like fresh air. He talked about the down-trodden laboring man, but not in the usual politician fashion; for the drift of his remarks was that while he loved the down-trodden laboring man, that down-trodden person had been trying to bulldoze him into voting against his convictions, and that he would not be dictated to. Which never did him a bit of harm, though it took courage to say it; for a man of courage loses nothing by letting it be known.

"It was a regulation Hanna speech, but it was accentuated by the appearance of Fairbanks immediately after him. Fairbanks came like a humming-bird after an elephant. He gesticulated with just the proper gestures; spread his hands in front of his face at the proper moment, clenched his fist when he was expressing indignation, uplifted his finger to indicate warning, and otherwise followed the approved elocution standards of the Boys' High School. And he closed every sentence with a rising inflection, whereas Hanna bore down on the last word of a sentence as if he were burying it six feet deep. It is needless to add that Fairbanks was strongly in favor of the down-trodden laboring man and ready to go any length to please him. [And not needless to add that, though Fairbanks with all his truckling never could make labor his friend, Hanna could.] These two Senators had often enough given specimens of two standards of oratory and two types of character, but never before in conjunction and in such interesting circumstances. It was an instructive contrast."

The quality of Hanna's statesmanship is shown in the fact that he made possible the Panama Canal. It shows his vision, his foresight; for the Panama Canal was as dead as Lazarus. He raised it from the grave. The Panama Canal waited five decades for Mark Hanna; if he had not come along it might have waited five more. In 1902 it was remembered as a joke long exploded; it was referred to only as one of the historical proofs of man's gullibility. It was usually spoken of as "De Lesseps' Folly"; it was used for purposes of rhetorical illustration, along with the South Sea Bubble and John Law's Mississippi Bubble.

The apparently eternal project for a canal was, as usual, before the public, but it was to be a canal across Nicaragua if we could ever get beyond the point of talking about it. Senator John Tyler Morgan, of Alabama, was the custodian and guardian of the Nicaragua Canal, as he had been for years; it was looked on as his personal property. Year after year Morgan used to bring it before the Senate and make interminable speeches about it, but it never seemed any nearer. In this year the Senate, to see whether Morgan could be induced to talk himself out if he got rope enough, turned over to him every afternoon for as long a time as he might desire, and Morgan consumed afternoon after afternoon without interruption. On one of these afternoons I went into the Senate Chamber after adjournment and sat down beside Senator Spooner in quest of information. While he was giving it to me Senator Elkins came up and, leaning his elbows on the desk, said:

"Spooner, when is Morgan going to get through with this speech, do you suppose?"

"We once had a spell of rain up my way," answered Spooner callously, "and some one asked an old woman one day, 'How long do you think this rain is going to last?' 'I don't know,' she said; 'all the rainstorms I ever saw came to an end some time or other, except this one.'"

On the prosings of Morgan and the inattentive apathy of the country, inured as it was to the belief that the Nicaragua Canal was a hardy perennial like the French Spoliation Claims or the lawsuits of Anneke Jans' heirs to the ownership of New York City, there suddenly intruded the figure of Mark Hanna. A man appeared who knew exactly what he wanted and was determined to have it, not some time in the far future, but right then and there. Also a man who, knowing what he wanted, knew just how to get it and was resolved to have no further talk about it.

Hanna had concluded that the Panama Canal was not a South Sea or Mississippi Bubble and was not De Lesseps' Folly. He resurrected the cadaver; he threw himself into the question with all his boundless energy. The Senate had acquired the conviction that when Mark Hanna set about doing anything whatever, it was going to be done. If anybody else had talked of breathing the breath of life into the carcass of the Panama Canal, the Senate would have smiled vaguely and said, "Yes, yes; go on." The moment Mark Hanna served notice that there would be a canal, a canal right away, and that it would be by the forgotten Panama route, the Senate leaped up and gave him agitated attention.

He shoved the Panama route through. Minister Herrán astonished the prosing capital of Colombia by a cable message; a thing which, as he told me one day, he was forbidden by his instructions to do; for, as Bogota never heard anything from Washington that was interesting, it did not propose to have the Colombian treasury eaten up by unnecessary and unprofitable cable tolls. Bogota began to stir. Secretary Hay and Minister Herran saw each other often. The Colombian Congress smelled money, much money, in prospect for that depleted treasury which could not afford to pay for cablegrams. The more positive became the outlook that the Nicaragua monologue was over and that the United States was really about to talk business, the higher rose the Colombian hunger, until it became certain that the purse of Fortunatus or of Uncle Sam would be inadequate to the final Colombian demands. Then President Roosevelt entered the situation. "I took the canal," he said later; and the horrified shrieking of the unco' guid never undid that fait accompli. It was in 1902 that Hanna ended the fifty-year monologue about a futuristic canal; it was in 1903 that Roosevelt "took the canal." Historically speaking, it was only a jiffy.

The clouds of misunderstanding had all blown away. There had come to Mark Hanna a rich reward, and one that was very soothing and grateful to his spirit. The baited man who had turned on me so savagely that Spring night in the White House grounds, when dogs were worrying his heels, had come to enjoy a tribute of respect and affection. The Senate was no more an awful place to him; it was like home. He had another reward, the understanding affection of those among whom he lived. As a thing written at the moment is more convincing, in such cases, than anything colored by memory, I will quote a letter I wrote from Washington the day after his death to a friend in Italy:

"Mr. Hanna's death yesterday was a painful shock to us here, although discounted by the fact that it was known he could not live. We were all very fond of him hereabouts, and nothing was talked of for days but his illness. Strangers would stop each other on the streets and ask about him. It was not so, of course, in other cities, where he was not so loved and appreciated. Everybody felt here a sense of personal loss; there is not another public man whose death would so affect people here—hardly excepting ex-Senator Vest. He was a fine man, Hanna was, and his death is a heavy blow."

BRYAN

CHAPTER III

BRYAN, AN OPPORTUNIST GALAHAD

BRYAN'S hold on the West lay in the fact that he was in himself the average man of a large part of that country; he did not merely resemble that average man, he was that average man. This is not true of the whole West, by a jugful, but it is true of what used to be the West and of what is still a good deal of it. The old Western type of mind is vanishing before culture, and in its vanishing the West gains something and loses something. In the regions where the old type was still the average type when you got a few miles away from the cities, there seemed nothing strange or funny in a Secretary of State who went solemnly from Washington to New York to sign temperance pledges, or went to Philadelphia to hold Billy Sunday's platform at his revival meeting. In 1915 it seemed queer to New York to see a Secretary of State undertaking to demolish the Darwinian theory, which to New York is a theory unrelated either to politics or morals. But, as New York afterward learned, there are plenty of regions where the Darwinian theory is regarded not as a matter related to science, but as a device of the devil to upset the Mosaic cosmogony. Chesterton says that Dickens never wrote down to the mob, because he was himself the mob; and Bryan never talked down to the prairie farmer, for a similar reason.

Bryan's vast influence was due to the fact that the uneducated and simple man, with all his mistakes and gaucheries, spoke in him, and that when that man heard his own thoughts spoken in Bryan's voice he knew the accent was sincere. Bryan did take up issues simply because they sounded to him like vote-makers, but none of them represented the least divergence from his course as a whole, which was always honestly bent in a certain plain direction. So, though an opportunist in issues, he was a consistent opportunist. He never hesitated to be in a minority and never dodged a fight. He was an innocent theorist, who frequently went wrong because of the simplicity of his mental processes; but he acted upon his theories with an intrepidity and a whole-hearted courage in which the ordinary man saw the qualities he himself would like to have, and sometimes dreamed he possessed. His mind was not broad, but it was strong; he was always sure he was right, and always ready to fight like a badger for his beliefs, and he kept his hold on his followers because he was not below them and not much above them, and because they believed he was honest and genuine.

William Bayard Hale once described him as "essentially a preacher, a high-class exhorter, a glorified circuit rider." There are vast spaces of our country still populated by men and women of the old-fashioned kind. Chesterton speaks of them as "full of stale culture and ancestral simplicity." Many of them still look askance on cards, dancing and the stage; they are the kind of folks who peopled the Mississippi Valley in Lincoln's day and Massachusetts in Cotton Mather's. Colonel George Harvey, with sarcastic intent, once alleged mendaciously that Bryan became a white ribboner because he heard a little girl recite, "The Lips That Touch Liquor Shall Never Touch Mine." There are regions which would accept that parable of Harvey as gospel truth, and much to Bryan's credit.

And whenever, in his recurring candidacies, he went

down to his customary defeat, epitaphs were written over his political grave; but Bryan never stayed dead, because there was something enduring in him. What was it? That same spokesmanship for the average man of many regions, the man of the little parlor with the melodeon or parlor organ, the plush-covered photograph album and the *History of the San Francisco Earthquake* bought by subscription from a book agent, and the grandfather's clock in a corner of the hall. The man, in short, who was not only average but preponderant before the invasion of the radio and the rural free delivery.

When Bryan died it seemed to me that almost half the critical appraisals of him contained the phrase "a simple man." But his character can not be summed up so abruptly. It had more complexities than were usually admitted; or perhaps it would be better to say that there were more sides to it. Then, and to-day, he was and is spoken of so often as a "crusader" that it might be well to mention that he was also a practical politician. Practical does not mean far-sighted or wise; most practical politicians are neither. And so here again there is a qualification to be made of his career, with its invariable (and never explained) ill-success at the polls. A politician to his finger-tips, he was yet, for the most part, a very poor one. Contradictory as such a phrase may sound, Bryan was an opportunist crusader. He prided himself on his skill in picking issues, but invariably he either picked the wrong one or picked the right one at the wrong time.

Bryan's tremendous hold on his following is usually contrasted with his failure to carry elections, as if a mystery were therein involved. The mystery disappears if we remember that, however great his influence, it was always over a minority. It is a bold thing to say that he never had the people with him; but if "the people" means the people who vote, the election figures prove it. He was constantly spoken of as the champion of "the masses"; but the people always voted against him—which can not mean anything except that they declined his championship.

Though he embodied in himself so much of the Middle West, the Middle West was not for him; there was something in the Middle West that he did not represent. For he could not carry a majority there. The Middle West, like Bryan himself, can not be summed up in a phrase; it comprises all kinds of people. His own old town of Lincoln contains as large a proportion of cultured people who know Europe even better than their own State as does New York. In my opinion, the proportion there is even larger.

Bryan, though popular in Lincoln, was not a typical Lincolnite. He was a product of a different Middle Western environment—that of Salem, a town which somehow reminds the visitor of Tom Sawyer's boyhood home. Salem looks as if it had always been what it is to-day. As you pass through its orderly little streets, with its little frame houses, all of the same kind and all neat and unassuming, with its dirt roads and its typical Town Hall, set correctly behind a correct little patch of grass in a neat square, you feel instinctively that the Darwinian theory must be avoided in your Salem conversation. You know at once that the same families have lived here for generations. So they have; one of them was Bryan's, and he was born there. Whenever I saw him in Lincoln I was struck by an indefinable feeling of incongruity; he did not seem in the right place, and I could not tell why; but when I saw him back home in Salem that feeling vanished. In Salem he was part of the picture; he belonged there; it seemed to me, and to the Salem people, and, unless I was greatly mistaken, to himself, that he had never been away a day.

He got away from Salem, physically if not mentally, as

early as he could. Salem did not offer much promise to a young man who felt that he was unusual and destined to eminence and intended entering upon a political career by way of admission to the bar—which was the prescribed route in the Middle West and South through the nineteenth century. Nowadays a Middle Western lawyer is expected to understand the law and work hard at it, just as is an Easterner, whether he goes into politics or not. In other days every lawyer was a jury lawyer, and if a boy had the gift of gab he was set apart to be the lawyer of the family; and the county court room was the practise field for the stump, the place where he could show his mettle as a talker. It was Abraham Lincoln's discovery that he could make a good speech which led him, after various tryouts at other occupations, to choose the bar as a career. Bryan, too, knew that he could make a good speech. He chose to try his fortunes farther west, in a more wide-awake community.

The tremendous Democratic landslides of 1890 and 1892, which almost wiped out the Republican Party in the House of Representatives, sent him to Congress from a district not over-partial to Democrats—as happened temporarily to a good many bright young Democrats who never were able to make use of that accidental opportunity as a springboard to further fame. Bryan was an exception, maybe *the* exception. At first there was no sign of it. In Congress he made a good impression, but did not become very well known to the nation—though one speech of his, on the tariff question, went all over the country. He was practising as a speechmaker, noting the effect of his phrases, discarding those which failed to make a hit and saving up those that did, until he combined the latter into a sort of anthology which became famous as the cross-of-gold speech, and is still popularly believed to have won him his first nomination for the Presidency.

No man was boss of that Convention of 1896, but the man who came nearest being a boss was its most powerful and outstanding figure, Governor John P. Altgeld, of Illinois. Before the Convention met, James A. Campbell, of *The Philadelphia Times,* was taking a drink with Altgeld's chief lieutenant, and as they parted after a short chat Campbell said, "Can't you give me some kind of tip on what's going to happen?"

"Only this, and don't ask me any more," replied the other after a moment's hesitation. "Keep your eye on William J. Bryan, of Nebraska."

Campbell pondered on what this might mean, and finally concluded that Altgeld intended to honor a bright young man by engineering Bryan into the chairmanship of some important committee, or perhaps that it had been decided to let him make an unexpected nominating speech. The idea of so obscure a man being nominated for President or Vice-President never entered his head.

So he telegraphed his paper to hunt up a photograph of ex-Congressman Bryan and have it in readiness for something, he did not know what. It was hard for his paper to find a picture of Bryan, he was so little known. But editors, if they are worth their salt, always follow implicitly the hunches of their convention correspondents, and finally, after a long search, a picture was dug up somewhere. And when Bryan suddenly blazed forth, *The Times* was the only paper in Philadelphia which was ready with a photograph of the new leader of the Democratic Party—the new leader who, though this was in the womb of the future, was to lead it such a dance for sixteen sorrowful years.

"I had the beat of my life right in my hands and didn't know it," said Campbell to me, mournfully. "Still, I can't blame myself. I would have been a damned fool to have docketed a high private for commander-in-chief on a tip like that. And anyhow," he added, cheering up, "we did beat the other fellows on that picture."

As a great many people now know, the men who were pulling the strings—for, though the Convention could not be bossed, it could be engineered, and was—had been at work maneuvering Bryan into the position from which he could attract national notice by his already prepared cross-of-gold speech, and thus step into the nomination. Few political secrets have been so well kept. The scheme was a good and sensible one. For all that has been written about the freakiness of that nomination, it was the only thing to do. Not the cross-of-gold speech nor anything else could have stampeded the Convention if there had been any available candidate who embodied the issue. The Democrats had an issue but no leader. "Silver Dick" Bland of Missouri personified the free coinage demand as no one else did, but he had no qualities of leadership and was not of Presidential stature. He got a plurality of votes, but not the nomination. The crisis, for it was one in political history, demanded the production of a new leader, and none was in sight. Altgeld and the other leaders had foreseen this situation, had finally settled on Bryan as the right man, and had given him the opportunity to convince the Convention that it had found what it was looking for. The mad enthusiasm over the Cross of Gold was not mere lunacy over rhetoric; it was largely compounded of relief at finding Moses unexpectedly.

The Democratic Party in the North and East was practically wiped out—not by Bryan's defeat in November, for defeats do not wipe out parties, but by the bitter civil war which had raged within the party from the day of President Cleveland's second inauguration, and there was no question of Bryan's permanent leadership. It is too much the Eastern fashion to assume that the Western and Southern Democrats were a pack of simpletons, believing fanatically in the free coinage of silver. Bryan's following included great numbers who took no stock in that economic heresy. But the West and South were in bitter revolt against conditions which gave the farmer and working man the worst of it, and the revolt, among labor men and their sympathizers at least, was beginning to spread eastward. It was President Roosevelt's keen perception of this—and he was alone among the party leaders in seeing it—which enabled the Republican Party to stave off the defeat which would certainly have befallen it if Roosevelt had not soothed the East and checked the West by his White House progressivism. The moment he took his hand off, the revolt sprang into life again, and in four years culminated in the apparent destruction of the Republican Party in 1912.

In 1896 all this was mercifully veiled from the eyes of the Democracy. Its spirit is excellently illustrated in the title Bryan chose for the book he promptly wrote about his campaign and his defeat—*The First Battle.* Neither he nor the others doubted that 1896 was only the Lexington and Concord of a war that would end with a Yorktown in 1900. I remember distinctly that the commonest saying among the militant and confident Bryanites was that 1896 was a close parallel to 1856. That was the year in which the Republican Party made its first nomination, and was not in the least cast down over Frémont's defeat at the polls, but on the contrary was eager for the victory it won with Lincoln four years later. The Bryan followers, East as well as West, had Frémont and 1856 always on their lips, and every superficial resemblance was accepted as a matter of course. The only deviation from the exact parallel, they fully believed, was to be that the Republicans had discarded Frémont for a new standard-bearer in 1860, whereas the Democrats in 1900 would stick to the candidate of 1896.

The intervening four years would be used for a campaign of education, and would give plenty of time.

Bryan had the Democratic Party in his hand. It was his to do what he pleased with. He was master. Now came his opportunity to demonstrate the quality of his leadership, and he at once demonstrated that, politician to the core though he might be, he was a very poor one. His first demonstration of it came in 1898. He had a superstitious belief (which never left him) in the power of politicians to make "issues," though all experience shows that it is the people themselves who do that. Free silver having failed as an issue in 1896, he cast about for another, and the Spanish War seemed to him to have dropped it providentially in his hand. He determined to make "imperialism" the issue, and he did; for, as I show in another chapter, it was Bryan who accomplished that feat by driving mutinous Democratic Senators to support McKinley's purchase of the Philippines, so that, the purchase once accomplished, he and they could depict McKinley as a new Cæsar and appeal to the people to overthrow the new Roman Empire. That period has become so dusty that I may be suspected of exaggeration, but for at least two years we heard more about Rome than about New York and Chicago, and more about Cæsar than about Hanna or Croker. The cartoonists were busy all those two twelvemonths with imperial robes, crowns, scepters and laurel wreaths, and McKinley always appeared in their products under the title "Emperor William I." If it is a little hard in retrospect to identify that honest gentleman with Tiberius and Nero, it is still harder to reconstruct the frame of mind in which anybody could have believed the American people would fall for such stuff. And they did not. McKinley was reelected by a majority almost too big to count, and we had had our first close-up of Bryan as a political seer.

The question now was what he would do about 1904. He did not leave anybody long in doubt. He had been defeated on two successive issues, free silver and imperialism, but he could not think of any other at the moment, so he resolved to make both of them the issues in the next campaign. The docile Democrats rebelled. They were tired of the wilderness and wanted to be led into Canaan. From the Southern leaders, especially, came a protest against being driven over another precipice. The intervening four years were busy with conferences.

I was acquainted with what was going on in these years of consultation, mostly consultation at Washington, and was occasionally able to give information and advice, especially when the Southerners wanted to know about the necessary East and most of all about crucial New York. They were not provided with any "paramount issue," as Bryan called it, but believed they could win without one; and it was a justifiable confidence, for campaigns are often won without any—more often than not, in spite of a widespread belief to the contrary. The only flaw in their generalship was that nobody could have beaten Roosevelt in 1904; but that, of course, they did not know.

They consulted Bryan, naturally, and he drove them almost to despair. He was darting to Washington and back again all through those years, and in all these conferences he showed that invincible firmness or obstinacy, call it which you please, that later came to be so well known. He insisted on a reaffirmation of imperialism and free coinage of silver at the sacred ratio of sixteen to one. The leaders balked. They were willing to reaffirm the imperialism issue, the more so since even after the capture of General Aguinaldo we still dragged on a weary and profitless guerrilla warfare in the Philippines. There was no more talk about Cæsar, the Empire, or the downfall of the republic, but the country certainly appeared to be tired of the white man's burden and the monotonous killings in the jungle. The leaders saw hope in this weariness. It was only a mirage, but it looked promising in 1902, when Senator Carmack of Tennessee and John Sharp Williams of Mississippi were skilfully jabbing the public's sensitive nerve. The leaders did not think much of imperialism as a "paramount" issue, but they were willing to reaffirm it in this altered shape. But they would not reaffirm free silver.

One of Bryan's true friends, a veteran in politics, Colonel O. O. Stealey, Washington correspondent for *The Louisville Courier-Journal,* urgently advised him to drop his insistence on this issue. "The folks down South like you," said Stealey, "but they are tired of going into the Post Office and having their mail handed to them by a Republican."

Bryan replied that it was a question of principle.

"That may be decisive with you, Mr. Bryan," said Stealey, "but how are you going to enforce your principles if your party doesn't get into office?"

"I think we can win with this issue," answered Bryan.

"Not in 1904."

"Well, then, in 1908."

"Not in 1908," declared Stealey, "and not in twenty-five years."

"Well, then, in seventy-five years," was Bryan's answer.

There sounded the crusader. But in a short time the politician got the upper hand and Bryan was hunting for a new paramount issue. After Judge Parker's crushing defeat by Roosevelt in 1904, Bryan, who had been momentarily shoved aside by the leaders, was again in unquestioned control and certain to be nominated in 1908. Seeing this, the Northern and Eastern Democrats, who were weary of the wilderness, were on the point of surrendering to him.

And things looked hopeful. Bryan had not had much to say about imperialism and had had nothing at all to say about free silver after the Waterloo of 1904. They cherished a hope that he was willing to put these issues aside. If he would only keep still about them—and there came, from sources apparently close to him, plenty of underground hints that he would—they would turn in and support him in the next election.

Bryan encouraged them by making a trip around the world and keeping mum. His first speech on his return was awaited with hopeful expectancy by all branches of the party.

He made it in New York in 1906 and tore the party wider asunder than ever. Bryan was, as had been reported by grape-vine and underground railroad, willing enough to subordinate the two sacred issues, but, with his usual ineptness at politics, he had decided that they must be supplanted by a new "paramounter." And he had picked, of all things in the world, the governmental control of railroads.

The roar of fury that went up from the North, the East and the Middle West seemed to astound him, and what dumfounded him still more was that it was not counterbalanced by any shout of approval from the Far West and South. The crusader rather hastily dropped his new paramounter. When he was nominated in 1908, he again had a divided party, and, for once, no issue at all.

I went through most of that campaign with him, and well remember how he brought out issue after issue, trying to find a good paramounter. They were all duds. The real issue had been made, as usual, by the people in their own minds. It was simply the question whether or not to approve Roosevelt's administration, which had established itself as being definitely progressive. The candidate was Taft, and Roosevelt assured the country that he would continue the Roosevelt policies and really believed it. That was what the people wanted. Bryan, with his usual political shrewdness, painted Taft as a mere Me Too for Roosevelt. If anything had been needed to insure Taft's election, that would have done it.

So Bryan lost again.

His further adventures in search of a paramount issue show that he never was able to learn. Exactly as he was in 1896, so he always remained. After 1908, however, he ceased to be a Presidential candidate and his paramounting was no longer so devastating in its effects. In later years it only bedeviled the party and its candidate, as when he nearly split the Convention of 1920 by insisting on a declaration in behalf of Volsteadism as a winning Democratic issue, but the effects, since he was not the nominee, were already gone when the Convention adjourned. His last appearance as an expert on issues was at the Convention of 1924, when he was influential in preventing the party from going on record against the Ku Klux Klan. It was appropriate that he should crown his career with that piece of political wisdom.

One day in 1900 I was in the Marble Room of the Senate, waiting for a Senator to come out in answer to my card. There were others waiting for Senators, and around one of these visitors, a distinguished-looking man, an eager crowd had gathered. Most of them were Democratic Senators, and they were hanging on his words. Puzzled by this, a moronic visitor approached me in search of light and asked if I knew who it was. "It's William J. Bryan," I replied.

"Bryan? Bryan?" repeated the moron vaguely. He cast about in his mind and then identified the name. "Bryan; ah, yes," he said, nodding wisely. "Free silver advocate." And, his mind at rest, he ambled away.

It was thus, however, that Bryan was regarded in those days when he and I were young, comparatively. It is hard to make this generation believe it. If my moronic friend of 1900 could have returned in 1925 and seen the same Bryan, he would have nodded again and said wisely: "Ah, yes. Prohibitionist." For, known so long to us oldsters as the champion of sixteen to one, to Flaming Youth to-day he is only the embodiment of the Eighteenth Amendment and the Volstead Law The fifteen years before his death were spent in such furious fighting in behalf of prohibition as to obliterate everything else. In the last year or two of his life he was evidently preparing to extend that field, and his premature death saved us from a political battle to legislate religious Fundamentalism into power through the ballot-box.

Therefore it is hard for Flaming Youth to realize that Bryan took up the prohibition issue late in life and not until it was evidently going to be a winner. The date was 1910. Prior to that time he never discovered, among all his paramount issues, the paramountcy of this one. He lived in or rather near Lincoln, the capital and second city of Nebraska. The first city was Omaha. Omaha's political king was James C. Dahlman, variously known as Mayor Jim and the Cowboy Mayor. Mayor Jim was reelected as often as he liked. He was outspokenly, defiantly, swaggeringly wet, and the Drys regarded him as a limb of Satan. He was Bryan's chief political ally; the two worked hand in glove, Bryan in Lincoln and the Cowboy Mayor in Omaha, and furnished each other with votes in every State fight. Mayor Jim had more votes to furnish than Bryan, for he ran a machine, but Bryan had influence with the unorganized plain people, so it was no unequal partnership.

By 1910 it was evident that prohibition was coming. State after State was adding it to the statute-book. Almost every time it came up at the polls it won. The momentum was obviously irresistible. Bryan came out for it, and from that time until his death he was, at any rate in the minds of the Wets, the whole front of prohibition in politics. Why he never took it up before I have often wondered; it was an indicated thing to do, for a politician. But, slow as he was in adopting it, he made up for lost time by the energy and uncompromising determination with which he fought for it. And the first thing he did was to turn on wet and wicked Mayor Jim and smite him hip and thigh. As, two years later, he called on the Baltimore Convention to purge itself of Wall Street alliances by throwing Thomas F. Ryan and August Belmont out of its membership, so now he called on the Nebraska Democracy to purge itself of all alliance with wetness by throwing the Cowboy Mayor into outer darkness. It was no short task, for that limb of Satan was firmly ensconced; but in the end the Christian soldiers conquered the citadel, Belial was hurled over the ramparts, and the Nebraska Democracy became as a pure and holy child. And from Nebraska Bryan proceeded outward, to overwhelm the hosts of evil in the other States and in the nation. It was the end of Mayor Jim. I was sorry, for I liked the Cowboy Mayor; for a son of Belial, a lost soul, he had some very engaging qualities.

CHAPTER IV

THE MAN OF THE CROSS OF GOLD

It was a wonderful thing to see Bryan in a fight, especially at a national Convention. Did you want drama? There it was. I don't mean melodrama, or theatricality. I mean drama, the fight of a cavalier against threatening hosts. To see him at such a moment was to see Bussy d'Amboise overcoming wave after wave of the Prince's assassins; it was to see the giant Porthos, single-handed, tearing up boulders and flinging them at the King's army; it was to see the Three Musketeers holding the Rochelle infantry at bay from their bastion. As the angry battalions fell upon him, to be tossed back with a flick of his wrist and a dart of his rapier, one seemed to see a poem translated into action. I have seen many a dramatic political fight, but never anything that remotely resembled one of Bryan's.

This may seem extravagant; it may seem that memory, years afterward, gives a rosy tint to prosaic political scrambles. So, to dissipate that impression, I will quote here something I wrote when I was fresh from seeing one of these extraordinary scenes. It was written when I returned from the Baltimore Convention of 1912, where, in the midst of a tumult of wrath and hatred, he had forced the nomination of Woodrow Wilson and saved the nation from the dreadful experience of having Hearst as President, with Champ Clark as his dummy in the White House, holding the title of President, in the years of the coming war with Germany. In a letter to a friend I wrote:

"He was the great figure of the Convention. He never was so great and he never was so victorious. Long as I have known Bryan, and many as are the aspects in which I have seen him, he was a revelation to me. The concerted onslaught upon him was a total failure, and the men who made it seemed like pigmies before him. He hurled them aside and brought them to naught with ridiculous ease. They beat him on the first fight, over the temporary Chairmanship, but this first victory was their last, and after that it was comic and pathetic to see the way he dominated them, quelled them, and played with them. Every new device, every craftily-planned scheme, that they sweated over and finally brought to birth, was turned by him to instantaneous account and he rode on it to new triumphs. Everything he undertook was a glorious success; everything they undertook was a lamentable failure. He left the Convention a conqueror, and a bigger figure than he had ever been in his life."

As an orator his effectiveness was due not so much to what he said as, first and above all, to a most extraordinary voice—which I can liken to nothing except a church organ, old as the simile seems—and, second, to an impressive presence. I have heard Bryan speak oftener than any other orator for the last thirty years. The best two speeches I ever heard him deliver were never reported, except perhaps in summary, but are far and away better than his more pretentious platform utterances. They were both spontaneous speeches. One of them was unpremeditated, and a moment before he had no idea of making it. And I think their tremendous influence upon the most hostile of his hearers was due to the fact that even the most skeptical could not doubt his sincerity.

The reason these speeches went unreported was that

they were both delivered at national Conventions at about two o'clock in the morning—the zero hour, when the correspondents have ceased to send anything but bulletins. One was delivered at the St. Louis Convention of 1904, the other at the Baltimore Convention of 1912. The first was a heroic struggle by a defeated man; the second was an effort to overcome the sudden rising of disaster after victory.

In 1904 the party leaders, determined to win back the North and East, and angered at Bryan's obstinacy in insisting on a free silver platform, humiliated him to the point of personal insult. Even physical force was, in one instance, involved. He was practically alone in his fight, and during those tumultuous days and nights had been everywhere at once,—in the Committee on Resolutions, in the Committee on Credentials, wherever there was a fight,—battling like a lion and speaking in different places for what amounted to about eighteen hours a day.

Finally, the fight over and Parker nominated, Bryan collapsed; he went to bed and was ordered by his physicians to take a month's rest, if he valued his life. It was 6:30 in the morning. That afternoon came Judge Parker's famous telegram saying that he was a gold man and that if the Convention did not like it it could take him off the ticket.

Both camps were thrown into the wildest confusion. All St. Louis was in a ferment. The Convention was not in session, having adjourned until night to give the delegates a chance to sleep through the day, but the news spread around and they came pouring angrily into the hotel lobbies. Parker was cursed up hill and down dale. There was every disposition to take him at his word, remove him from the ticket and nominate somebody else. Ollie James, afterward Senator from Kentucky, was on every street corner making stentorian speeches in his bull voice and calling on the delegates to throw Parker off and "nominate old man Bryan."

In this ugly mood the Convention reassembled at night, and for hours the storm raged. With infinite address and tact John Sharp Williams set about allaying the fury of the throng, and was succeeding at last when there was a sudden uproar. Down the aisle came Bryan, white-faced, ghastly, his brow covered with sweat, but his eyes gleaming with the old fire. The news had come to him on his sick-bed, despite the efforts of the doctors to keep it from him. He had defied their orders, had canceled his reservation for a train to take him to some rest cure, and had come there to seize the opportunity Parker's telegram had given him.

A United States Senator, Carmack, of Tennessee, and the leader of the House of Representatives, John Sharp Williams, tried to force the sick man into his seat when he mounted the platform. They had just got the angry crowd into a fairly quiet mood and were heartsick at having Bryan make ducks and drakes of their work. Carmack put himself between Bryan and the delegates, and when he tried to pass Williams dug his elbow into Bryan's ribs. But he burst from between them and delivered such a speech as I never heard before or afterward. He spoke with difficulty, but his voice rang through a hall seating twelve thousand people. His white-hot passion, as he pleaded with the delegates to stand by their convictions and not to bow to "this god of gold," so wrought upon his hearers that even those most resolved to defeat him were deeply moved.

This speech may be taken as the continuance and climax of the one he had delivered the day before to the same effect; the two may be taken as one speech. The first one, also delivered late at night,—or rather early in the morning,—was equally moving. I happened to be near that iron old machine boss, Jim Guffey, who was implacably determined to throw Pennsylvania's immense vote against Bryan the moment the time came. Believe it or not, at the climax of this oratory I saw tears come into that hardened old cynic's eyes. Of course, an hour later, he was throwing Pennsylvania's vote in Bryan's face, in the most businesslike way. But, all things considered, I believe that momentary display of emotion on the part of one of his enemies was the greatest oratorical triumph I ever saw Bryan achieve.

It was Sunday morning when Bryan's battle ended in final defeat. It had lasted many days and nights. All that Saturday night he fought on incessantly; beaten at one point he would turn to another, and all this in the breakers of a human sea. And at last, when the long hours of toil and tumult were over, he went to his hotel and fell again into his sick-bed. We often hear of the "triumphs" of oratory, but oratory has its defeats. In this night of defeat Bryan the orator was greater, to my eyes, than he ever was in his moments of triumph.

Eight years later, after Bryan had rejected Champ Clark at Baltimore and guided Wilson to victory, the majority of the Convention was in no pleasant mood—for be it remembered that a majority had voted for Clark. In the post-midnight hours, when nominations were being made for the Vice-Presidency, a delegate from the District of Columbia delivered a speech proposing that all party divisions be healed by giving Wilson a running-mate worthy of him, and concluded by naming Bryan.

This proposal was meant in no friendly spirit; it was designed to shelve him. If the Convention had had time to think, the proposal would have been rejected without question. But in the sudden silence that fell over the Convention at the name of Bryan, the look of uncertainty that was on almost every face, there was the premonition of one of those sudden impulses that sway conventions, especially on Vice-Presidential nominations. Between those who wished to shelve Bryan and the unthinking Bryan followers who were always ready to vote blindly for him for any office, there was a moment's real doubt whether the wild suggestion might not cause a stampede. At any rate, Bryan thought so; and the Convention was momentarily stunned. Anything might have happened.

The maneuver was clever, for Bryan could not asperse the Vice-Presidency or give the impression that he thought himself too big for it. There was only one thing that would be certain to crush any danger there might be, and that was to tell the truth. He sprang to his feet and, in a marvelous speech not three minutes long, he told it.

He declared three successive and overwhelming defeats had taught him that however large his following might be it was not large enough to carry an election. He would be a source of weakness rather than strength to Wilson, and their Presidential nominee ought in fairness to be allowed to go before the country on his merits, without any of the remains of the factionalism of the past to handicap him.

The blunt truthfulness of this speech and its ring of sincerity, coupled with an almost desperate determination and the sheerest kind of oratory, swept the Convention. Marshall was nominated.

Bryan certainly spoke his convictions in that unpremeditated speech. There are plenty of people who still insist that he went to Baltimore to get the nomination for himself, as there are still plenty who hug the delusion that Roosevelt was scheming to get the nomination for himself when he nominated Taft in 1908. There is no arguing with such people; the only answer to them is a smile.

Bryan, who was a witty man in private,—though he carefully concealed the fact in public because he knew that a reputation for wit would only damage him in politics,—

had put the whole thing in a nutshell two weeks before at the Republican Convention in Chicago. He was there as a newspaper man, reporting the nomination of Taft. The Republicans were fighting each other like cats and dogs and howling down their speakers with fairly maniacal rage, but they always softened instantly at the sight of Bryan. The only gleams of sunshine in that black tempest were when he or Job Hedges appeared, and Hedges only came into the limelight once. Whenever Bryan came in to take his seat at the press tables, the Republicans would forget for the moment their mutual hatreds, and join in cordially applauding him. One day, the applause being unusually hearty and long-continued, I said to him as he took his seat just behind me:

"If the Democrats give you as good a reception at Baltimore as the Republicans are giving you here, you'll get a fourth nomination."

"My boy," said the Commoner with a paternal smile, "do you think I'm going to run for President just to get the Republican Party out of a hole?"

And that witticism, expanded, was just what he told the Democrats in his thrilling three-minute speech at Baltimore, two weeks later.

He had left his old ambition behind.

CHAPTER V

BRYAN'S DARK SECRET

"TELL me a funny story," said I to John Sharp Williams, of Mississippi. Williams had not yet become a Senator, but he was the official leader of the Democratic Party in the House of Representatives and was occasionally mentioned for President of the United States.

"I will if you won't print it in your paper," said Williams.

"I won't," I said, "but why the prohibition? You have a national reputation as a wit."

"I know I have," replied Williams bitterly, "and it has been the curse of my public life. When I was young and was first elected to Congress, Henry Watterson gave me some advice about how to conduct myself so as to make my budding Washington career a success, and he concluded by saying earnestly:

"'One thing more. I have noticed in you a tendency toward both wit and humor. When you get to Washington, John, curb it; strangle it, kill it.'

"Then he paused, looked reflectively past me, and added: 'But, John, if you find that this curse is too strong for you; if a time arises when you feel that you positively can't help saying something funny, then, John, say it with a slight nasal twang, so that you may be suspected of New England ancestry.'"

A few weeks after he told me this story Williams was

chosen by the Democratic National Convention of 1904 as chairman of the committee to notify the candidate for Vice-President, Henry G. Davis, of his nomination. Forgetting Watterson's warning, he delivered a satirical speech, satirizing and ridiculing the Republican Party and Roosevelt's administration. It almost blighted his career, and it was some years before he could make a speech on any subject that was not met with a universal chorus of jeers. The notification speech itself aroused not mere disapproval, but a blast of actual anger, amounting almost to fury, from all over the country. Nothing more was ever heard of nominating him for President.

Bryan was wiser than Williams. In the preceding chapter I said that he carefully concealed his humor because he knew that it would only damage him in politics. It will probably astonish ninety-nine one-hundredths of Bryan's followers and foes to be told that in private he was full of humor, but it is true. In public he never permitted a hint of this damning fact to escape, but in a small circle of friends he exuded humor at every pore. He had wit, too, though not of the restrained British type, and this dark secret he also concealed. In addition he had the power—in private—to drive his point home by a funny story, as apposite and pat as any of Lincoln's. (I say "in addition" because many people confound humor with telling or appreciating jokes, a thing with which it has nothing to do.) But by the time he was of age he came to the wise decision that it would be suicidal for him to let the public know these things, and all his life he was astonishingly successful in keeping them hidden from all but his friends. This is one of the reasons, though of course a minor one, for the continuance through so many years of Bryan's tremendous hold on that club of hero-worshipers, the great middle class.

In public he was always as solemn as a sexton. Only

once or twice, and then under the influence of strong emotion, did he permit a hint of his secret powers to escape him One such occasion was in the riotous scenes at the Baltimore Convention of 1912, when his move to outlaw the Wall Street wing of the party had unloosed the wildest passions. While he was speaking from the platform the reactionaries were trying to yell him down, and a hundred men with raucous voices were bellowing at him at once. Ex-Governor MacCorkle of West Virginia, finding that Bryan was steaming ahead without paying the least attention to them, planted himself directly in front of the Commoner and began waving his arms and jumping up and down and yelling: "Are you a Democrat? Are you a Democrat?"

Bryan hesitated, thrust his palm-leaf fan straight at the empurpled face of the gyrating MacCorkle, and let loose his thunderous voice with this annihilating sarcasm:

"My Democracy has been certified to by six million and a half Democratic voters. But I will ask the secretary to record one vote in the negative if the gentleman will give me his name."

"If the gentleman will give me his name!" And this to an ex-Governor of a great State. MacCorkle sat down, wilted. The yelling mob in the aisles fell silent. For a few minutes Bryan was not interrupted. In two sentences he had compressed the whole issue—that he was the spokesman of the party and that the Wall Street crowd were flies on the wheel. This was not humor, it was wit, wit of a grim and menacing kind. Usually Bryan no more displayed his wit than he did his humor, but the temptation was irresistible and the opportunity was magnificent.

There was in Omaha an organization called the Knights of Ak-Sar-Ben, the last word being Nebraska spelled backward. Their initiation ceremonies were pretty rough and very hilarious. I was present when Bryan, then a candidate for President, was initiated; in fact I was initiated that night too, along with a number of others. In view of his distinguished position the usual horseplay was omitted in his case, but, of course, they did have some fun with him; nobody could be initiated without having to ride the goat to some extent. He was called on to make a speech, and started for the platform, but before he could get there a Knight of Ak-Sar-Ben, made up to look exactly like him, appeared upon it, thanked the chairman for his kind words, and proceeded to deliver a speech in perfect imitation of Bryan's well-known style. Bryan had to sit down, and the crowd was in convulsions. When the bogus Bryan left the stand the chairman turned to the real Bryan and said, "Now that we have heard from Mr. Bryan, we will extend the same courtesy to his Republican opponent for the Presidency. We have with us to-night Mr. William H. Taft, and I now request him to take the platform and reply to Mr. Bryan's remarks."

The thing was a surprise to Bryan, but he instantly mounted the platform, and, assuming the character of Taft, delivered the speech called for, every sentence of which was such a finished product of wit, humor or satire as to keep the crowd roaring. He could do this with perfect safety, because the proceedings of Ak-Sar-Ben were not reported. Newspaper men were there in plenty, but honor-bound. I shall never forget the anxious humility with which, as Taft, he apologized for this or that omission in his discussion of the issues on the ground that he had not yet had an opportunity to find out what Roosevelt thought about it, and so on. It was never put as baldly as that, but deftly suggested. He and I happened to leave the hall together, and as we went out he turned to me with a wide grin and said, "I put one over on them, didn't I?"

Another thing not generally known about Bryan is that

some of the best stories making fun of him and his constant ill-success at the polls originated—in private, of course—with the Commoner himself. The best-known example is the famous story of the drunken man who tried three times to get into a dance hall, was thrown down-stairs each time, and on landing in the street after his third attempt picked himself up and, regarding the building with owlish sagacity, said wisely: "They can't fool me. Those fellows don't want me in there."

The appositeness of this story lay in the fact that Bryan told it when he was making his third attempt to get in. He invented the yarn after his nomination for President in 1908, and he evidently viewed with serenity the prospect that he too would be thrown out a third time. The story got into print and went all over the country, but only a few of us knew where it originated. This motif, "Those fellows don't want me in there," was a stock saying in Bryan's home near Lincoln that year. One day I was on a trolley car which was coming near Fairview—Bryan's place—and saw his young daughter Ruth sprinting for it. It was a run of a quarter of a mile down the "rising ground" where the place was built to the road where the trolley ran, and Ruth was all out of breath when she swung on board. She had made it just in time. As she dropped into a seat beside me she pantingly said: "I seem to be the only member of the Bryan family that ever ran for anything and caught it."

He could not only make a joke against himself, but he could see one. He was constantly caricatured, and he reveled in the cartoons. When one of them struck his fancy, he would write the artist asking for the original; and I have seen him get them at his home, Fairview, pleased as punch. He would pounce on the package, crying, "Here's that cartoon I sent for!" and open it, and then exhibit it proudly to those present, laughing like a boy over its cleverness.

He had them framed, and they hung on the Fairview walls and were the first thing to strike your eye as you came in.

It reminded me of John Hay, who took the same delight in having himself burlesqued in cartoons and did pretty much the same thing with them. It was wholly out of the character most people imagined to be Hay's, for he was supposed to smart under ridicule. He did not hang them up to strike the chance beholder's eye, as Bryan did, but he planted them around his study, to which he always took his visitors, and which was the most prominent room in his fine house. It was also supposed, and was frequently printed, that Hay, having become a highbrow, was ashamed of his youthful indiscretions, "Jim Bludso" and "Little Breeches," and disliked to be reminded of them. The fact was that the first thing you saw, as you entered Hay's house in Washington, was a great oil painting covering most of the entrance wall, of Jim Bludso "holding her nozzle agin the bank till the last galoot's ashore."

The more I saw of Bryan the more my admiration mounted for his strength of will and command of himself in respect to his humor. It took self-knowledge and tenacity for a man to remain so much in the public eye for so many years and still keep the public in the dark about a side of his character which would assuredly have damned him from the beginning if it had been known. For we Americans do not love humor in our statesmen. No other nation prates so incessantly about its sense of humor and has so little of it. In England they relish humor in a public man, and in France they relish wit. Here it is nearly as damning to have humor as to be a poet. In England a statesman can even write a novel—Disraeli did; in America, when John Hay wrote *The Breadwinners,* the best seller of the year, he published it anonymously, and his reason was that if it were known he was so frivolous his political career would be at an end. And he kept the secret to the end of his life; he was under suspicion, but they could not prove it on him.

Abraham Lincoln had a reputation as a story-teller, and it is generally the notion that he was helped by it, but it was a detriment to his advance. It counted heavily against him. It created the impression that he was flippant and light-minded. At the outbreak of the War of Secession *Harper's Weekly* printed a cartoon showing two Quaker women in conversation. One was saying, "Martha, who does thee think will be successful, Abraham or Jefferson?" "Jefferson, Rachel," replied the other. "And why does thee think so, Martha?" "Because Jefferson is a praying man." "And so is Abraham a praying man, Martha." "Yes, Rachel, but the Lord will think Abraham is joking." After the dreadful Union disaster at Fredericksburg it published a terrific cartoon showing Columbia demanding from Lincoln what he had done with her slaughtered sons and the President replying with a complacent grin, "That reminds me of a little joke."

The deification of Lincoln to-day, the progressive and industrious effort to strip him of all his own traits and pretty nearly of all human attributes as well is of course stripping him of his humor. Increasingly the soft pedal is being played on it. We can not endure that the canonized Lincoln should be thought of as being so low. So Lincoln is now always the Man of Sorrows; it is always the sad Lincoln that is depicted, never the jocund Lincoln. When his story-telling can not be escaped, it is always qualified by the apologetic explanation that he told stories only to drive home some great moral truth, as Christ did. Which I take the liberty to doubt. I doubt it even about Christ, who showed more than once that He had humor among His other human attributes.

In 1893 I heard Robert G. Ingersoll say: "Hundreds of people are now engaged in smoothing out the lines on Lincoln's face—forcing all features to the common mold—so that he may be known, not as he really was, but, according to their poor standard, as he should have been." The work has been greatly accelerated since he said that.

Certainly his reputation as a humorous man hurt, not helped, him in politics, as it always does. It may have contributed to his unpopularity, for in spite of the general idea to-day that he was a popular President, he was not, until John Wilkes Booth made him so. The supercilious contempt which the Republican leaders felt for him does get into history, without being explained by the historians; I think the general impression of his levity had much to do with it. Senator Charles Sumner's disgust with him because he was always joking and Sumner could never get him to be serious is recorded, but always in an amused way, as if Sumner were denser than others, as if he were the only man so dull as not to see that he was standing on holy ground when he was in the inspired joker's presence.

The political coast is strewn with the wrecks of public men who did not throttle their sense of humor in time, as Bryan did and as Watterson counseled Williams to do. A conspicuous example was Job E. Hedges of New York, who should have risen to the highest honors, and whose career was thwarted and demolished. He was a man of great ability, who had an almost preternatural skill in getting at the core of things—knowing which shell the pea was under. His power of doing this in advance of other people nourished his natural bent toward satire, and as our public makes little distinction between satire and jesting, Hedges became to the popular mind a buffoon, which is about the furthest possible remove from what he really was. In truth he was a political philosopher, and if he had been grave and portentous instead of witty in stating the deep truths which his quick mind unerringly perceived, there is no office to which he might not have aspired. He discovered this at last, but only after it was too late. He was actually nominated, in 1912, for Governor of New York, and was instantly caricatured everywhere as a clown and even in the costume of a court fool. The public would not take him seriously. He was Job the Joker. In truth he never, so far as I remember, either made a joke or told a story; he clothed his philosophy in epigram, but that damned him. His promising career ended with that campaign.

Perhaps a year after his defeat I called on him to get an interview on an important public question, and did not get it. Hedges told me that his reputation as a clown was so firmly established that anything he said would be misinterpreted, and his one desire was to keep his name out of the papers until his false reputation could be lived down. The subject I wanted him to talk about was perfectly serious, but that made no difference; nor did Hedges ever again say anything for publication until just before his death, in 1924, when I got him to analyze the Coolidge-Davis-La Follette Presidential campaign. He did it with his customary insight and sagacity and with his usual power of lucid statement; and with his usual wit. His enforced silence during all those years was a distinct loss to the body of clear-cut thinking and intelligent criticism on political subjects, which is never so large in America that it can afford such losses.

Woodrow Wilson was extremely witty and humorous, but though he was not so secretive about it as Bryan, the public was not permitted to know much about that side of him. In the campaign of 1916 the Democratic National Committee got out a campaign book entitled *The Wit and Wisdom of Woodrow Wilson.* If it had contained many samples of Wilson's real wit it would have been a dangerous experiment, but the witticisms were carefully selected from the more obvious and simple of his epigrams and consequently did him no harm. Even making this allowance the "wit" in this volume was in very small ratio to the "wisdom," which again shows the acumen of the National Committee. In his first campaign Wilson made very few displays of his incisive wit, generally not going much further than a satire on the Republican Party which he had concocted and which was based on *Alice's Adventures in Wonderland*. After he became President he could afford to be witty without so much danger, since public attention was bound to be focused mainly on his achievements in the office and therefore much could be forgiven him. Even then, however, his public displays of wit were few indeed compared with his constant scintillations in private. He was another man who, though chiefly a wit, had also plenty of humor.

To this day it is a common saying, constantly repeated, that Roosevelt had no sense of humor. It is idiotically false, for he was as full of humor as an egg is of meat, but the saying is merely another example of the fact that if anything, however obviously untrue, is repeated often enough it will pass into history. The queer thing is that Roosevelt did not take any great pains to disguise his sense of humor, and the only explanation I can think of is that he laid so much emphasis on solemn and serious things, repeated the verities so often and so trenchantly, that that side of him overpowered the other in the popular imagination and even obliterated it altogether. However, it is a fact that he was rather moderate in his exhibition of his humorous powers until the Bull Moose campaign of 1912. In that historic fight he cut loose. At first I was somewhat startled by the reckless prodigality with which he revealed that none-too-well-advertised side of the Roosevelt character to his public, but as it kept up day after day I got reconciled to it and quieted my apprehensions for him. I think the explanation was that he enjoyed that fight more than any other he had ever been in. I noticed it in him as early as the Convention which nominated him, in August. He was gay, exuberant and hilarious, and was having the time of his life; so he bubbled over into spontaneous humor on every occasion.

McKinley was the most solemn President since Washington and was much beloved by an awestruck people. I used to notice that handshakers came out of his presence with bated breath and almost on tiptoe, as perhaps Nicodemus came out of the presence of God. McKinley did not conceal his humor, because he had none to conceal, and as for wit he had none of that either. It was easy for him to defeat Thomas B. Reed, his rival for the nomination, who was a great man and who was vastly nearer being the leader and protagonist of the Republican Party than was McKinley. Reed was not a humorist, but his tremendous powers of wit and sarcasm made people vaguely uncomfortable, distrustful and uneasy. Reed had the ability to compress pages of argument in a short sentence and wither the enemy with it; in a dozen words he could annihilate the entire campaign material of the opposition. Thus, when the Democrats made an issue of Republican extravagance and charged that Reed had been the Czar of "a billion dollar Congress" (for that was a great deal of money to spend, in 1890 and 1892), Reed made the whole issue profitless by one sentence: "It's a billion dollar country." He could give the history of the Democratic Party completely in another sentence: "The Democratic Party is like a man riding backward in a railroad car; it never sees anything until it has got past it."

These utterances of Reed were so complete and annihilating that they lived; but to give an idea of his more sustained manner I will quote two of his characterizations which I copied down at the time, 1894. Here is one: "It is true that the present House of Representatives [which was Democratic] has refused its privileges, and shirked its duties, and led a gelatinous life, to the scorn of all vertebrate animals." And the other, made at the same time, thus perfectly summed up the character of the Democratic Party in that year—and in some others:

"While Mr. Springer [the Democratic leader] has at all times formed and expressed a great variety of opinions on a great variety of subjects, he has never been by his friends or his enemies regarded as in the least degree bigoted. History has justified the confidence which the Democracy have in Mr. Springer. He has been a Democrat. The party can contemplate his work of this session with the calm certainty that there is no intellect so subtle, no mind so broad, no sympathy so delicate, as to detect therein the slightest trace of a principle of economic science or a system of revenue; and the Democracy certainly do enter the next campaign unembarrassed by their immediate past, and with great power of being natural, that is, of being all things to all men."

Off the platform he was precisely the same as he was on it. In the days of his "Czardom" as Speaker of the House he was furiously denounced as a tyrant and a despot who was riding roughshod over the rights of the minority. When the committee which daily framed the conditions under which bills should be considered and debate conducted met, Reed would announce to the Democratic members what was about to befall them that day in these words: "Gentlemen, William and Joseph [McKinley and Cannon, the other Republican members of the committee] and I have decided to perpetrate the following outrage."

It must be remembered that this was habitual and constant with Reed. The lightning-like flashes of his intellect illuminated everything they touched. What is unusual with wit, it powerfully convinced. A Reed epigram was worth tangible votes; many more than a solemn McKinley speech. It excited not only laughter but thought. But it killed Reed as a Presidential possibility. Even while they laughed, people were uncomfortable and afraid; at any rate they looked askance at him. It did not seem fitting to have a joking President in the White House; no, not even though his jokes were really sermons.

I was young then and took my politics more to heart than I do now, and it was a bitter disappointment when Reed lost the nomination to McKinley. Looking back, I can see that the things for which I liked Reed most were a detriment and a handicap to him. The people may admire a witty man, but they adore a solemn one. McKinley's portentous gravity was no small factor in making him the idol of his country; for that, hard as it may be for this generation to believe it, is exactly what he was.

I hope it is not necessary for me to explain that I have no intention of trying to prove that elections are decided by the candidates' possession, or lack, of humorous powers. That matter, however, is a factor like others and, slight as it seems, is not to be sneezed at.

CHAPTER VI

THE FROLICSOME BRYAN

ONE of the penalties of being either a President or a Presidential candidate is that people of leisure go without sleep thinking up bizarre presents to give you. They run from the Lord's prayer engraved on a pebble up to an apple pie six feet in diameter. Bryan got the usual assortment; and about a month after his 1908 nomination he looked up from his mail inquiringly and addressed the correspondents thus:

"Here's a Minnesota man who says he's going to present me with a bucking mule. Says the mule has taken three prizes at county fairs. It's on its way now, and ought to be here before the end of the week. What in the world shall I do with a bucking mule?"

"Send it to Mr. Taft," I suggested. "Nobody can stay on the deck of a bucking mule for half a second. There are no limits to the distance you can travel perpendicularly. You might be elected unanimously if you could get Taft to ride the mule."

"He says," said Bryan, disregarding the well-meant suggestion and referring again to the letter, "that nobody has ever succeeded in riding the mule yet. He has thrown the best riders in Minnesota. I suspect the man's a Republican and has an evil motive. Still, he says he cast his first vote for Samuel J. Tilden."

He ruminated. "I'll have to send the mule to some

circus," he said. "Nobody can ride him and I can't keep him on exhibition here at Fairview. These people seem to think candidates have nothing to do but think up zoos and aquariums and aviaries to send their ostriches and electric eels and elephants to."

"I'll ride yo' mule fo' you, Colonel Bryan," said Major J. J. Dickinson of *The New York Herald*.

Major Dickinson was a Kentucky gentleman of great girth, large weight and dignified speech. He was no longer young. Though a Kentuckian, he came by his military title virtuously, having got it in the army. His impressive appearance and gravity of manner masked the fact that he was an inveterate kidder. He was not satisfied to josh now and again; he joshed incessantly, in everything he said, and he never abated a tittle of his owlish gravity.

Bryan's eyes lighted. "Do you mean it, Major?" he asked eagerly, though he knew very well that Dickinson was kidding, as usual.

"Did you evah know me to say anything in jest, Colonel Bryan?" inquired the Major in a wounded tone.

"On next Friday," said Bryan with wolfish joy, "we will assemble in the alfalfa patch, march on the stable, and you shall ride the mule. And I'll see that you ride it with all the pomp and paraphernalia. Any time between now and Friday that you want to back out, say the word; but I shall be disappointed in you. Remember, Major, your honor is engaged."

Thereafter, each day, Bryan would look at Dickinson with hungry anticipation and remind him that one more day had gone by. The Major would nod defiantly and say indignantly, "I tell you, sah, I'll ride yo' mule."

He was still kidding, of course, and he supposed Bryan was, but Bryan was not kidding the least bit in the world. On Friday morning he met us at Fairview with his face beaming all over, and announced that the mule had arrived the previous evening and he had had a special stall built. "He's there, awaiting you, Major," he said triumphantly, "and you'll find that I have made every preparation to do you befitting honor. Come on, everybody!"

He had indeed made every preparation. When we got out to the stable we found he had provided an élite audience. It included fair ladies and distinguished men, the fashion and intellect of Lincoln. Prominent in the van of the assemblage were several photographers, armed with the weapons of their calling. A burst of applause greeted us as we approached, with Bryan and Dickinson leading the procession arm in arm. And then, at a sign from Bryan, the stableman led out a dour and gloomy mule.

Not until that moment, as Dickinson afterward told me while the surgeon was fixing him up, did he really suspect that Bryan meant him to board that creature and butcher himself to make a Lincoln, Nebraska, holiday. We all expected him to back out, but the old boy was game. For the honor of Kentucky, by all the memories of the blue-grass and the Dark and Bloody Ground, he must bestride that waiting volcano and rise with it. That, at any rate, was what I later gathered from the remarks that emerged from his bandages.

The animal—it was really a baleful-looking quadruped—regarded him agnostically as he walked up. The cameramen unlimbered. The Major made a few confidential remarks in the mule's ear. The brute listened attentively, but with what I thought was a skeptical air, boding no good. However, when the Major finished whispering he had done all he could to propitiate his critic, and he swung one large leg across the main deck and paused to see if there was any protest.

There was none. The mule stood as if carved out of

rock. Bryan applauded, and incited Dickinson. "You've got him tamed, Major," he cried. "He may buck the best riders in Minnesota, but he falters before a man from Old Kentucky."

Dickinson's manner indicated to me that he regarded this encouragement as an impertinence. He followed his leg with the rest of his considerable person, and was poised on the mule's back for, as nearly as I could estimate, one-twentieth of a second. The creature did not seem to move at all. But the Major rose straight up in the air and seemed to us to keep on rising for a long, long time. Then he turned over and descended more rapidly, with his feet pointing directly toward the empyrean.

It was at this point that it dawned on everybody that the thing was not so funny after all. The horrified photographers forgot to click. Bryan's face went white. The Major landed on the top of his head, six inches from a rock; the only rock I ever noticed in Nebraska, though of course there were others somewhere. He did not get up, though he tried to.

White as a sheet and with wild eyes, Bryan tore over to him and put a hand under his shoulder. "I'm all right," said the Major, feebly but sportily. "Just give me a hand and I'll be able to get up."

Bryan raised him gently, and half carried him to the house. His joke had exploded, and he was frantic with self-reproach. But the Major smiled weakly and told him it was all right, and so it proved, though Dickinson had to spend a couple of days in bed.

However, as soon as we found he had only been temporarily lamed and not seriously hurt, the ludicrous side of the thing came uppermost again. On his bed in the Lincoln Hotel the Major received deputation after deputation of solicitous inquirers for his health, all bursting with laughter and interrupting their anxious questions with irrelevant shouts. The Mayor headed a delegation of citizens; the Elks and the Country Club, to both of which Dickinson belonged, came in by battalions. Mayor Brown finally started a subscription list and purchased a bouquet of cabbages, squash and turnips, tastefully arranged and labeled:

FROM THE
AMALGAMATED MULE RIDERS OF AMERICA
TO OUR HERO.

It hung suspended from the light fixture and charmed the eyes of the Major's constant parade of visitors. The correspondents all sent a short account of it, a paragraph or two, to their papers; and when, a week later, Bryan took us into Iowa on a stumping trip we found that we had made the Major famous. Wherever we went the local reporters met us, and their first question was not, as usual, "What are Mr. Bryan's plans for to-day?" but, "Please point out the man who rode the mule."

In each city the newspapers photographed Dickinson before they snapped Bryan himself. He even had the distinction of being cartooned. On the front page of *The Chicago Tribune* appeared a cartoon by John T. McCutcheon, representing a number of reporters with note-books in hand, poising pencils and waiting patiently for something to happen which they could write down. They were all gazing up toward the sky, toward which was traveling with incredible velocity a diminishing figure. Only one of them was taking notes, and what he was writing was this: "The correspondent is still in the air. It is as yet too early to predict the result."

"Did any of you ever write a song?" asked Bryan, who had entirely recovered from his scare and his remorse.

"I'm going to give you a chance to make some money. I'll give a cash prize to whoever writes the best song entitled, *When the Major Rode the Mule.* It ought to be rather martial and stirring, something like *Sheridan's Ride* set to music. I think it would be a go."

Spellbinding through Kansas, Bryan and his party climbed aboard a train. The car was a day coach, of course; when Bryan was a candidate no power could induce him to ride in a Pullman. So the party had to take its chances on finding seats. Bryan and most of the party got seats together, but I was the last on board and had to take a seat far up the car. Looking around, I saw Bryan beckoning to me. I got up and went back to him. "Have a seat," said he hospitably, wagging his large knee; so I sat down on it. The other passengers stared; some of those up front, unable to believe their eyes, verified the strange spectacle by twisting their heads around and wondering at the sight of the (possibly) next President riding with a short reporter perched on his knee. But Bryan paid not the least attention; such things never ruffled him. "You've been a very good boy," he explained when I asked why he thus distinguished me.

I did not stay with Bryan through the whole of the 1908 campaign. Some of the other reporters who had started out with him had returned to the East, and after a while I followed. When I left him we were in the midst of a campaign tour, and had reached Kansas City. Having got my ticket for Washington, I started to say good-by to the rest in the union station, but Bryan stopped me. "We'll escort you to the train," said the Peerless; so he and I marched out on the eastbound platform, with the rest following. I said my good-bys and climbed aboard the car. As I turned to wave at them, the Peerless clapped his hands.

"Speech! Speech!" said he gravely.

The others took it up. The crowd on the platform stared uncomprehendingly and solemnly. Bryan would not be denied. So, making the best of it, I started on a burlesque speech in imitation of Bryan's style from the car platform. He listened with the most profound gravity, and whenever I reached a period he would applaud vehemently and sometimes cheer. He never altered his pose, which was that of an enthralled listener greatly moved by an eloquent orator. When the train began to move I hurriedly concluded, and Bryan broke into a stentorian cheer—taken up, of course, by his weaker-lunged companions—and applauded till it seemed as if his hands must be sore. The last I saw of the station, as the train passed on, was Bryan waving his big black sombrero at me in a slow rhythmic manner, and the crowd on the platform studying him in a sheeplike effort to divine the meaning of his extraordinary behavior. They say, however, at least some people say and seem to believe it, that Americans are notable for their sense of humor.

Coming into Omaha one day when he was running for President, we stopped amid a wildly excited mass of several thousand enthusiasts all crowding the platform and pushing to grab the hand of Bryan. It was a hard battle to force one's way through that mob of madmen. The police were holding back the crowd with difficulty, or Bryan would have been swept off his feet. Bryan was the care of the policemen, and of the citizens' committee headed by Mayor Jim Dahlman; the rest of the party had to fend for themselves as best they could. The committee had planted several automobiles at the station, ready to take us to the Omaha Club, and we were struggling to get to them.

I was sick, but it was a case of every man for himself and nobody had time to look after me. I was lugging a heavy suitcase down the platform and making heavy weather of it. Bryan was ahead, in the clutches of the excited committee and the Board of Trade, which had butted in on the Mayor; the rest of our party, except myself, was almost on his heels. Suddenly Bryan broke from the crowd, wheeled and darted back to me, leaving them staring after him open-mouthed.

"You're too sick to carry that suitcase," he said, taking it out of my hands. "Let me carry it."

And off he went, suitcase in hand, to be engulfed again by the rival boards and committees. The others had been too busy to think of me, but Bryan, the busiest of all, thought of everything.

That night we were initiated into the Order of the Knights of Ak-Sar-Ben. As I remark elsewhere in this book, there was nothing conventional about the initiation ceremonies in this organization. The man who was initiated was usually thankful and a little surprised to find that he was still alive. In Bryan's own case the Knights did not offer any physical violence, because he was a Presidential candidate, but nobody else in the party was an exception to their inflexible rule. I was still sick, and was wondering how I could stand being tossed in a blanket or hurled off a cliff; for, though I had never before been in the toils of Ak-Sar-Ben, I knew what awaited me.

But as the night wore on and I saw all my friends and many others go through the inferno, I became aware that an invisible hand was stretched over me. Every time I was about to drop down a precipice three hundred feet high and land on a feather bed, at the last moment it was not I but one of my fellow-initiates who made the ridiculous descent. I could not understand it. I saw Charley Cotterill of the Associated Press led into a large cage, from which he looked around inquiringly to find out what he was there for; when he was suddenly enlightened by having a hose turned on him.

I saw my portly and dignified friend, Major Dickinson, hurled airily off an imitation mountaintop on to a pillow far below. But, though I always seemed to be about to experience one of these calamities, it invariably changed its course just as it was approaching me, veered off and struck some one else.

As I was going out I received, as did all the others initiated, a certificate of membership in the order. That completed my astonishment. I turned to Victor Rosewater, the editor of *The Omaha Bee,* and asked him how it was that I and nobody else had gone through the fires and come out unscathed. "Why," said Rosewater, "didn't you know? Bryan told the initiation committee that they could haze every man in the party to their hearts' content except you, because you are sick. He said he wanted you to become a Knight of Ak-Sar-Ben without having to go through the ropes. I thought of course he'd told you, or that you had asked him to."

And of course he hadn't told me. That was not Bryan's way. He had no notion I would ever hear of it, and I never would have if I hadn't happened to ask Rosewater. Bryan's adversaries delighted to picture him as a man of no delicacy, but he showed strange delicacies to those who knew him well; in some things he had the delicacy of a woman. I tell this story not because it illustrates his kindness, which it does obviously enough, but because it illustrates his thoughtfulness. He was the busiest man in Omaha that day, but Bryan was never too busy to think of others.

When I came to leave him in that campaign I was in another sort of trouble. I had been out West for several months for *The World,* and my funds were low. At the moment I received orders to start for the East I did not have money enough to get me there. I telegraphed *The World* to send me some, but got no answer, and I could not wait. I did not say anything to the other members of the party about it, but I was doing a lot of figuring on how to make my money last until I got to Washington, where I could cash a check. I finally made out that I could get there by eating only one meal a day and not tipping the porter or buying any cigars.

At the union station in Kansas City there were two ticket offices, one selling tickets for eastbound trains, the other for westbound. Bryan was going west, so he, with his secretary and the reporters, was at the western ticket office, while I crossed over to the eastern. While I was waiting my turn I felt a heavy hand fall on my shoulder. I turned, and beheld the Peerless Leader.

"I was watching you in the train," he said, and I was surprised, for he had seemed to be doing nothing of the kind. "And I noticed that you were counting your money and looked worried. Do you need any?"

"Well, I could use about ten dollars," I said.

"Here's twenty," said Bryan, shoving it into my hand. Over at the western ticket office the others were still buying tickets. None of them had noticed that I was "counting my money and looked worried." Nobody had seen it except the Peerless. But nothing of that kind ever escaped Bryan.

On a campaign trip, as I have said, Bryan would never ride in a Pullman, but always in a day coach. Alton B. Parker did the same. The idea was that it would show how democratic the candidate was, how he was a plain rough fellow and one of the people. I never could see that it had that effect at all. The proletariat voted against Bryan and for Taft, who not only rode in a Pullman but didn't receive any visitors, if he could help it, while he was riding; and against Bryan and for McKinley, who wouldn't even go out among the plain people at all, but held that it was more dignified in a Presidential candidate to stay home. As for poor Parker, he couldn't have convinced the proletariat that he loved the horny-handed if he had hoofed it over the ties.

The only thing this democratic style of progress did accomplish was to make the existence of the men who had to travel with the candidate ten degrees more unhealthful and uncomfortable. It was hard enough in a private car, with Wilson or Roosevelt. It did not bother Bryan much, partly because he possessed the uncommon ability to go to sleep at will. Once, starting out on a campaign trip from his home town of Lincoln, he reached the station at midnight and found the train three hours late. He sat down on a bench and was asleep on the instant, while the rest of us sat bolt upright on hard seats for three dragging hours. When the train did arrive he woke instantly, bright and lusty, and charged cheerily aboard, as wide awake as a morning rooster. But his berth had not been made up, and the porter asked him to step into the smoking compartment for a few minutes. "Certainly," said Bryan; he stepped in, sat down, and was immediately asleep again. Three minutes later, when the porter awoke him, he was instantly broad awake, undid his raiment, plunged into bed, and was asleep as he hit the sheets.

The result was that Bryan could always get eight hours' sleep, but nobody else in the party ever could; for, in order to get in as many dates as possible, Bryan would frame up all sorts of train combinations which required him to leave his train several times a night at some way station or junction to make connection with another train.

Once we were going out of St. Louis to Salem, Illinois, and the original program was that we should leave at six A. M. We had to write our reports of his St. Louis speech and telegraph them, but we figured on finishing by one A. M. and getting about five hours' sleep before making the train to Salem; and we needed it, for Bryan had kept us up all the previous night with his devilish ingenuity for cooking up new train combinations. But just as we were pounding out our last few paragraphs Bob Rose, Bryan's secretary, came rushing in with the announcement that the Peerless had succeeded in finding a train which left at three A. M.

It was after one when we finished, and we decided that a mere two hours of sleep would make us feel worse instead of better; so we boarded the train, with the idea that we could get some sleep on the way to Salem. Did we? Not at all, but Bryan did. While he was peacefully slumbering, we tossed about on our hard seats on that jerky train, until, about an hour later, Rose loomed up with the glad news that we were to get out. "Why?" we shrieked as one man. "Because," explained Rose, grinning, "the Peerless has found that we can get to Salem earlier if we get out at Jacobus Junction and make connections with another train. And we'll be at Jacobus Junction in half a minute."

Jacobus Junction wasn't its name, but it was something like it and just as improbable. We got out dizzily in the dark, and found ourselves on a station platform with some tracks running aimlessly around it and no houses in sight, no seats on the platform and a cold wind blowing. Bryan leaned up against the side of the station and went instantly to sleep; but we stood around and walked for an agonizing hour until the train came along. Bryan's speech was to be delivered at two P. M., so we ought to have had the morning to rest in; but Salem was his birthplace, so his arrival was a great day for the town, and a general holiday and a big program had been scheduled. The morning was one long nightmare of the Peerless darting from reception to reception, greeting old neighbors, making offhand little speeches all over town, and all this had to be reported and was far harder work than merely listening to a speech and making notes. Finally he made his speech and we rushed to the hotel and banged out the story. We were to take the eight o'clock train out, so we thought we could get three hours' sleep after we finished writing. But just as one of the reporters rose from his typewriter, stretched himself and said, "Now I can snatch forty winks, and how I'll enjoy it," Bob Rose came charging in, shouting, "Everybody out!"

"What's the matter, Bob?" cried somebody, aghast. "The train doesn't leave until eight."

"Oh, yes, it does," responded Rose. "The Peerless has discovered another combination. The train he's going to take leaves in ten minutes, and if you don't hustle you won't catch it."

I never saw a Convention more dully serious than the Republican one in 1920, which nominated Harding; and the only gleam of comedy which irradiated it was Bryan's conscientious effort to act like a reporter. His usual course hitherto had been to sit at the press tables and write nothing but thoughts. Now, for some reason, he tried to be a real reporter and set about observing and imitating the professional behavior of those toilers. Having observed that most of them were wearing caps—a tribute to the fierce wind that blew from the Lake all through that Convention—he donned a cap too, and daily darted from headquarters to headquarters asking to see the candidates. He had noticed that the real reporters did this, so he did it; what he had not noticed was that they had a reason for doing it and that he had none.

He began by visiting Governor Lowden. Subsequently I asked that candidate what news he had imparted to the new reporter. "Didn't tell him any," said the Governor. "Didn't have a chance. He did all the talking, and when he got through he put on his cap and left."

Leaving Lowden, the busy journalist hustled over to General Leonard Wood's quarters for an interview. That short-spoken warrior gave the scribe exactly one minute and a half. Bryan came out into the anteroom, placed himself in a chair and viewed interestedly the pictures on the wall. General Wood, emerging and noting with apparent surprise that the reporter had not gone, saluted in military fashion and passed wordlessly on. Bryan, though only a Colonel, did not return the General's salute. His early training in the Third Nebraska in the bloody days of the Spanish War had done him no permanent military good. He departed for the headquarters of Senator Hiram Johnson, and found the California candidate holding a levee for reporters, who were all firing questions at him.

Cap in hand, Bryan took a prominent position in the midst of the circle. Johnson looked at him inquiringly. The new reporter explained that he would not try to ask anything just at that moment; he would remain after his colleagues had gone and "gather up the fragments."

"I thought that was what you were going to do at San Francisco," replied Johnson in mild surprise. San Francisco was where the Democratic Convention was to be held and Bryan was going there to raise all the Cain he could. As Johnson gazed upon him with bland innocence, Bryan for once in his life had no comeback.

CHAPTER VII

THE MIND OF THE GREAT COMMONER

It is customary to make two errors about Bryan: First, that he was the champion of the people, the voice of the masses; second, that he was high-minded in an unusual degree, a sort of modern chevalier.

He was not even the spokesman of the Middle West, as the Middle West proved on election day. The Middle West is made up of all sorts of people. The farmer is no such open-mouthed gosling as the urbanite pictures him; he is as intelligently keen on his own interests as any other man, and if he sometimes chases rainbows, why, so does the sophisticated city-dweller who could be persuaded in two elections to vote for a moronic blatherskite like Mayor Hylan of New York or an impudent and brazen fraud like Mayor Thompson of Chicago. In the long run the voter is likely to exercise good judgment. In that respect the Middle West shows up to better advantage than New York, for it never did vote for Bryan, while New York was eight years in finding Hylan out. The two were of the same stamp intellectually, hard as this saying may sound. In other respects, of course, there was not much resemblance.

Bryan lived at first in Lincoln, Nebraska, and as he grew richer bought himself a place four miles outside the city, on a hill, and named it Fairview. But he was not a typical Lincolnite, and the knowing and seasoned citizens of that up-to-date town always looked upon him as a rather queer fish, though they liked him for his personal qualities. Lincoln is far from being a "hick" town. It is above the average eastern city of its size in culture and worldly wisdom. Bryan, in his big black sombrero, driving his horse and buggy into town and passing farmer-like greetings with Tom, Dick and Harry, was a popular figure in Lincoln, and yet looked at rather quizzically as somebody a little gauche. He did not fit into the Lincoln picture.

The nickname "Main Street" is so overworked that I dislike to use it, but it portrays Bryan's mind and character. After his defeat in 1904 he went around the world. Everywhere he was received as a great American citizen. Europe and Asia turned themselves inside out for him. Every source of knowledge was at his command for the asking. He was seeing the Old World in a way to electrify the imagination of a clod. No man capable of receiving cultural impressions could have had such an experience without receiving great mental stimulation. Such a man would have broadened; and also he would have had things to say to his countrymen which would have been new to them and of value.

But Bryan wrote a book on the order of Baedeker. He could have written it without stirring from his library at Fairview. He had made his world trip without receiving a single impression. He was a progressive who never progressed—mentally. I never saw the least indication that he ever learned anything, either in Europe or at home, at any time in his mature life. As for this matter of the book, it may be said that Bryan preferred, as a politician, to keep out of print the new ideas he had received abroad. But if he kept them out of his book, he also kept them out of his conversation. He often talked about his trip, talked with exuberant pleasure, and nothing gave him more enjoyment than to take us through his home just out of Lincoln and show us the endless lot of curious and valuable presents that had been given to him by the great and less-great whom he encountered in Europe and Asia. But never, in his highest moments of delight, did he drop a word to show that he was anything more than a Cook's tourist who had had the luck to get a quantity of souvenirs.

His political maneuvers were of the cheapest order. He could not rise to anything above smart and petty tricks. Quadrennially, whenever his own nomination was not forecast, he would bring out candidates for the nomination. They were always a herd of unknowns; once a Tennessee Mayor named Head, once a North Carolina Judge named Clark, and so on almost endlessly, until in 1924 he reached his climax with a Florida college President named Murfree. To Bryan's mind this seemed a clever stratagem. Whenever he began to pull rabbits out of his hat in this conjurer fashion, the reporters would always, in a bewildered manner, try to find out what it portended; what ingenious political combination Bryan was planning. There never was any ingenious political combination, and it never portended anything. It merely represented Bryan's idea of a clever maneuver; and in every case the Convention, after trying to puzzle out his meaning, simply shrugged its shoulders, gave it up, and dismissed the subject from its mind. He never learned anything from this, of course. In the last year of his life he actually tried the same maneuver in the election of a Moderator of the Presbyterian General Assembly. The Presbyterians, as the Democrats had so long been accustomed to do, simply shrugged their shoulders and gave it up. After twenty years of failure with this pet device of his, he was still ignorant of its futility, and his friends in the General Assembly were reluctantly obliged to ride over him and leave him spread on both sides of the road.

At the Democratic Convention of 1904, after bringing out his usual parade of nonentities for several months, he turned at the last moment, the night before the Convention adjourned, to Senator Francis M. Cockrell, of Missouri. To his shallow mind this seemed the best bet, because, the Convention being in St. Louis, he thought he could stampede the galleries for a Missourian. He was not, to be sure, the only politician who never learned that stampeding the galleries has no effect on the Convention, but among all the politicians who could not rise to the height of that fact, he is the only one who has ever been thought big enough for the Presidency.

His account of this in his memoirs is curiously false. He flatly states that he had two reasons for seconding the nomination of Senator Cockrell. The first was that Cockrell endorsed his views and the second was that he was an ex-Confederate soldier and might break into the Southern delegations.

The real truth is that a plan to stop Parker with Cockrell and get him the nomination if possible had been very carefully engineered, that it did not originate with Bryan, who came into it only at the very last moment, and that the Cockrell managers relied chiefly on a stampede which was to be started by the galleries, packed with Cockrell men. It was a desperate plan, foredoomed to failure, but it was undoubtedly the best political move the opponents of Parker could make. The stampede was carefully planned, and, if it had been a stampedable Convention, should have succeeded. When Champ Clark put Cockrell in nomination, thousands of flags appeared as if by magic throughout the hall, the band broke loose, and an easy majority of the crowd filled the air with every noise that human ingenuity could invent. It was all, of course, by prearrangement. No device to set a torch to apathy and turn it into enthusiasm was neglected. The madmen who were yelling for Cockrell pervaded the floor and tried to thrust flags into the hands of Parker delegates; one of the maddest of them even rushed up to Colonel Jim Guffey with starting eyes and flushed face and tried to force a flag on him. The hard-boiled, ironclad old war-horse had some difficulty in pushing the maniac aside.

Still, this artificial stampede evoked the only real enthusiasm of the whole Convention. Bryan had kept out of it, refusing to declare for his candidate; but he was there, saw the wild demonstration, grasped at it as his last hope, and promptly sprang up and seconded the nomination. Whatever Bryan says in his memoirs, these are the facts. It is a frightful strain on the imagination to believe that when he came to the aid of Clark and the galleries he was as innocent of the situation as—twenty-one years later—he said he was.

What spoiled the stampede was the fact that the delegates were hand picked. David B. Hill and William F. Sheehan, of New York, with their Southern allies, had seen to that months before. It was the best-planned stampede since Bryan's own nomination in 1896—much better organized and thought out than Jonathan Bourne's quite similar attempt to stampede the Republican Convention of 1908 for Roosevelt. Bryan knew about the Cockrell movement long before he came flying into it at the twelfth hour, but he kept aloof from it until his eyes and ears told him that if he were to beat Parker at all, that was his only chance.

It was this inability to rise above the ground that led him to leave the camp of the Third Nebraska Regiment, of which he was Colonel in the Spanish War, and hurry to Washington to dragoon Democratic Senators into voting to ratify the peace treaty against their convictions. That treaty provided for the annexation of the Philippines, and to his opportunist mind it would provide the Democrats with a winning issue in the campaign of 1900—that of "imperialism." The election of 1896 had shown that the party was too badly split to win with free silver as the issue, and the war seemed to have providentially opened up a new one. He could not understand why some Democratic Senators balked at the treaty. Some Republican Senators did, too, and there was danger that it would not pass. So the Colonel of the Third Nebraska descended upon Washington, and cracked the whip. He could do it, because he was the leader of the Democratic Party and its destined candidate for the 1900 nomination.

This simple-minded strategy seemed Machiavellian to him. His idea was that if he could get the treaty ratified, the people would blame McKinley for it, since it was a McKinley treaty. If anybody remembered that Democrats had voted for it, the answer would be, "Why, we voted for it because it was a *peace* treaty. We wanted to end the war. We are as horrified over the new Empire as you are, but you wouldn't have us keep the country at war, would you?" He had his way, the treaty was ratified, the Philippines were annexed, we became an "Empire," and Bryan happily prepared to fight imperialism and Philippine annexation and take his seat in the White House in 1901. For a short time it was actually believed in some quarters that he had succeeded in uniting the Democrats on a winning issue and even in capturing the anti-imperialist Republicans. *The New York World,* which had consistently opposed him, printed a cartoon by the brilliant Charles G. Bush, depicting Bryan and that rock-ribbed old Republican Senator Hoar clasping hands on the new issue. Hoar was one of the Republicans who voted against the treaty.

This elation did not last long, at least among the discerning. Bryan remained happy over his great stratagem, and the "imperialism" he had done so much to plaster on the country was slated as the "paramount issue" in 1900. The Republicans did not think it so paramount as all that.

Led by Mark Hanna, they decided that the paramount issue was what they called "the full dinner pail." Perhaps the voters agreed with them. At any rate, after all his devious and wondrous strategy over the peace treaty, he got one hundred and fifty-five electoral votes to McKinley's two hundred and ninety-two—McKinley beating him nearly two to one—and was in a minority on the popular vote of nearly nine hundred thousand. Incidentally, Theodore Roosevelt became Vice-President.

The workings of Bryan's mind are illuminated by his reaction to the *Lusitania* massacre, as recorded by his wife. She says that as soon as he heard of it he exclaimed, "I wonder if that ship carried munitions of war? I will have Lansing investigate that! If she did carry them it puts a different phase on the whole matter! England has been using our citizens to protect her ammunition!"

Knowing his mental processes as I do, as I did for a quarter of a century, I recognize him instantly and thoroughly in this authentic utterance. Whatever happened, his mind immediately pounced upon it and dissected it to see if it could be made useful on his side of the political argument. If it could, it was campaign material; if not, it was not of importance. That was the microscope he applied to the *Lusitania.* In this appalling event, as in all other cases, he thought only as a partisan. Not as a Democratic partisan, understand; the country was then divided between pro-Allies and anti-Allies—pro-Germans, they were indiscriminately called then, but that word is too inclusive. Many of them merely hated England with no love for Germany, and others were pacifists of that peculiar school which knew we might get into war with Germany but hardly with the Allies, and therefore thought it safe to take the German side at every turn of the war that affected us. Bryan was a member of what may be called the Pacifist Party (since that was the real party division among Americans in 1915), and as usual with him was scrutinizing every occurrence to see how it could be turned to partisan account. His mind had been trained and focused along that line all through his adult life, and now responded promptly and almost mechanically to that stimulus. I had seen it work that way for many years, but he never summed his mind up so completely as he did in this unconscious self-revelation so eternally and damningly and faithfully reported by his adoring wife.

In 1913, when Bryan became Wilson's Secretary of State, he showed an unsuspected side of his character to the country. In fact, he showed it to his friends too, for to those who had known him longest and best he seemed to be acting directly contrary to that character. He effaced himself in Wilson's interest; he became a loyal subordinate, accepting second place cheerfully and laboring with might and main to make the Administration a success. It is chiefly due to his efforts that it was such, for the first two years. The new President was unknown to most of his party, and the legislation he recommended was squarely opposite to the ideas most of the Congress leaders held. This was particularly the case with the Federal Reserve bill. Wilson's legislative program would have been ditched in his own party if it had not been for Bryan. The Secretary not only told inquirers that he was for it; he went down to Capitol Hill and lobbied for it openly, driving his recalcitrant followers in the Senate and House into line. He whipped them into harness even for measures so repugnant to them—and, hitherto, to Bryan himself—as currency reform. In the two years that followed, ending with Bryan's resignation from the Cabinet, Wilson became a definite personality and acquired a following of his own; he no longer needed Bryan's aid; but his initial successes were due to the intervention of Bryan, to Bryan's interpretation of him to the critical and suspicious party leaders. But for Bryan he might have had to face a party as divided as did Cleveland in 1893, and might have seen his Administration wrecked from the outset as Cleveland's was.

Bryan hoped to make an enduring name for himself as Secretary of State. In the years that had elapsed since he was Colonel of the Third Nebraska he had become an ardent pacifist, and he dreamed of going into history with a title greater than that of any other statesman who ever lived—for such, surely, would have been the meed of the man who abolished war. That mind of his, strong but not broad, saw everything as simple, not as complex. Is there a wrong? Why, then, abolish it; it is as simple as A B C. War is wrong; therefore let us stop it. How? Why, get everybody to agree never to fight without taking a year to think it over. And he busied himself drafting and negotiating treaties with all the world promising to adopt this certain and simple remedy. The "glorified circuit rider" was at the head of the State Department of the United States. If anybody had suggested to him that there were some nations which no treaty could bind, he would have answered, in the style of the prayer-meeting exhorter, "Ah! I have a higher faith in human nature." So he worked on happily, building himself his niche in the temple of fame, and meanwhile the greatest war in history broke out.

One month after the sinking of the *Lusitania* Bryan left the Cabinet, saddened but not disillusioned. When he had been Secretary of State two months he said he would not have taken office "if I thought there was to be a war during my Administration." It was a little more than a year before Serajevo. "I believe," he added, "there will be no war while I am Secretary of State, and I believe there will be no war so long as I live." It did not come out that way; it might so easily have come out that way if only Germany had signed that peace treaty of his! Then, of course, she would not have been able to attack France. But he was not disillusioned; nothing could ever disillusion him; his ideal was always just a day or two ahead of him. One more effort, my friends, and we shall grasp it at last!

> "Forward, on the same old journey, let us follow
> where she leads,
> Let us chase the beckoning glory of the Vision that
> Recedes."

But if there was a comical wistfulness about Secretary Bryan's statesmanship, there was a comical tawdriness about the political side of his activities. The plague of office-seekers that fell like a cloud of bats on Washington when the first Democratic Administration since Cleveland's was inaugurated appalled and disgusted most of Wilson's Cabinet, but not Bryan; he enjoyed it. He reveled in it. He was in his element. There were two sides to the job of Secretary of State, but in Bryan's mind the duties of statesman were evidently wholly subordinate to those of patronage dispenser. Eighty-odd years before a similar swarm of the hungry and thirsty had befallen Washington, and the new Administration's stalwart defender, Senator William L. Marcy, had said, to prudes who groaned about it, "They" (the Jackson Democracy) "see nothing wrong in the rule that to the victors belong the spoils of the enemy." That sentence and all it meant politically had been harped on so constantly for eight decades that in 1913 the successors of Jackson and Marcy were sensitive about it. It was no longer fashionable to be a spoilsman. But though Wilson and most of the new Cabinet were tender on the subject, Bryan was not. He took to the situation like a duck to water. He was having the time of his life.

I am not imagining Bryan's state of mind or trying to reconstruct it from the evidence, for I saw it in operation. I was with him in Washington daily and never saw a man so happy in the benevolent exercise of power. Lest it may be thought I am viewing him through the mists of memory, I copy something I wrote at the time for *The New York Times*. It incidentally gives an idea of what that pestilence of office-seekers was. It may be supposed that every new Administration has to encounter such a flood of appetites, but it is not so. It drove Lincoln wild, and angered and worried Cleveland, and William Henry Harrison died of it in a month; but such ferocity of onset is not the rule. What I wrote was this, and I wrote it after Bryan had been Secretary of State a week:

"Yes, yes, there is a little bit of a crowd in the White House these days—about a hundred a minute. Also there are crowds in the anterooms of the various Cabinet officers, each unit of the multitude elbowing his neighbor and looking askance as if to say, 'Who is this person?' But neither in the White House nor in any Cabinet office east of Seventeenth Street is there any such crowd as is gathered in the office of William J. Bryan, Secretary of State.

"Secretary Bryan has had no chance to eat comfortably or sleep creditably or give a thought to the problems before the State Department. [The gravest of the problems was left on his door-step; Madero had been murdered a few days earlier, and the whole world was watching anarchic Mexico with anxiety.] Even the surging multitude at the doors of the White House is a mere handful compared with that which swarms at the doors of the Secretary of State.

"Senator Tillman yesterday made a Biblical quotation with regard to the horde of office-seekers. It was as follows:

" 'The wild asses of the desert are athirst and hungry; they have broken into the green corn.'

"Today Senator Tillman came into Secretary Bryan's office and saw on one side of his desk a crowd of office-seekers and on the other a group of reporters. He glanced over both groups and then turned to the Secretary with a quizzical smile. 'When I said that thing yesterday, Bryan,' he said, 'I didn't know you had two herds of wild asses to handle.'

"The Secretary grinned. So did the reporters, but the office-seekers looked serious. It is fair to say, however, that the crowd which fills every moment is not wholly made up of office-seekers. There are many men in Washington who followed Mr. Bryan through his campaigns, and before they leave town they want to call on him and congratulate him. Besides the men who want a job in the State Department and know they must see the Secretary himself to get it, there is the great army of those who do not want a job in the State Department but do want one somewhere else, and who have the idea that Mr. Bryan's voice will be potent in their behalf if they can get him to raise it. These three main divisions make up the mass which clogs his doorway and makes it impossible for even Senators and Representatives to see him, even such men as his old running-mate John W. Kern.

"It is no wonder that he sends out dispatches indorsing Henry Lane Wilson without reading them. [Henry Lane Wilson was the American Ambassador to Mexico, holding over from Taft's Administration; the Wilson régime was at loggerheads with him, and Bryan had aroused the country's wonder and laughter by signing an indorsement. It turned out that he had not read it.] The wonder is that he has time to read anything whatever, or to know what he is signing. The man who invented the word 'busy' had never heard of William Jennings Bryan."

It was not Bryan's delight in the congenial job of pap-dispenser which disgusted the country, but the way he dispensed it. His letter ordering a subordinate in the West Indies to find jobs for "deserving Democrats," and many other illustrations of his obtuseness to the public interests when there were handouts to be had for the faithful, are well enough remembered. But what has not attracted so much attention is his idea of a "deserving Democrat." A deserving Democrat was a man who had done something for Bryan. This might have been a pleasant exhibition of gratitude, if Bryan had been rewarding the deserving incompetent—and incompetent they often were, but it made no difference to him—out of his own pocket. But he was rewarding them out of the taxpayer's pocket, and that, as Abe said to Mawruss, is something else again. The taxpayer, the man who paid the bills, had no reason to feel gratitude toward the deserving Democrat, whether Bryan had or not. If a Democrat, the taxpayer might have had the comfort of feeling that his money was at least going into the pocket of a fellow-partisan who had earned reward; but this poor consolation was denied him. The deserving Democrat was not being rewarded for service to the party, but for personal service to the Secretary of State.

These appointments showed no relation between the recipient and the duties he was to perform, and so many of the deserving Democrats were grotesquely miscast. In the State Department at Washington Bryan placed a deserving Democrat whose duties were such as to make him Bryan's intermediary and representative with Senators and Ambassadors. The man, however, was an uncouth, mannerless, mentally inadequate individual whose gaucheries in dealing with diplomats and statesmen caused American onlookers, proud of their country, to writhe and tingle.

His appointment sheds much light on Bryan's character. In 1896, when Bryan invaded what he called "the enemy's country" and tried to convert the East to free silver, he had rough going in some places. At Ithaca, New York, a crowd of Cornell students attended his meeting with intent to break it up. Their method was to raise such a din of discourteous noises that he could not finish a sentence; and each noise was introduced by one of those disconcerting questions which youth is adept in inventing for the discomfiture of its elders. Not all the Cornell boys approved; some of them even tried to get a hearing for Byran. Seventeen years later, when Bryan was in a position to reward his friends at government expense, he sought out the leader of these friendly youths of 1896 and gave him the best job he could find in the State Department.

It showed a long memory for favors. But it was regrettable that Bryan did not reward the man with a job where he would be out of sight. The years had not dealt softly with him. He was not a shining success in life; he was not the sort of man to go out from the university and conquer the world, or to make a Henry Ford anxious over the advent of a dangerous competitor. It was nice of Bryan to reward him,—or to compel the taxpayer to reward him,—but he could have found a less conspicuous place. That he did not is simply due to the fact that Bryan did not see anything unpresentable about the man. He seemed all right to Bryan. This fact reveals the quality of Bryan's mind.

The atmosphere in the State Department under him was cheap and vulgar. There was no dignity. The place resembled a county campaign headquarters, not one in New York or even in Akron, but in the foot-hills of the Ozarks. Foreign Ambassadors who had to go there never got over the novelty of being received by a coatless, vestless Secretary of State, who gestured at them with his inseparable palm-leaf fan while he talked. His subordinates presented a similarly disorderly appearance, especially that official who had championed him at Cornell in 1896. The office which Root, Hay, Olney, Blaine and Seward had made impressive in appearance as well as in reality was filled with streams of "deserving Democrats" clamoring for offices and favors.

The Secretary's dealings with diplomats were unconventional. A single example: Once Mr. Takahira, the Japanese

Ambassador, came to the department to see him, but another diplomat was in conference with him at the time and Takahira had to wait. When the other diplomat was ushered out, Bryan, handkerchief in collar, opened the door and bawled out to Eddie Savoy, the colored doorkeeper who had served such dignified gentlemen as John Hay, "Eddie, show the Jap in!" Not a quiver of a muscle showed that Takahira heard, if he did; his face was as impassive as that of the long-suffering Eddie, a diplomat himself and now past the stage of being astonished at anything in this strange new world in which his new chief had placed him.

When he made himself famous in an hour with his cross-of-gold speech, he dazzled the eyes of millions who saw in him a man inspired. Even his adversaries, who were venomous, looked on him as a star-eyed crusader, and wondered angrily at the source of the inspiration. The universal belief, that of friends and foes alike, was that the young man had gone to the Convention with no expectation of the nomination, had been roused by the effort of the gold men to override the West, had flamed into indignant eloquence, and had been rewarded by a nomination as surprising to himself as it was to the country. We know better now. Bryan himself, in his memoirs, frankly tells how he attended the Republican Convention, held earlier, "ostensibly in the character of a newspaper man," but "as a matter of fact" to collaborate with Senator Teller, Senator Pettigrew, and the other Silver Republican leaders who subsequently nominated Bryan for President on a third party ticket, after the Democrats had made him their candidate.

The Cross of Gold, so long imagined to be spontaneous, was a mosaic of smart sentences which for years he had observed were successful in catching the ears of the crowd. Other sentences, not so successful, he had discarded. He had carefully noted his most telling phrases—he could do so by repeating them to his audiences and seeing which ones were most effective—and made a private anthology of them. Now he collected and rearranged the gems in his collection, added a few more phrases, and stampeded the Convention. In his memoirs he calls the speech extemporaneous, but is honest enough to add, "That is, extemporaneous insofar as its arrangement was concerned." What he means by this is shown by an equally candid sentence, "I fitted my definition of the business man at the place that I thought best and kept my cross of gold and crown of thorns for the conclusion."

In the minds of Bryan's worshipers he was a stainless knight heroically battling against the bosses, who to them were the personification of evil. I never was able myself to see wherein their deviltry consisted. They played politics with their cards close to their chests, but so did Bryan. However, this likeness was withheld from the eyes of his idolators, who regarded him not as a politician but as a man sent of God. The three great bosses of the Democratic Party were Roger Sullivan, of Illinois, Thomas Taggart, of Indiana, and Charles F. Murphy, of New York, and to the pro-Bryan mind these three were children of Belial against whom the noble Commoner was waging a war of extinction.

But when Bryan emerged from Lincoln for a quick trip to Chicago, it occurred to an alert editorial mind on *The Evening Post* of that city to wonder if it could be possible that he had come there to see the iniquitous Roger Sullivan, the great boss of Illinois. It seemed a wild, crazy speculation, and yet—— And yet, if by a hundred-to-one shot it happened, how interesting it would be. Editors learn that nothing is impossible, and this is why weary reporters, sent out on wild-goose chases, curse the editorial tribe. The editorial mind on *The Evening Post* beckoned to Percy Hammond, and a moment later Hammond was grouchily making his way to Bryan's hotel. This is the same Hammond who now (1928) adds such brilliancy to *The New York Herald-Tribune* as its dramatic critic.

Bryan himself opened the door of his room, and when Hammond asked if he had seen Boss Sullivan, the Commoner answered in his splendid baritone, "No, I have not seen him. And what is more, I will not see him." He then closed the door, but Hammond did not go away. He was too good a reporter. Instead, he picked out a window-seat at the end of the corridor, pulled a book out of his pocket, and settled down to while away the evening in reading. In about ten minutes Bryan's door again opened, and the wicked Sullivan slipped out of it and hurried away.

In the campaign of 1908, when Bryan and Taft were running against each other for the Presidency, I was in Lincoln as correspondent of *The New York World.* One night I was called to the telephone in my hotel room, and found that the call was from Bryan, speaking from his home four miles away. He was cautious until he made sure it was I, and then turned loose. After first pledging me to secrecy, he told me he had something on his opponent, Secretary Taft. It was to the effect that while Governor General of the Philippines Mr. Taft had been a grafter. Bryan gave me all the details and felt sure it would make a big "story." But aside from getting it into print, his main anxiety was that nobody should suspect the "tip" had come from him. He kept impressing this on me until I could hardly speak to him politely. Over and over again he explained his plan for keeping his own authorship of the story dark. It was that I should print it, not as a dispatch from Lincoln—for in that case he probably would be suspected—but as a local New York story, supposed to come from some unnamed New Yorker who was conversant with conditions in the Philippines.

I did not write it. I did not even inform *The World* privately that such a story had ever been suggested to me. To Bryan's small-caliber mind it seemed a great opportunity, and he picked *The World* out as the medium for this underhand assault on his square and honest rival because *The World* was the only important New York newspaper which in that campaign was supporting him for the Presidency.

ROOSEVELT

CHAPTER VIII

WHERE MACGREGOR SITS, THERE IS THE HEAD OF THE TABLE

WHEN Roosevelt died there was a feeling—one noticed it everywhere in the week following his death—which, strangely enough, had to wait for an Englishman to put it into words. The Englishman was "E. T. Raymond," (Edward Raymond Thompson, editor of *The London Standard*) and his words were: "Mr. Roosevelt, a very human type, had many enemies, but also hosts of friends who felt for him as Bardolph for Falstaff—'would God I were with him.'" He was writing particularly of Roosevelt's lifetime, but it was actually true of his death; there were many who in that week felt about Roosevelt in the identical sense in which Bardolph meant the words.

When Daniel Webster died, Charles Graham Halpine (afterward celebrated as "Private Miles O'Reilly") wrote a poem, the last verse of which is:

"Gone! We are like old men whose infant eyes
Familiar grew with some vast pyramid;
Even as we gaze, earth yawns, and it is hid—
A long, wide desert mocks the empty skies."

There never was precisely that feeling from the time of Webster's death to the time of Roosevelt's.

No man could meet Roosevelt and go on hating him; that is, of course, unless he met him in a fight. During the

Barnes-Roosevelt libel trial in Syracuse, I ran across James J. Montague, who was then a reporter on a highly anti-Roosevelt newspaper, walking up and down a hotel lobby and cursing. I asked him what moved him to these expletives. "Roosevelt, damn him," exploded Montague, jerking a shoulder to the Colonel's unconscious figure on a settee: "I can't keep hating him if I get within twenty feet of him, and, damn it, I'm always forgetting and doing it accidentally. He's spoiling my story."

The Colonel never won over any antagonist by blandishment. On the day he died I wrote: "He was often said to have 'used' the reporters, especially the Washington correspondents. Well, if he used them it was by an old magic, with no black art in it. He never flattered or palavered or went out of his way. I knew him very well for many years, and he was always the same to everybody. I saw the magic in action; it was the magic that can only be conjured with by a large, joyous and generous soul with real manliness at the back of it. And something else, which I can best express by saying that no man who knew Roosevelt would have been willing to let the Colonel know that he had done something mean or dirty. But no man could use that magic as Roosevelt could. Men loved to be put under that spell; and there will be many sore hearts for the lack of it now."

Voluminously as he spoke and wrote, the power of his words was astounding. I mean their practical power, their power to do work. He knew this power of his, as he knew all his powers, measured it and counted on it.

In 1912, when he was the Progressive candidate for President, he went on a month-long swing around the circle. His special train was crossing Illinois on its western way when it was boarded by some Progressive leaders, whose mission was to get the Colonel to swerve off to Chicago and make a speech. The Colonel refused; his itinerary was made up, the whole weight of the campaign rested on his single personality, he could not personally cover the whole country and had to go where he could do the most good. Illinois was safe.

The Progressive leaders explained the situation in Illinois. It was safe for Roosevelt, but unsafe for the Progressive candidate for Governor, Frank Funk. The Republicans were spreading the story that Funk had been a supporter of Lorimer, the disgraced Senator who had been the center of a vote-buying scandal and whose name was anathema to the liberal element in the State. The story was doing Funk so much harm that his chances were growing slimmer all the time, and despite the most vigorous counter-propaganda the truth did not seem to be making any headway. The Colonel was immovable. "But," he said, "without going to Chicago I will fix that matter all right for Funk."

The next stop was a "rear-end" stop; that is, a brief pause at a little hamlet, where the Colonel would come out on the rear platform and talk for three or four minutes to the villagers, just that they might see him. There were perhaps a hundred or two at this place. The Colonel had time to speak only a few sentences before the train started. He spoke in generalities, and then, just as the train began to move, he called out as if it were an after-thought:

"And while you're voting for me, don't forget to vote for Frank Funk, the most vigorous, honest, and relentless opponent that Lorimer ever had."

That was all. The train pulled out, the little crowd cheering the Colonel, who waved his sombrero till they were out of sight. "Now," said he, turning to the crestfallen Progressives, "you'll find that not another word will be said from any source about Funk being a Lorimer man." Naturally, they could not believe him. But it was true. The offhand sentence, tossed to a handful of people by the wayside, did what columns of argument and speeches without number from other men had failed to do. This is what I mean by the practical power of his words.

This was not due to his position. It was due to the force of his personality. In any scene where he appeared, he was remembered afterward and the others were forgotten. While he was there, he was seen and the others were eclipsed. In 1910, when the whole country was agog over the great prize-fight between Jack Johnson and Jim Jeffries, *Puck* published a cartoon by the younger Keppler, entitled "If Roosevelt Should Go to the Fight." It pictured the immense arena, with the thousands of fight fans. Far down was the ring, so distant that the two pugilists looked like dwarfs. Away off in the rear of the vast crowd was Roosevelt in an obscure seat; and the limelight was on him, not the fighters, and everybody was looking at him.

In 1915 I was at Sagamore Hill with George Meyer, the ex-Secretary of the Navy. In the course of the afternoon Meyer picked up a book and began turning the pages, while Roosevelt and I talked on. Presently we got on the subject of the celebrated libel suit, which William Barnes, the Republican boss, had brought against him.

Meyer looked up from his book.

"By the way," he said, "it's funny, but I've forgotten how that case came out."

"Why, I won it," said the Colonel.

"Oh, I know that," said Meyer, "but I can't remember how much damages you got."

The Colonel regarded him with a look of fatherly benignity. "Would you mind saying that again, George?" he inquired, in a soft, purring, silky sort of voice. Innocently, but uneasily, Meyer repeated it. The Colonel walked over to him and placed his hand, with a look of infinite pity, on Meyer's head.

"My dear fel-low," he said, parting his syllables with great care and speaking as one who instructs a very backward urchin, "*I* was the de-*fend*-ant."

Still, I could not blame Meyer. Roosevelt had so dominated the trial with his personality, had swept Judge, jury and spectators with him so irresistibly, that Barnes did seem not to be the plaintiff, but a careless fellow who had been foolish enough to get in Roosevelt's way when the Colonel was in a hurry.

Many people imagined that Roosevelt was rash in his talk, given to reckless, impulsive, unpremeditated statements. No man ever counted the effect of his words more closely or knew more exactly the precise weight of each one of them. As his slightest word was sure to be pounced upon, dissected, and, if possible, distorted, he could not be careless and be safe. He spoke with heat and violence, to be sure, but that is not the same thing as rashness or recklessness. A man may be violently accurate.

Anyway, he was; and this set pitfalls for many commentators on him, who kept falling into them with regularity as long as he lived. They saw the violence and assumed the rashness, and had fully committed themselves to the assertion that he was wrong or mendacious before they found out that he had been exactly right.

In the heat of a campaign the Colonel made some remarks on certain inequalities and injustices in the law. He was not a lawyer, and the first response was a chorus of derision at the expense of this would-be expert on matters beyond his knowledge. Then came a settler. Simeon E. Baldwin, the Chief Judge of the highest court in Connecticut, a lawyer of national reputation, issued a statement, calm and judicial in tone, declaring that Colonel Roosevelt's version of the law on that subject was entirely wrong.

Then what a chorus of jubilation over the rash meddler

who hung his mouth on a hair trigger and let it go off by itself. The Colonel repeated, with somewhat more emphasis, his original statement of the law. More jeers; here was an amateur actually entering the lists on a question of law with one of the most eminent Judges in America. The laughter was Homeric. But within a few days Judge Baldwin voluntarily issued another statement, saying that on further examination of the point of law in question he had found that he was wrong and Colonel Roosevelt right. It was an awful moment. The only thing to do was to bury Judge Baldwin's honorable confession on the inside pages under an unobtrusive caption, but the chorus of jeers dropped so dead that one could have heard a pin drop in the dense, opaque silence.

He was called impulsive, and I have no doubt that by nature he was; but he had this trait, if it was indeed his, so thoroughly under control that he never said a public word or did a public act from impulse. I say this deliberately after searching a memory of Roosevelt that goes back to the Spanish War. To understand him one must bear in mind the fact that he had made himself over; he was, in an entirely new sense, a self-made man. He was a weak puny boy and youth. He resolved to make himself not merely a strong big man, but a man surpassing most others in size, strength, and the ability to use this strength in a great variety of directions; and he did this. Similarly he resolved to bend his mind in the direction in which it ought to go, and he did that, too. He could not make for himself a new mind, as he virtually made for himself a new body, but he planned out coolly for himself the limitations and the expansions which that mind should manifest in action, and he accomplished that feat as he accomplished the other. He could not cut impulsiveness out of his nature, but he could so control it that it should never influence his actions; and in the same way he organized his mind in every direction, just as he had organized his once weak body.

If one reflects that Roosevelt could not have been over twenty-one when he thus set about the reorganization of his mind and body, one must be astonished at the concentration of will and energy which such a decision and its inveterate fulfillment show.

There were, no doubt, times when Roosevelt's action in a given case seemed impulsive, but that was because of the startling suddenness with which the thing was done; it had been carefully weighed and calculated before he sprang it on the public. We all know now that that was the case with the "grabbing," as his opponents called it, of the Panama Canal Zone, which seemed to thousands to be the sudden outbreak of an enraged child. Well, if we know it in that case we can assume it in others; but, as a matter of fact, we do not need to assume it. It is simply a fact.

If this is misunderstood to mean that Roosevelt staged his plays in advance for mere dramatic effect the misunderstanding must be willful. Wilson was praised for thinking out his moves in advance—it being assumed that he did so. By the same token it is no discredit to Roosevelt if he thought out his moves in advance; and he most certainly did so. The difference lay in the fact that whether Wilson thought out his moves in advance or not, and there were assuredly occasions when he did not, he always seemed to do it, while Roosevelt, by his dashing way of doing the thing, seemed to his contemporaries not to have thought of it at all.

It is true that Roosevelt is better understood now than he was in his lifetime, but the old errors about him still persist, and are repeated so often that if they are not unremittingly scotched they will get into history and mislead it. As I write these lines I have just read a book that came out in March, 1928. It is by a responsible and well-known writer,

M. R. Werner, and is a history of Tammany Hall. In a chapter dealing with De Witt Clinton he endeavors to explain that statesman's character, and says, "He was brusque, sometimes haughty, and inclined to lose patience with those who disagreed with him on abstract questions. In general character he resembled the late Theodore Roosevelt." If Clinton's "general character" is correctly described here, he did not merely fail to resemble Theodore Roosevelt; he was the direct antithesis, the polar opposite, of Theodore Roosevelt. Roosevelt was never haughty, he was never brusque except in a fight, and he was patience itself with those who disagreed with him not only on abstract but concrete questions. No man ever lived more ready to be shown that he was wrong. Since this old misconception persists, and persists in books intended to be historical, it is a duty to that too-confiding Muse to set her right.

It belongs to this side of his character that he was never interviewed, in any proper sense. That significant fact will give an idea of how thoroughly his governed mind controlled his warmth of temperament. (Nothing is harder than to avoid being interviewed; the temptations are too much for almost everybody.) He gave out many statements, some of them in the form of interviews, and sometimes, too, he was actually interviewed, but in such cases he always directed the form the interview should take. Now, a real interview is an unpremeditated thing, in which the reporter asks what questions he pleases, and takes the answers with merciless accuracy. There is no escape even in saying, "I refuse to answer that question," for that sentence may have a world of significance if the question is rightly framed. The best type of the real interview is the colloquy between reporter and public man in a railroad station as the public man gets off the train. It may be short, but it is spontaneous and revealing. No one ever heard of an interview being given by Roosevelt as he got off a train or entered a hotel corridor—unless it was something he had determined to say, like the famous "My hat is in the ring," and then he never said one word more than he had already decided to say. All this, though no man ever talked more freely to reporters—not for publication.

Editors seemed never to learn of this peculiarity, and continually sent reporters to interview him. The Colonel never responded unless he had thought what he wanted to say and wanted it published. He could not be badgered or worried into an interview, he had himself under an iron control, no matter how exasperating or exciting the state of affairs might be. Impulsive? The thousand reporters who have tried to catch Roosevelt off guard and make him say something he did not expect to say will laugh at that idea. Yet no doubt his naturally impulsive nature was all the time beating vainly against the stone wall of his will.

And he never was trapped into uttering that sentence that has damned so many who have used it, "I refuse to answer." If a question came that would have jammed the works, he would explain candidly but confidentially why he could not answer it, make the reporter see his position, and neither the question nor the avoidance would be printed.

Furthermore, he would not talk freely, even under the seal of secrecy, with reporters he did not know. The extent of the acquaintance might be short, for among the qualities the determined youth had forced to full growth in the character of the man was a powerful faculty of appraisal. He could size a man up very quickly. There was something psychic about the way he could tell, on almost no acquaintance, whether a new reporter would fit in with what he called the "Oyster Bay atmosphere." That atmosphere was a very real thing—almost tangible. It consisted in mutual respect, confidence and friendliness.

I wish to emphasize that word "friendliness," for it bears hard on another quality of Roosevelt. He was the most democratic of men, and many were shocked by what they considered the undignified demonstration of this democracy, as in slang phrases, or shaking hands with the engineer and telling him that he had made a bully run. But the Colonel had his own notion of dignity, and any one who crossed the boundary of that dignity did so at his peril. People who thought his democracy meant that he had no care for what he considered his dignity never made the mistake twice, for they never had the chance. He never forgot that he had been for seven years the head of the Nation, and he never did or permitted an act that conflicted, in his opinion, with that fact.

A new reporter was added to the Oyster Bay contingent, just as the Presidential campaign of 1912 was closing, and went with the rest of us to Sagamore Hill to see the Colonel on the eve of election. The Colonel, as he came into the room, looked at the new man with a glance which meant nothing to the latter, but was full of meaning to the rest of us. It was the appraising look, and the first report it brought back to the Colonel's mind was unfavorable. The expression that came over his face was the one we recognized as distrustful; and when he spoke, his tone had a certain restraint in it.

The new arrival did not take long in fixing the Colonel's opinion. Throwing one leg over the other, for he had read much of Roosevelt's democracy and knew from his reading how much the Colonel would enjoy a free-and-easy, hail-fellow-well-met salutation, the misguided man said:

"Going to vote the Democratic ticket on election day, Colonel?"

There was a brief blaze behind the Colonel's glasses. After a moment he requested, in his grimmest voice, that the question be repeated. The newcomer repeated it, with a little less confidence.

"I have come here to answer any sensible questions that may be put to me," said the Colonel, in a hammer-like tone, "but I have not come here to answer any idiotic questions."

That was the end of the interview. We all knew there was not a word to be got out of the Colonel while the newcomer was there. Lucius Curtis of the Associated Press asked a formal, genial question for the purpose of covering our retreat, got a pleasant answer, and we all bade him good night and went out. There was a taxicab outside, and in it was the newcomer's wife. He had brought her up so that after he had got acquainted with the Colonel and had got real chummy with him, he might bring her in and introduce her. It was really a sad and tragic thing. "What did I do to offend him?" he kept saying over and over.

Later on, together with Curtis and Jack Pratt of *The New York American,* I went back to Sagamore Hill and was received by the Colonel with open arms. "But that new fellow won't do," he said. "I felt creepy as soon as I saw him. I knew right away he didn't have the Oyster Bay atmosphere and couldn't get it. I don't care whether a man is for me or against me: I don't care whether he even dislikes me personally, so long as he has the Oyster Bay atmosphere. Now, you take D——. He's been here six months. He is a violent Democratic partisan just from the South, and had been trained to regard me as a limb of Satan. He came here hating the assignment and full of prejudice against me. So far as I know he's never gotten over it. But you have seen how welcome I've made him, and how I have confided important political secrets to him. It's because, as soon as I met him, I knew he was an honorable, high-minded gentleman, with sense and judgment, and would fit right in with the Oyster Bay atmosphere."

As he talked on Curtis, Pratt and I were staring in astonishment. As he finished Pratt gave an amazed yell. "Why, Colonel," he cried, "how under heaven did you know all that about D——? We've never given a hint of it. In fact, when he came here he bound us not to let you suspect it, because he thought it would prejudice you against him and cramp his work."

The Colonel smiled amiably. "Oh, I usually know those things," he said.

He did, too. Five or six years before, when he was President and I was Washington correspondent of *The New York Times,* I left that paper to take charge of *The New York World's* Washington bureau. As I went to the White House I debated with myself uneasily how I should tell the President about it. *World* correspondents did not go to the White House any more. He and *The World* were at swords' points; *The World* was conducting a furious campaign against him, and that very week was industriously trying to convince its readers that he had gone mad and was headed straight for an insane asylum. He was bitter against the paper,—in fact, a few months later he was trying his hardest to put Joseph Pulitzer behind the bars,—and I felt it my duty to warn him to be careful what he said, since I was now employed by his worst enemy. I was going to open the conversation with this confession, but I never got a chance; he began talking in his most explosive manner the moment he came into the room, and to my horror he dashed into the most confidential revelations. I tried several times to break in, but he steamed ahead, growing every minute franker and franker, opening to me wider and wider vistas of his confidence.

Finally, to my astonishment, I heard him say, ". . . of course, what I've been telling you is not exactly in accordance with the view your people on *The World* take of——"

I cut in, with the same astonishment Pratt displayed five years later at Sagamore Hill. "Good Lord!" I cried. "How did you know I was on *The World?* I've been trying to tell you that for fifteen minutes."

He smiled wisely. "I knew you had," he answered. "As for how I know it, I know those things."

The reason Pratt, Curtis and I went back to Sagamore Hill without the others was that they had elected us. We three happened to be on closer terms with Roosevelt than any of the others, and so they picked us out to represent them and see if the newcomer's catastrophe had left any permanent ill effects. The others preferred to have us as envoys until things had quieted down. As we went back to Oyster Bay we debated how we should break the news to the child of misfortune that he couldn't go to Sagamore with us any more, because, of course, though the Colonel would receive him, not a scrap of news would come our way while he was in the room. But he saved us the trouble. He was still shivering from his experience, and begged us to do the interviewing in future. The Colonel knew that we would give the new man whatever news we got from him; he had no objection to that; he just didn't want the man around.

Here is another illustration of what I mean by the democratic Colonel's care of his dignity. When Roosevelt sued the Michigan editor, Newett, for libel, Newett having charged him with drunkenness, Newett threw up the sponge as soon as the Colonel's witnesses had finished, offered none of his own, retracted the libel and apologized in court. The Colonel immediately announced in court that he would waive the ten thousand dollars damages he was suing for, and by his request the jury awarded him the stock damages of six cents. I went over to where the Colonel was receiving congratulations, added mine, and said, "Are you and Newett going to meet?"

The Colonel looked me over with an expression that was at first surprised and then slightly sardonic.

"Not if the advances are to come from *me,"* he said.

Perhaps I lay too much emphasis on Roosevelt's idea of his dignity. If so, it is only because the conception of his democracy as comprising a rough-and-ready, slap-on-the-back carelessness of what was due him has been so wide-spread. It was the crowds that called him "Teddy"—not even his relatives called him anything but "Theodore." In the days of his intimacy with Taft it was "Will" (not Bill) on his part and "Theodore" on Taft's; although I do remember just one occasion in the White House when Taft, then Secretary of War, started to enter the room and then, seeing others present, drew back. "Come in, Big Bill," cried the President, stepping forward and drawing Taft's arm through his own. But this was a novelty, such a novelty that it surprised Taft, who gave a shout of laughter at hearing the President echo the nickname which the papers had already given him.

No, his democracy was the true sort. It was not indiscriminate, and there was an aristocracy to which he paid tribute in his own mind—the aristocracy of Worth. Where he did not find it he was never at ease; he could use unworthy men (not for unworthy purposes, however) in the vast continental game of politics he played, as a party leader must, but never without contempt, and he always felt happy when he could get rid of them. A President or the leader of a national party must work with such instruments as the people choose to give him in Senate, House and party machine, and the people do not always pick out saints.

It was his keenest joy to find this aristocracy of Worth in what to most people would be unexpected quarters. When he found it, he recognized an equal, whether the man was a wolf-killer, a cowboy, or a statesman. Neither did he care if public opinion were set against the man's worth, so long as he himself had found it. He did not care much, as a rule, for political bosses; but he was not afraid, in defiance of the universal opinion, to tell of the fine qualities of Matthew Stanley Quay, the incarnation of bossism and machine government. A point to be noticed is that he did this years after Quay's death, when there was nothing whatever to be gained by it and something to lose.

It was always strange to me to see how the solemn profundities and the unco' guid among our varied population used to regard this trait of his as something discreditable to him. He received visits from John L. Sullivan at the White House! He entertained Booker Washington at the White House! and Jack Abernathy! He counted among his friends Archbishop Ireland—for political purposes, of course—and Viscount Bryce and Sir Cecil Spring-Rice; and Bill Sewall! He was a friend of boxers and actors! With what a sneer would they pronounce the words "Jack Abernathy, a wolf-killer," and "Bill Sewall, a guide," in listing Roosevelt's friends. Mean minds, incapable of imagining that a man would do anything except for advantage, cast about for Roosevelt's motive. It must be that he had a motive; by which they meant a selfish one. They hit on it—it was spectacular drama to impress the crowd, or demagogic ostensible democracy to get votes. It was not possible to suppose that he actually liked these boxers and wolf-killers and reporters and wanted to be with them.

They would have been still more scandalized if they had heard something he once said to me at a time when a steady stream of corporation magnates was flowing in at the White House doors.

"It tires me to talk to rich men. You expect a man of millions, the head of a great industry, to be a man worth hearing; but as a rule they don't know anything outside their own business. You would be astonished to know how small their range is and how little they can talk about that an intelligent person wants to hear.

"They're not all of that kind, of course. There's ——, and ——, and —— [he mentioned the names of three railroad Presidents], who are well-read men and have studied life besides. But take the run of them, and they're just about what I have described. I have to see them, but I don't enjoy their company."

And he turned with relief to Jacob Riis and Bill Sewall, who had studied life in their so different ways and could tell him things. When he first chummed with Riis, Riis was a humble reporter and he was President of the New York Police Board. Their friendship ended only with Riis's death.

Therefore, I wondered much at the mean-minded who could find fault with this side of his nature. But I had long noticed that the men who hated him for any cause were generally petty, and their real grievance, if they had known it, was that they were not capable of understanding him. That, indeed, is the chief reason why he was continually surprising them. He "was always doing something unexpected," which meant that he was always doing something unexpected by those who had charted his course for him by the mean motives they supposed were actuating him. They reasoned that in his place they would do so-and-so. He did exactly the opposite, because he was not actuated by the motives that would have actuated them had they been in his place; and that, of course, surprised them. To the day of his death he kept astonishing the Oswald Garrison Villards.

Thus and not otherwise did he acquire his power of frightening the Republican leaders into believing that he could do miracles; that he had an uncanny power. It ought, for instance, to have been as plain as the nose on one's face that he could not be nominated in the Republican Convention of 1916; that he could not even muster a respectable vote there. But he allowed the use of his name as a candidate,—indeed, he took delight in encouraging it, though he had not the remotest intention of running,—and instantly the politicians were thrown into fits of panic. They never had understood the source of his miracles, but they were sure he had done them and could do them; therefore the impossibility, a "Roosevelt stampede," seemed possible to them.

That was because they never doubted that he was actually a candidate. But he was not. His purpose was simply to frighten the bosses into saving the good name of the Republican Party by coming out for "preparedness and Americanism," by rousing the country out of its happy sloth, the work nearest to his heart and for which in those months he had made that marvelous speaking tour from East to West. He wanted to scare the ostriches into taking their heads out of the sand and looking up at the storm. He wanted to accomplish that feat because he loved his country. And, casting about in their lesser minds for a motive, they never hit on love of country as a possible one. If they had they would not have been scared. So you see they never understood Roosevelt, even up to the end.

CHAPTER IX

WHAT ROOSEVELT WAS NOT

THEODORE ROOSEVELT was bitterly hated, but the people who hated him were people who hadn't met him. He was accused of insincerity, but not by people who knew him. He was accused of opportunism—by people who did not know him. There were many who believed that his course was always dictated by a desire to get votes, but such people were not acquainted with him.

He was called a poseur, but he was a poseur in the same way that Tom Sawyer was. That is, scenery appealed to what Mark Twain called "the circus side of my nature." The people who didn't know him and who hated him were usually, when of the male sex, persons of a feminine cast, to whom the rip-roaring masculinity of Roosevelt was a continuing shock. Very few women hated him. If that seems a paradox, it isn't. And a personality that is so rip-roaringly masculine simply has to have a circus side to it.

There comes before my eyes a mental picture of a scene out at a lonely jerkwater station in Arizona. The Colonel's special train had stopped there so that a few of the Rough Riders could come to it from their ranches and shake hands with their old commander. It was at the height of a great campaign, and the itinerary was ordered from headquarters at Washington. Applications from every town and city were flooding headquarters to have Roosevelt stop and talk, if only for a minute, and most of them were being refused.

But here Roosevelt insisted, though there was not a vote to be made by it, and the train stopped in a wild-looking, desert place amid half a dozen scattered houses. The Rough Riders cantered in, some of them forty miles, and they were waiting on the plank in front of the hut that served as a railroad station when the special train puffed itself to a stop. Aside from the station agent and the Rough Riders there was not a human being in sight, nor the faintest hint of a town or village in the clear sun-dried Arizona landscape.

The moving-picture man in Roosevelt's party—whom the Colonel had frivolously christened "Movie," and also "Dare Devil Dick," his name being Richard J. Cummins—saw a great opportunity and yelled to the Colonel, who was standing in front of the hut talking to his old comrades. The Colonel turned around, saw the point, and grinned widely. His face was all aflash with animation. Turning to the astonished Rough Riders, he arranged them all in beseeming attitudes, and then, with his arm thrown around an Arizona shoulder, he began talking away like a steam engine. "Throw a little ginger in, Colonel!" shouted Movie, and the Colonel began throwing in the appropriate gestures, while Movie stood on the other side of the track grinding the crank. The picture must have indicated to those who saw it subsequently that the Colonel was recalling the brave days of '98 to his old comrades, fighting over with them the "crowded hour" in Cuba, but this is what he was saying:

"Barnes, Penrose and Smoot—do you remember that charge up San Juan?—in favor of the initiative and referendum—Jack Greenway, one of the best men in my regiment—recall of judicial decisions—the man with the muckrake—Alice in Wonderland is a great book—Bob Evans took the fleet into the Pacific——"

All this to the most furious gesticulation; any nonsense that came into his head, talked at the rate of sixty miles a minute. The Rough Riders had nothing to do but look impressed, and did it badly, the more so as we of Roosevelt's party were laughing ourselves sick behind the camera.

"That'll be a corker, Colonel," said Movie, stopping the crank, and the Colonel, released from duty, joined the rest of us in our roars of laughter. "By George!" he gasped, mopping his brow. "I haven't had so much fun in a week." If that is posing, make the most of it.

He was not a vote-hunter, except in the sense in which every man in politics must be. He never compromised a conviction for a vote. He always made it a point to denounce in its presence and to its face anything he thought wrong. If, for instance, he had been a free trader he would have picked out Pittsburgh as the place in which to denounce protection; if he had been a Ku Kluxer he would have sailed to Italy and attacked the Pope in Rome. In that sense he was less of a vote hunter than any other man I ever met in politics.

On his stumping tour, as the Bull Moose candidate for President, he never said more than a perfunctory word against the Democratic Party until he got into the South, its home, where it is not only wicked but anti-social to speak against the Democrats. His most blazing denunciations of pacifism in his great campaign for "preparedness and Americanism" early in 1916 were reserved for Henry Ford's home, Detroit, which under the leadership of its local deity was then the pacifist hotbed par excellence. It was the same on his trip abroad in 1910—not that that has anything to do with vote getting, but it shows the consistency of his character. It was in France, the paradise of the birth controllers, that he denounced race suicide, and it was in England and nowhere else that he lashed her for her vacillation in Egypt. Always he picked out sin's home town to lambaste sin. These are not the methods of a mere vote-getter. In fact, his going into the South at all in 1912 was quixotism; he knew he could not get a single electoral vote there, and the whole Progressive campaign depended on his voice reaching as many vulnerable spots as could be found. Yet he side-tracked himself into the South, for he dreamed that he could break up the one-party system there and relieve the South from an incubus; not in one campaign of course, "but," he said to me, "I have drawn the furrow, and whoever comes after me won't have to go over that furrow again."

When the Convention of 1916 was drawing near, I asked him, one night at Sagamore Hill, if he thought he had a chance at the nomination. "Not the least in the world," he said decisively. "If I had, I killed it by my tour of the West advocating preparedness and Americanism. Those issues will be taken up; but when it comes to making nominations, a Convention will always pass over the pioneer, because he has made too many enemies by his pioneering. I've been the pioneer; I have forced those issues to the front, and even if the Convention adopts them, it will nominate somebody else who is safer. It's the invariable rule in politics." And, of course, he knew that invariable rule when he made his tour; but it didn't stop him, or weigh with him for an instant.

He had the most delicate and sensitive perception of what would get votes and what would repel them, but he would not angle for votes and he had utter scorn for those who did, his own supporters as well as his opponents. Bryan, the vote-hunter, Bryan, the opportunist, was, as I have said, essentially consistent, for his main object was ever the same. In his farthest excursions in search of votes, Bryan never lost sight of his main road. He did not really compromise his convictions for votes. But Roosevelt could not have done as Bryan did. To hunt around for some clap-trap "issue" to tickle morons with—why, Roosevelt would almost as soon have been unfaithful to his wife. Perhaps his good-natured contempt for Bryan arose partly from this, although it seemed to rise chiefly from his insight into Bryan's mental inadequacy and his lack of fineness. But there were others entitled to less credit than Bryan; others who would do anything for votes, which could never be said of Bryan. Some of them were in Roosevelt's own camp, or at least pretended friendship for him. He understood them perfectly—and humorously.

Senator William E. Borah was between two fires in 1912. Nobody knew where he was going to flop when the split between Taft and Roosevelt became imminent; but when Roosevelt began to loom up in the West in a threatening manner, the Western Nicodemus came out for him. He was one of the lustiest Roosevelt shouters when the Convention met, was in the van and forefront of the Roosevelt fight until it was over and Taft nominated, and then withdrew into the silences. When the Bull Moose Party was formed and Roosevelt nominated, Borah was not there.

There was a Senatorial election in Idaho that year, and it was for Borah's place. As everywhere else, the Republican Party was split between Taft and Roosevelt. As everywhere else in the country, men in Idaho were asking each other: "Under which king, Bezonian? Speak, or die!" Borah undertook the seemingly impossible task of running for the Senate as a kindly and interested friend of both the Republicans and the Bull Moosers, of both Taft and Roosevelt. It is the highest imaginable compliment to his agility and his deftness that he succeeded. He did actually walk the tight-rope over the raging river and did not fall.

Of course he did not reach port without difficulty. Men's passions were high in that year. Idaho was not pleased. It was remarkable to see, day after day, with what dexterity Borah avoided the reefs each sunrise brought to view, how he threaded his way veering ever so little to the right to catch the Taft breeze to-day, ever so little to the left to catch the Roosevelt breeze to-morrow. Nothing like it was seen anywhere else in the United States throughout that lurid campaign.

But he was getting away with it when the whistle of Roosevelt's special train began to sound ominously in Idaho ears as it tore through the Mountain States. Borah would probably have given anything but his seat in the Senate to keep that train out of Idaho. If it once got to Boise, how could he keep his precarious position astride the fence? Nobody had been able to tease out of him a single word for or against either Taft or Roosevelt since he had been so valorous in Roosevelt's behalf in Chicago; and those days were far back in June; and now he was running for the Senate on the Republican ticket and smiling kindly on the Bull Moose voters.

The Roosevelt train swept past Idaho, and Borah, I surmise, thanked his god. It entered Montana from North Dakota; left it, and went on to the Pacific Coast. Borah read tranquilly of the big fuss in Washington and Oregon as Roosevelt stormed southward through those States. He was thankful for his mercies, for the Idaho situation was growing ticklish. The party leaders in that State were becoming mutinous; they were threatening to bolt him unless he came out for Taft and against Roosevelt. Under this prodding it was taking all his heroism to keep his mouth shut.

And then came a thunderbolt. Instead of continuing south down the Pacific Coast, the Roosevelt train suddenly turned eastward and headed straight for Idaho. The news that Roosevelt was going to speak in Boise was a severe jolt to Borah. As the State leader, as the man who had been in the van for Roosevelt in the thickest of the Chicago fray, and above all as the candidate for Senator who needed Bull Moose votes, it was inevitable that he must preside at the meeting. How he could do that, and how he could make an introductory speech without alienating the Taft voters and the State organization, was a question that would have been unanswerable by anybody less astute than Borah.

He rose to the occasion. When the train entered Idaho Borah boarded it, and rode with Roosevelt all the way to Boise. I saw them in consultation, but did not know what they said; although I suspected strongly that Borah was pleading with Roosevelt not to make his position on the fence impossible by demanding that he declare where he stood, when they faced each other on the platform that night in Boise. I did observe that when the train stopped Borah wore a satisfied look; but I also noticed a peculiar twinkle in Roosevelt's eye. I had seen that twinkle before, and every time I had seen it something happened.

When we got to the hall we found it packed to the roof with a happy and expectant audience, whooping its head off at the sight of "Teddy." Borah introduced him in a dexterous speech. He steered as adroitly as ever between the Taft and Roosevelt Scylla and Charybdis, and concluded by saying that if Roosevelt had received the Republican nomination at Chicago the party would have swept the country. Then he waved Roosevelt to the front with a charming bow.

The Colonel stepped forward, the twinkle there again. He quoted that last sentence of Borah's, and thanked him warmly for it. "So I will explain," he said, with careful distinctness, "just why it was that I was *not* nominated.

And," he added with a joyful grin, "I will ask Senator Borah to corroborate me."

The crowd howled. Borah tried to smile, but it was the most unsuccessful smile he ever negotiated. The issue Roosevelt was making in every speech in the West was that the nomination had been stolen from him; that the Taft faction had unseated his duly elected delegates and had seated men not elected but defeated by the Republican voters, so that they might vote to nominate Taft. He now took up each State in turn, showing how it had elected delegates favorable to him and how their places had been stolen from them and given to others who would vote right. He dwelt with special emphasis on the Western States. As he concluded each recital he would turn to the petrified and dismayed chairman and say, with innocent and eager politeness:

"Isn't that so, Senator Borah?"

And that unhappy man was forced each time to nod his head and look as if he liked it, while any one could see he was undergoing the torments of the damned. He could neither refuse his nod nor qualify what the Colonel said, for it so happened that in the Chicago fight he had taken the lead in the matter of exposing and denouncing the theft of the delegations. He was obliged to sit and listen while the Colonel made him an involuntary party to a speech arraigning the Republican organization as a band of thieves.

The audience greeted the first question and Borah's first nod with a yell of pure joy; but as time went on and the Colonel recited robbery after robbery, its happiness beat against the stars. It came to watch for the Colonel's inevitable courteous turning from the speaker's stand to the hapless man in the chair, for the inevitable "Isn't that so, Senator Borah?" and for the inevitable tortured nod, and to greet each repetition with an ever-increasing volume of mirthful jubilation. At last, after securing Borah's tragic endorsement of every charge he made, the Colonel concluded with an air of indescribably bland innocence, as if he were laying down a general axiom of no special application to anybody:

"Any one who is acquainted with the facts and does not condemn them is blinded to the light and has a seared moral sense."

The Colonel went back to his railroad car in high glee. I tarried long enough to ask Senator Borah what he thought of Roosevelt's speech. "It was great," he said sadly.

CHAPTER X

THE JOCUND COMPANION

ON ROOSEVELT'S thirty-day swing around the States, when he was running for President in 1912, I developed an infected finger which gave me such serious trouble as to affect my general health. The Roosevelt party was like a big family, and everybody was deeply concerned. I couldn't write my dispatches, so the other men used to take turns at my typewriter while I dictated. The Colonel was anxious about me. One day in Portland, Oregon, he showed his interest rather remarkably, and I tell this story only because it illustrates his character so well. The city turned out to greet him, and the Portland Hotel, a splendid and spacious one, was packed with people, while other thousands jammed the street. Presently, as the great crowd waited to see the Colonel, he came out of a dining-room on the mezzanine floor, surrounded by all the bigwigs in the State. The multitude broke into rapturous cheers and wild excitement as the reception committee of eminences progressed along the floor on their way to the broad stairs.

Half-way along the mezzanine the reporters from the *Sunbeam*—the name of our car—were standing, observing the scene and making mental notes for their dispatches. As the Colonel passed he smiled and nodded; then, catching sight of me, he threw the reception committee into consternation by suddenly stopping the procession, leaving his place in the middle of them, and darting over to me. The committee didn't know in the least what was going on;

neither did the wondering multitude below. The Colonel was inquiring anxiously whether I felt better or worse; he hadn't seen me that day. "Don't you think you'd better go back to New York?" he inquired. "I wouldn't for anything have you risk your health, and it's in pretty risky shape," and so he went on questioning and advising, while the crowd wondered and the eminences fretted. Finally he returned, reassured, to his place, and the stately cavalcade moved on. It was highly Rooseveltian.

The party traveled in two private cars, the *Mayflower* and the *Sunbeam,* which sometimes were hung on to regular trains and sometimes made the nucleus of a special train. In one car lived the newspaper men, the moving-picture man and the representative of the New York Central. In the other lived the Colonel, with his two secretaries, his cousin, George Roosevelt, his physician, Doctor Scurry W. Terrell, and Colonel Cecil A. Lyon, of Texas (afterward General Lyon), who stage-managed the trip. Lyon had been for years the boss of the Republican Party in Texas, had led the party into the Bull Moose camp, and he and Roosevelt were great chums.

Every night there was a poker game in the second car, and all in the first car, except Roosevelt, knew it and used to drift in and join it. The difficulty was to think up a plausible excuse for deserting the Colonel; not that he would have been shocked by a poker game, but it looked rather raw to let him know that his friends preferred a game to his conversation. My finger, and the Colonel's interest in it, supplied Colonel Lyon with a bright idea, after he had finished planning the next day's program with Roosevelt.

"Colonel," said Lyon, with an air of expansive benevolence, "do you know, I think it might be a gracious thing for me to step back into the *Sunbeam* and see how Charley Thompson's finger is getting along."

"Fine! bully! great!" shouted the Colonel. "That very thought had occurred to me just this moment. We'll both go."

A look of panic crossed Lyon's face. "Oh, no, that would look sort of ostentatious," he said hastily. "I'll go, and I'll let you know how he is."

"Do," agreed the Colonel. "Cecil, I'm rather worried about that boy."

Lyon departed into the second car, and the Colonel picked up a book. He had read about a page when in came his cousin, George Roosevelt, to report on the matters of which he had charge. When he and the Colonel finished their discussion, George said, with the look of a man who had just been struck by a clever idea, "Wonder if it wouldn't be a good scheme to ask how Charley Thompson's finger is getting along. You haven't heard how he is to-night, have you?"

"No," said the Colonel, regarding him curiously. "It would, indeed, be a gracious act, George. Don't fail to let me know how he is."

George promised, and vanished. Then in came Doctor Terrell. It was his duty not only to watch over the Colonel's health in general, but specifically to examine his throat every night, spray it if necessary, and protect it from the ravages of stump-speaking, which is a terrific strain on any man's throat. After he had finished his professional duties he sat around a bit uneasily for a moment or two, and then said, "Colonel, I lanced Charley Thompson's finger this morning."

"So I heard," said the Colonel with a questioning look.

"Yes," said the doctor, "and I think I'd better see if it needs any further attention. I'll just go back and see how that finger is getting along."

"By all means," said the Colonel, relapsing into his

book. He was all alone now, for the two secretaries, McGrath and Martin, didn't need to give an excuse; their work was done and they had been back in the *Sunbeam* for an hour. The Colonel waited ten minutes, which he judged would give plenty of time. Then he closed his book, rose, stepped out on the platform, and entered the *Sunbeam's* door.

At the head of the table sat Colonel Lyon, dealing, with George Roosevelt on his right and McGrath on his left; all the rest were present and accounted for, and all holding hands except the doctor and myself. At the sight of Roosevelt framed in the doorway, a mighty shout went up. Lyon threw down the cards and waved his long arms wildly, yelling, "Who's the Benedict Arnold?"

"Gentle-men," said Roosevelt, carefully biting his words into syllables after his wont when he sought effect, "I just dropped in to see how Charley Thompson's fin-ger was get-ting along."

In a flash he was gone, and we saw him no more that night. But he never got over it. He christened us the "Charley Thompson Finger Club," and used to stupefy solemn strangers by referring to it by that name in casual conversation, as if they knew all about it and it were the name of some famous social organization which everybody ought to be acquainted with. The flight of time did not dim his joy in it. Three years later he introduced me to one of his daughters-in-law whom I had never met before; and seeing that my name meant nothing to her, he expostulated. "Why, Belle, you know who Charley Thompson is," he reasoned; "the President of the Charley Thompson Finger Club, you know." And Mrs. Belle Roosevelt registered enlightenment.

And in reading Jack Leary's book, *Talks with T. R.*, I find that in his last conversations with the reporters who in the course of years succeeded the Oyster Bay squad to which I had belonged, he was using the old name and addressing this new generation as the "Charley Thompson Finger Club."

A few days after that night we were approaching the Oklahoma border when the Colonel approached Lucius Curtis and me and said, "As soon as we get into Oklahoma we'll be boarded by prominent citizens."

"I know we will," said Curtis.

"Yes," said the Colonel seriously. "And I'm going to warn them to be careful how they talk, because we have a bad man on board. Four-Finger Charley."

One night on this trip, when we returned to the train I stopped in the car behind ours to make friends with an unusually attractive baby about a year old, and the delay had consequences. When I finally reached our car it was locked. All my ringing of the bell produced no answer. The poker game was on. They heard me ring, but did not know who it was; somebody merely said, "Gxlc." That was our code word for the official committees which invaded the train at every stop, swollen with self-importance, and was a telegraphic abbreviation of "Great Excitement! Local Committee!" "Gxlc," said one of them, comfortably; "just another of the pests. Go on with the deal." So I slept in an upper and had to reason for half an hour with the conductor to get that.

There was considerable kidding next day, in which the Colonel took the lead, about my supposed slumbers on the roof. But the next morning the Colonel woke before anybody else, and as the train was whirling through the wide open spaces and there were no inhabitants to gaze upon him, he stepped out on the platform in his pajamas to enjoy the dawn breezes. When he tried to return he found the door had locked itself. He rang for twenty minutes and woke one or two of his fellows, but Lyon only said sleepily to Doctor Terrell: "Gxlc. How did those creatures get aboard so early? Confound their impudence." Finally a porter got inquisitive and poked his head out of the door, and the marooned bystander got in. Later in the morning, when I went in to the *Mayflower,* he sprang up, thrust out his hand gripped mine fervently and said impressively:

"Welcome, fellow-member of the Order of the Outside Rest!"

Of all the candidates I have ever traveled around with on campaign tours, Roosevelt was the most thoughtful and forehanded; he made our work several tons lighter. For instance: A candidate always repeats again and again certain of his speeches. Sometimes he does not repeat the whole speech, but takes parts of several speeches and "wangles" them in together, as the Londoners say. Of course the reporters do not report these repetitions; they only report the new stuff, and in a trip of this kind the candidate may make a dozen speeches a day, in only one of which will there be anything new and therefore newsy. But the reporters do not know which speeches will be old stuff and which will contain something of head-line size. So they have to pile off the train at each stop, scramble into automobiles, buffet their way through the shouting crowds, gain a place of vantage near the speaker, weigh every word he says, rush for the telegraph office if he says anything new, make hurried arrangements for wires, rush for the train and typewrite furiously. Repeated a dozen times a day this is hard grinding work; and in eleven cases out of the dozen it is all for nothing and the reporter might as well be back there in the train resting up from his strenuous work at the last town. For it is no pleasure for him, whatever it may be for the audience, to hear the great man speak; he is tired to death of it. As *The New York Times* remarked when Grover Cleveland repudiated an interview and said he didn't know that George Bailey, of Texas, was interviewing him, "For what purpose did Mr. Cleveland imagine the reporter left Texas and journeyed to New Jersey to see him? Reporters would not travel a block to feast their eyes on a public man. Except in the line of duty, they would not cross the street to see the Czar of Russia, the Ahkoond of Swat, or even the Governor of North Carolina and the Governor of South Carolina expounding their celebrated theory of irregular intervals."

I never knew a candidate, except Roosevelt, who seemed to sense the immense amount of toilsome and unnecessary work the reporters have to do in this way. But traveling with him was a pleasure, not a burden. He abolished unnecessary work for us. Whenever he returned to the car after a speech he would round us up and say, "Now the next stop will be at Blankville. You don't have to bother about that; I'm going to get off the usual thing." Or, "At Dashtown, where we stop next, you'd better be on the job. I'll have some new stuff there." Sometimes he would even tell us in the rough what the new stuff was to be, so that we would watch for that point in the speech. In this way he not only saved us useless physical and mental work, but economized our time and systematized our schedules. It also aided the editors at home to plan out their work without uncertainty, for we could telegraph them, "Don't expect anything from me before the Dashtown speech," or "Big story coming when we reach Blankville."

As with all candidates, we knew the Colonel's stock speeches by heart. In the Bull Moose campaign his argument that discontented voters should support him and not Wilson always contained this as its most telling phrase: "It is no advantage to change the Barneses, the Guggenheims and the Penroses for the Murphys, the Sullivans and the

Taggarts." In his informal "rear-end" speeches, that is, talks from the car platform wherever the train stopped, he always said the same things, using the phrases that experience had taught him would catch the crowd. For instance, he would say to the children who always flocked on the railroad track, "Children, don't crowd so close to the car; it might back up, and we can't afford to lose any little Bull Mooses, you know." He said this the first time on the spur of the moment, but it made such a hit that he kept repeating it, and the crowd always roared with delight. Women with babies in arms used to be prominent in the crowds, and one day after the glad news had come that Ethel Derby had an heir the Colonel found a particularly lovely baby gazing up at him from a distance of about five feet. The baby smiled; the Colonel grinned back, and said to the mother, "I like babies; I'm in the grandfather class myself now, you know." The crowd received this so gustily that he added it to his repertoire and got it off whenever a baby was near enough. At another time a Grand Army man stood near the car, and the Colonel looked down and caught his eye. The sight of the Grand Army button always stirred Roosevelt's emotion, and he said directly to the veteran, "Comrade, you who wear the button——" Then he had to stop to let the crowd get through cheering. After that he always used that phrase whenever a veteran or several veterans of the War of Secession were prominent around the car.

I had noticed years before, when campaigning with Bryan,—who, like all other candidates except that poor devil, Alton B. Parker, had his stock speeches and stock phrases,—that no matter how often these sayings are repeated they are always received by each crowd as brand-new. If you think a moment you will see how impossible it is for a candidate to make a new speech every time. Making speeches is hard physical work, and it is a strain on the mind. A candidate makes from five to fifteen speeches a day. If he were to try to be original and also say something important each time, he would be a driveling idiot at the end of a month. Also there would be no sense in it, for if what he says is not new to the reporter, it is new to that particular crowd. Of course, after it has been uttered once, the reporters never send it in again, so every successive audience thinks it is hearing something spontaneous.

The thirty-day swing around the circle in 1912 was hard work, and when we began to travel up the Atlantic Coast from Alabama to New York on the last homeward lap the constant anxiety and alertness fell from us for the first time in a month, and our spirits soared. The Colonel had tipped us off that we wouldn't have anything to worry about in the remaining speeches of the trip. There was a frolicsome spirit, an air of relief. We—not only the reporters but all the Roosevelt party—began to sing, "We're going home, we're going home," and finally one man, taking the center of the car, assumed the Colonel's voice and manner, imitated his gestures, and got off one of Roosevelt's stock speeches word for word—the one about "social and industrial justice."

We all knew it by heart, and applauded him uproariously. When he sat down another man arose and got off the speech about "the Barneses, the Guggenheims and the Penroses," still giving an exaggerated copy of the Colonel's voice and manner. He was followed by a third, who delivered the appeal about "little Bull Mooses." A fourth sprang up and began, amid great enthusiasm, the address to "Comrade, you who wear the button."

As he finished the Colonel emerged from his compartment at the other end of the *Mayflower*. He was so far away and the train was making such a racket that we had not supposed he had heard us, but he had. He marched into the midst of us, wagged his big forefinger at the circle, and crowned the performance by giving a speech in imitation of himself. It was a screamingly funny burlesque of his own style, and combined all the stock phrases.

"Comrade, you who wear the button," he began, pointing his minatory finger at Colonel Cecil Lyon. Then, exaggerating his own voice and gestures, he tore through the "social and industrial justice" paragraph, warned us with great intensity about "the Barneses, the Guggenheims and the Penroses," and finally, with an expression of anxiety and alarm, he leaned toward Jack Pratt and Lucius Curtis and implored them piteously, "Children, don't crowd so close to the car; it might back up, and"—in his highest falsetto—"we can't afford to lose any little Bull Mooses, you know."

That was his peroration. It may not have been the greatest speech he ever made, but I'll swear it was one of the most successful.

CHAPTER XI

DEATH PASSES BY

NOTHING shows more sides of Roosevelt's character than the time when the moron assassin, John Schrank, shot him. And, as some of them are among the less known sides, a few pages on that occurrence are desirable.

The shooting was in Milwaukee, in October, 1912. Roosevelt and his party were leaving his hotel to go to the Auditorium, where he was to make a speech as the Progressive candidate. His automobile was waiting; back of it were other cars for the rest of the party. On the opposite side of the car was a crowd waiting to see and cheer him, held back by the police. The front rank of the crowd was kept twenty or thirty feet away from the automobile.

When the party came out of the hotel Roosevelt and Colonel Lyon walked ahead toward the curb. Lyon carried an automatic in his pocket and had guarded Roosevelt with sleepless vigilance throughout his westward swing. He saw the ex-President into the automobile, where he stood acknowledging the cheers of the crowd. Lyon stood beside the car until its purr told him the chauffeur was about to start. Then he turned to get into his own car, which was immediately behind. As he did so Schrank, who was in the front rank of the crowd on the other side of the automobile, shot Roosevelt.

The bullet struck him in the left breast, and he staggered, but did not fall. The pistol was an old-fashioned one. If Schrank had had an automatic he would have killed Roosevelt, for he did not rest with one shot. He was pressing the trigger again when something flew from the sidewalk clear across the automobile and the intervening space, and fell upon him, carrying him to the ground. It was Elbert Martin, Roosevelt's stenographer, who had been standing on the sidewalk on the other side of the car.

To make a jump like that between two pistol-shots, even when the pistol is an old and slow one, is such a unique feat that nothing accounts for it except the quickness of Martin's mind. He had actually started his leap before Schrank fired the first shot, having seen the glint of his pistol as he raised it and put his finger around the trigger; and he was flying through the air while Schrank was shooting. His flight was over the tonneau, and would have been impossible if Martin had not been an athlete; he landed on the man like a ton of brick.

Getting Schrank under his knee on the pavement, and fighting until he got control of his pistol hand, Martin dug his fingers into the assassin's throat and started to strangle him to death. "I wasn't trying to take him prisoner," he told me afterward; "I was trying to kill him." The police had their hands full dealing with the surging crowd. Lyon, horrified and furious, was dancing around like a madman with drawn revolver, trying his best to get in. The police captain, Girard by name, came running up with one of his men and yelled to Martin, "Give me that man's revolver!" Martin, still choking the wretch to death, shouted back over his shoulder, "I'll be damned if I do." The two policemen rushed on Martin, when Lyon swung his .38 caliber on them and roared, "If you advance another step I'll kill you both!" They recoiled, and the crowd started to surge forward. Lyon turned his gun on them and shouted, "Get back there!" The crowd wavered and fell back, and at that moment Roosevelt, still standing up in the car, called out to Martin:

"Bring him here; don't hurt him."

Sorely disappointed, the stenographer reluctantly dragged his captive over to the automobile. Roosevelt looked down on him with an indescribable expression, in which there was no anger, and said in his ordinary tone of voice: "What did you do it for—oh, what's the use? Turn him over to the police."

And then, to everybody's stupefaction, he ordered the chauffeur to take him to the Auditorium, where he made his speech to the waiting crowd. No one, himself included, knew whether the wound was mortal or not. The X-ray showed that it had stuck between two ribs. Its force was lessened by the notes for the Auditorium speech, which Roosevelt had put in his vest pocket and which were right in its path. I still have one of the pages, with the tear made in it by the bullet as it went through.

When the party got out of the cars at the Auditorium, Roosevelt found himself side by side with the man who had saved his life. "Martin," he said, gripping the stenographer by the hand, "I'm mighty glad it was one of our crowd that saved me, instead of an outsider."

When he made his speech the crowd did one of those things which make a reflecting mind wonder about the human race. Before Roosevelt arrived the chairman of the meeting told them what had happened, having been informed by telephone. He let them know that Roosevelt had been shot, that no one knew whether the wound was fatal or not, that this might be his last speech, that he might not finish it. The crowd was horrified and sympathetic. And yet, when Roosevelt finished and started to leave the hall, they rushed forward to pump the wounded man's hand. It seems incredible, but it happened. The insensate creatures were held at bay with difficulty. It was nothing to them if they killed him, so long as they might be able to boast, "I was the last man to shake hands with Roosevelt." The mind of man is the proud possession that distinguishes him from the beasts that perish. Or so they tell us.

As the purpose for which I am writing of this incident in Roosevelt's life is to display certain phases of him which are not so well known as others, I shall here copy two of the dispatches I sent from the Mercy Hospital, Chicago, where the injured man was carried from Milwaukee, to *The New York Times*. Written the very day of the scenes they describe, they give a better idea of his reaction to the experience of an attempted murder than anything I can write sixteen years after the event. Here they are:

"Chicago, Oct. 17.—The boss of the Progressive Party sat in Room 308 of the Mercy Hospital today and ruled it with a firm and unyielding face. All the bosses that had gone before her—Quay, Platt, Hanna, and Hill—were amateurs to her. She was Boss Edith Roosevelt, and she ruled the occasion with an iron hand.

"That sedate and determined woman, from the moment of her arrival in Chicago, took charge of affairs and reduced the Colonel to pitiable subjection. All day today he had not dared to say his soul was his own. Up to her advent he was throwing bombshells into his doctors, telling them that he cared not one continental what they might say and directing his own plan of medical campaign without regard to them. The moment she arrived a hush fell upon T. R. After that he became as meek as Moses. Today not even Mrs. Longworth could tease him into a snicker.

"Now and then the Colonel would send out secretly for somebody he knew and wanted to talk to, but every time the vigilant Mrs. Roosevelt would swoop down on the emissary as he was on his way back and drive him away. No such tyrannical sway has ever been seen in the history of American politics.

"Mrs. Roosevelt remained in her room and never showed her face outside, but every underling in the Mercy Hospital had orders to bring every card and letter that arrived to her, and not to him. The Colonel, lying two doors away, pleaded vainly for the privilege of passing on the missives handed in. But the Boss was inexorable. One glance at that determined face was enough to scare off a United States Senator.

"She is the Boss, and the best boss any political party has had for some time. Whether the redoubtable Colonel really believes in women's rights, as Miss Jane Addams thinks, or whether he has been forced into it, as Mrs. Ida Husted Harper says, there is no doubt that there is one household where women's rights is the rule. He has been as meek as a lamb since the Boss arrived and began to run the machine in the Mercy Hospital.

"For the rest, he is the same kindly soul he has ever been since he took his place here. He does not seem to think of himself at all. If he has a word to say, it is always for 'Jim,' or 'Mike,' or some attendant. Their eyes fill with tears when they talk of him. The puncture in his chest is the least of his concerns.

"Yet as he tossed on his bed he would say every now and then, 'Ethel, I don't see why your mother won't let Jack come in,' or 'Jim,' or 'Joe,' or whoever might be hammering at the portals at the moment. But it was no use. Mother was inexorable. Ethel would soothe the warrior, and after awhile he would grumblingly subside.

"At the present moment the Colonel is apparently very grouchy over the way in which he is being bossed, although very fond of his boss.

" 'This thing about ours being a campaign against boss rule is a fake,' he remarked today. 'I never was so boss-ruled in my life as I am at this moment.' But he grins fondly at his wife as he says it, and it is evident that the Great Unbossed likes being bossed for once.

"Chicago, Oct. 18.—Colonel Roosevelt obeyed the orders of his boss today with reasonable patience until evening. Mrs. Roosevelt wouldn't let him see anybody but Governor Johnson, and she went in with him and asserted her power over the second in command of the Progressive Party, as well as the first, for she wouldn't let him remain more than ten minutes.

"But in the evening the Colonel led a new bolt against boss rule. Somebody told him that the 'Old Guard'—as he calls the newspapermen who have been with him throughout the campaign—were in Dr. Terrell's room and he refused to take orders any longer. Mrs. Roosevelt protested in vain. John McGrath, his secretary, came into Dr. Terrell's room looking frightened and guilty and told the 'Old Guard' that the Colonel wanted to see them.

"They went in and found a particularly lusty-looking Colonel sitting up in a chair, with a dressing gown on and a book in his hand. If it hadn't been for the chair and the dressing gown, and the fact that he asked them not to shake his hand too hard, there would not have been a thing to indicate that it was an invalid Colonel whom they saw instead of the husky person whom they had accompanied so long and of whom they had grown to be so fond.

"After the first few hand grips and small talk had passed over, somebody got down to cases by asking the Colonel about his plans for the future. From the next room an apprehensive face was to be seen peeping around the door every few minutes with a look in it that said plainly, 'Don't make him talk too much.' It was Mrs. Roosevelt. But the Colonel's back was toward her and he talked ahead with all his old fire.

" 'I want to get out of here on Monday if I can,' he said. 'I don't know whether the doctors will let me or not. You see, I'm not in such bad shape as you might think. My rib is broken, but if the edges can get together so that I can breathe a little easier, I can talk, and if that happens I intend to make some more speeches in this campaign.'

"Here the Colonel began illustrating with his fingers the situation of his wound, and it is impossible to give an idea of the eerie feeling that possessed all of us as we saw and heard him diagnosing his own case with the impersonality of a medical professor in a clinic.

"'You see,' he explained carefully and dispassionately, as if he were talking of some third person miles away, 'there are only three possible dangers—pleurisy, pneumonia, and blood poisoning. If we get safely past these three there isn't a thing in the world to prevent me from resuming my campaign. The bullet does not amount to anything, in itself, but it's possible that the breaking of that rib might result in pleurisy and put me out, or lead to pneumonia. The blood-poisoning possibility we have pretty well discounted, but still it might come along. Outside of that I don't see any reason why we shouldn't board a train for the East next Monday.'

"He grinned as though he were discussing a matter of no concern to him—the probable recovery of some patient somewhere of whom he had heard, and in whose case he took a sort of academic interest.

"'If the edges of that rib hitch together,' he added, 'I expect to make some speeches in this campaign that will interest a lot of people, particularly those of the other side. It is very nice of Governor Wilson to offer to let up on account of my condition and I appreciate it, but Mr. Bryan is right; I don't ask for quarter.'

"The Colonel laughed, and we stood there waiting for him to explain the joke.

"'I was thinking,' he explained, seeing our bewilderment, 'of the position Governor Marshall (the Democratic candidate for Vice-President) is in. Mr. Marshall doesn't know whether to go on attacking me or not. Now, his whole campaign is built up on the proposition that I wasn't at San Juan Hill at all. That occurrence at Milwaukee has taken his breath away, but he'll get it back in a week, and then he will be assuring his audiences that he has indisputable proof that I wasn't shot at Milwaukee, or that if I was it was only birdshot, and that it hit somebody else instead of me, and that, anyhow, I was in Oshkosh that night and not Milwaukee.'

"Mrs. Roosevelt looked warningly around the door and shook her head, but the Colonel didn't see her and plunged on.

" 'It's curious to note how a little infection will spread,' he said, using his finger to indicate the smallness of the spot. 'Still, I don't believe there is going to be anything further. Dr. Lambert wanted to go back to New York today, but the other doctors made him stay, just on the chance that there might be something doing.'

" 'How did you feel while you were making that speech at the Auditorium?' asked one of the Old Guard. 'We were running around in circles there like crazy men, but you seemed to be perfectly calm.'

" 'Well,' said the Colonel, opening his eyes very wide, which is a habit he has when he wants to say something very serious, 'the fact is that I didn't feel any pain while I was making that Auditorium speech.'

"This sounded queer, in view of the fact that he almost collapsed while making it, but he went on to explain.

" 'Every time I tried to take a deep breath,' he said, 'it made me gasp, but there really wasn't any sharp pain.'

" 'Didn't it give you a shock when you pulled that manuscript out and saw the bullet hole in it, and realized how narrow an escape you had had from death?'

" 'No,' said the Colonel matter-of-factly, 'but it did amuse me to see that manuscript and the smashed spectacle case.'

" 'Amused you——,' said somebody in a smothered tone, while all the rest stared at the wounded man.

" 'Perhaps I should say,' said the Colonel, grinning, 'that it interested me.'

"He inquired as to the chances of people coming around the train on his way to New York and insisting on seeing him.

" 'You know,' he said, rather appealingly, 'that I honestly can't get up and talk to them, much as I'd like to. They're good fellows, but lots of our good American folks don't seem to realize that a man with a bullet in him can't do everything he'd like to. Why, at Milwaukee, when I got down from the stage at the Auditorium, they surged around me, calling out "Handshake, handshake," and, much as I'd have liked to oblige them, you know that it is impossible for a man with a bullet in his chest, which for anything he knows may be mortal, to shake hands with any approach to real cordiality.'

"Here Mrs. Roosevelt leaned across the doorway again and shook her head still more decidedly, and the Old Guard cut the interview short and filed out, though the Colonel was evidently willing to continue it until the cows came home."

In this account there is one prevarication. I gave the impression, in writing it, that it was the first time any one of us had seen the Colonel in his sickroom, though I did not actually say so. This was not for the purpose of misleading the public. It was, I regret to say, for the purpose of deceiving my fellow-correspondents. My only defense is that I was forced to do it. While the ban was still on against visitors the Colonel had ordered Doctor Terrell to slip me in when Mrs. Roosevelt was catching forty winks in the next room, and the doctor, in much perturbation and deep fear of the boss if she should catch him at it, had obeyed. He had come into the press room in the hospital, invited me to take a walk, and when we were in the corridor had sworn me to secrecy and spirited me into the sickroom. Mrs. Roosevelt never knew anything about it. In the beginning the Colonel was too weak to talk at all, and the doctor limited him to one sentence. The Colonel feebly spoke it to me, as follows: "I'm not allowed to see anybody; but I had to see you, you old trump." Then the frightened doctor rushed me out.

Also there was one omission in this account. When the Colonel was picturing Thomas Riley Marshall's probable demonstration that the Milwaukee shooting was just another solar myth, he told us of something Doctor Alexander Lambert, his principal physician, had said. In New York, on his way to Chicago and his patient, Doctor

Lambert had met a man who told him he knew for a fact, on the most unimpeachable authority, that the shooting was a frame-up. This man assured the doctor that Roosevelt had arranged the whole thing himself and had been shot with a wax bullet. Schrank was an employee of the Colonel, and would be released, well paid, as soon as the hubbub was over.

It was our custom, when we returned to the room the hospital had allotted to us for an office, to hold a council, sort over the things we had been told, and arrange with each other how to treat them. On this day, we came in due course to the story about the imaginary wax bullet. Somebody remarked that that was the best story of the day, and several were noting it down, when Lucius Curtis of the Associated Press said: "Hold on. If we print that it will do the Colonel harm. Don't you know that the United States is populated largely by damned asses? If we publish that, some infernal idiot will start the story that it really was a wax bullet, and all the other idiots in the country will take it up."

So we all struck it out. So far as I know, it never did see the light of day.

CHAPTER XII

LET THE CHIPS FALL WHERE THEY MAY

THE brilliancy of his service in the New York Legislature is not well remembered now; it has been obscured by the greatness of his later life. Besides, if to the end of his career there were plenty of people who did not understand him, it is easy to see how he must have been misunderstood in that early period. Joseph Bucklin Bishop, in his *Theodore Roosevelt and His Time,* gathered together some of the newspaper comments which illustrate this. In one paper he is described as "young Mr. Roosevelt of New York, a blond young man with eyeglasses, English side-whiskers, and a Dundreary drawl in his speech." Another referred to him editorially as "the exquisite Mr. Roosevelt," but he was no more the exquisite then than when he was a Rough Rider, and it is impossible to imagine him with a Dundreary drawl. It was simply that an imaginary picture was drawn of him; he was a dude legislator, and in describing a dude legislator, as in describing any other type, there are certain ironclad conventions that must be followed. Once he was so classified, a perfectly sincere Albany correspondent could honestly describe him precisely as he was not. I have observed this curious freak of the human mind a hundred times, displayed with regard to all sorts of public men from Anarchists to Archbishops.

Yet at the end of every session the newspapers joined in a chorus of sincere praise for Assemblyman Roosevelt and what he had accomplished. He entered the New York Legislature at twenty-three, and a year later he was the Republican leader. Partisanship was much more violent then than it has been in the newspapers in the past few years; that is to say, nowadays newspapers in great cities, except on the lower part of the Pacific Coast, make an effort to treat the other party with some pretense of fairness, a thing which they did not do in those early 'eighties. Nevertheless, Democratic newspapers united with Republican ones, except in the smaller cities, in giving Roosevelt full credit for the astonishing record of good legislation he had made as the Republican leader. It is true that this record was non-partisan, which undoubtedly had a good deal to do with it; for Roosevelt from the earliest, partisan as always, was concerned mainly with the improvement of the condition of the people when it came to legislation. In those years I was interested in the cartoons of him and preserved them; and in looking over them now I see that Nast and the *Puck* cartoonists, who were the only important cartoonists of that time, generally associated him with a Democrat, Governor Cleveland, as two men who were working for the public welfare without regard to machines. In those days such an attitude was wholly unfamiliar.

It is a curious thing that when he was being considered for Assistant Secretary of the Navy his path should have been so easy. Senator Lodge wrote him a letter on March 8, 1897, reproduced in Bishop's book, telling him that Secretary Long "spoke in the highest terms of you," and said only this word of criticism: "Roosevelt has the character, standing, ability and reputation to entitle him to be a Cabinet Minister—is this not too small for him?" Hay, as one might expect, had "written and spoken and urged in the strongest way at all opportunities." More surprising than Long's attitude was this, "Hanna is entirely friendly and wants you here. Platt is not lifting a finger against you." More on the same line from other surprising quarters—Cornelius N. Bliss and Vice-President Hobart. It is interesting to remember that this same Hanna was Roosevelt's most vigorous opponent when he became President, and lent himself to a business men's conspiracy to defeat Roosevelt for the 1904 nomination; although before Hanna's death the two men came to understand each other. As for Platt, in three years he had got so sick of Roosevelt that he was trying to get rid of him by boosting him into the Vice-Presidency—the worst mistake Platt ever made.

Consistency was one of the main keys to Roosevelt's character, and yet in his lifetime the public generally regarded him as an inconsistent, impulsive man who could not be calculated upon because he was likely to do anything. Of all the men in public life whom I have known, I never met one who was so consistent, who hewed so steadily to the line. The explanation of the misapprehension that was so general may be found in a letter he wrote in 1906 to George Horace Lorimer. It was on a different subject, but what he said in it about his two attitudes toward bosses—different but consistent—was true of his attitudes toward other things. He said:

"I have had on occasions to fight bosses and rings and machines, and have had to get along as best I could with bosses and rings and machines when the conditions were different. I have seen reform movements that failed and reform movements that succeeded, and have taken part in both, and have also taken part in opposing fool reform movements which it would be a misfortune to have succeed."

In the same manner, it was just after he had "muck-raked" the packers that he came out with his famous denunciation of the man with the muckrake. There was no mistake and no inconsistency, though at the time it was said there was. The packers deserved to be muckraked, and the outcome of his raking was not only government inspection of prepared meat products, but the Pure Food and Drugs act. But the man with the muckrake raked everything and wrote articles on "The Treason of the Senate" and "The Shame of the States." That speech of the President's smashed muckraking as an industry, and up to that time it had been one of the most prolific in the United States; muckraking was all the rage. The individual he had especially in mind was David Graham Phillips, though Phillips was only the most flagrant of the many muckrakers. Rather curiously, that speech was not for publication. It was made before the Gridiron Club, the dining organization of Washington correspondents, whose rule is that no speeches at their dinners shall be reported. Consequently public men can speak their minds freely and in safety. I was a member of the club and heard the speech. It impressed the Gridironers so profoundly that they told the President—privately, after the dinner—that it was a public duty to put it in print. He finally agreed to write it out and give it to the press, and it crushed the muckraking trade, necessitated a hasty revision of the year's editorial program in many a magazine office, brought about a saner and healthier mode of public thinking—and added a new word to the language.

So, too, it was of a large branch of his own supporters in the Progressive Party that he spoke in 1913 when he said, "Every reform movement has a lunatic fringe." Not even the excitement of a campaign in which he was a candidate ever swayed this critical perception of the good in the worst of us and the bad in the best of us. One day in 1912, when he was running for President as a Bull Moose, he got a vociferous reception from a crowd he addressed in Colorado, from the rear platform of his train. Coming back into the car amid the tumult of cheering, he said to me, grinning broadly:

"By George, Charley, I almost think I'll carry Colorado. And why not? Colorado has voted for everything crazy, including Weaver."

Weaver was the Greenback candidate for President in 1880 and the Populist candidate in 1892 and stood for all the "isms," including free silver.

Ambassador Bryce compared Roosevelt—in a letter he once wrote him—to Jefferson, a comparison which may have been little to Roosevelt's liking, since he said there was no President he despised so heartily as Jefferson. But the resemblance Lord Bryce detected was "in range and variety of interests," and he added: "You are unlike him in this, that he lost nearly all his friends, and yours draw always nearer to you and prize your friendship more." Which was true of him in a special, peculiar sense, as of no other man I ever knew. Jefferson was Roosevelt's *bête noire,* but he admitted one good point in him, which was that Jefferson stood for the people. Here is the explanation of Roosevelt's course, always directed toward a consistent end; he aimed at the good of the people, but was too far-sighted to suppose that that good could be attained by worshiping the particular kind of "consistency" Emerson meant when he wrote, "*A foolish* consistency is the hobgoblin of little minds, *adored by little statesmen* and philosophers and divines." It almost seems as if Emerson must have been thinking of Roosevelt when he added, "The voyage of the best ship is a zigzag line of a hundred tacks. This is only microscopic criticism. See the line from a sufficient distance, and it straightens itself to the average tendency. Your genuine action will explain itself and will explain your other genuine actions. Your conformity explains nothing."

Roosevelt further believed in going first after the thing

which was immediately attainable. For instance, he always favored woman suffrage, but while it was not a major issue he declined to weaken the fights he was making for other reforms by taking that on, too. Still, from the time he entered politics he did what he could do for woman suffrage; and it was rather curious that when he made a major issue of it in 1912, when the Republican and Democratic Parties still side-stepped it, he was accused of being a new convert who was using it for votes. That was the year when the Progressive Party nominated him for President. I myself did not know of his previous record on the subject until one day in Portland, Oregon, when some suffrage leaders visited him at his hotel. In the course of the conversation I was surprised to hear them mention that he had been for suffrage twenty-eight years ago.

Their leader was Mrs. Abigail Scott Duniway, an old lady who was recuperating from a long illness and had to be carried in the arms of several of her followers from her automobile to the second floor of the hotel. She was the suffragist leader in the State. The Colonel came up to her, grasped her by the hand, and said, "This is indeed a very great pleasure; if I remember rightly, the last time I saw you was in Albany a good many years ago."

"You are quite right," said Mrs. Duniway. "It was in 1884, and a party of us asked you to present a woman suffrage measure to the Legislature. It took a good deal of courage in those days for a rising politician to espouse so unpopular a cause, but you rose to the occasion, and I remember saying at the time, 'There is a great man.'"

It did take a lot of courage, though this generation may find that hard to believe. In 1884, as I remember very distinctly, it was enough to damn a man to be suspected of favoring woman suffrage, much more to be accused of doing anything for it. He was immediately set down as a ridiculous person, somewhat flighty, a crank. I do not remember any one of prominence in politics who advocated suffrage without being laughed at, except George William Curtis, whose position was assured; but even Curtis was regarded as having given intellectual hospitality to an eccentric vagary. And Roosevelt was the Republican Party leader in the Assembly, a position in which a politician has to watch his step.

It may be thought that this phase of Roosevelt—holding to main convictions, but emphasizing at first only those which could be immediately realized—was the product of long years of political experience. However, it dates back as far as you can go, back to the days when he was just entering politics. I did not know him then, but from those who did I have learned enough about it to see that in this respect there never was any change in him. For illustration, there is the well-known story—it may have been told first by Joe Murray, but I first heard of it from Francis E. Leupp—about his first campaign for the Assembly, in 1881, when he was only twenty-three years old. His managers took him around to the saloons to get solid with their managers and customers, as was the practise in those days. The trip ended with the very first saloon, where the proprietor opened the conversation by saying he thought the existing license fees were too high. The candidate replied that he did not think them high enough and would endeavor to make them higher. The interview was getting stormy when Roosevelt's friends got him out of the place on the plea of another engagement, but they did not take him to any more saloons.

Yet—and here is the point—although Roosevelt as a candidate thus risked and undoubtedly lost the votes of the Sixth Avenue part of his district, he did not introduce a high license bill until his third term, when he was leader of the Assembly. He did not consider the time ripe till then, and even at that time he was premature, for the bill was beaten. His idea in such matters, as he often explained to me, was never to be too much in advance of the time, but always to be a little in advance. And this was not for the sake of making a bid for popularity; it was for the sake of accomplishing something, which by a different course would not be accomplished. Incidentally, this is the difference between a progressive and a radical; but I never saw it illustrated in any man as it was in Roosevelt.

Nor did he ever sidestep, from the time he met that saloon-keeper in 1881. He scoffed at the idea of being the Presidential nominee in 1916, because, he said, he would not pussyfoot, and he felt certain the Convention was going to do that very thing. This was the meaning of his much-misunderstood remark that it would not nominate him "unless it was in a heroic mood." He knew it would not be; his strength was all exerted to keep it from being too spineless and groveling. When he said he would not pussyfoot, he meant that if he were nominated he would declare in favor of the Allies in the war, and that declaration, of course, would play hob with a pussyfooting campaign. In more despondent moods he used to say to me that the people were probably with Wilson in his effort to be "neutral in thought." "They have got soft," he told me over and over again. After 1910 he felt that they had got tired of him, and that opinion he never changed. One day in 1915, when I was visiting him at Sagamore Hill, the talk turned to the next Presidential nomination, and the name of Colonel George W. Goethals came up. Roosevelt's face lighted.

"By George, I'd do anything to make Goethals the candidate," he said enthusiastically. "Anything! I'd either come out for him or oppose him, whichever would do him the most good; and," he ended, rather grimly, "I guess it would be better for me to oppose him."

He knew, however, that, like Bryan after 1908, he had strength enough left to make himself a power, and he used it to force the stolid and sordid Republican Convention of 1916 into taking something like an American attitude toward the war. In this he only succeeded to the extent that the platform was not so bad as it probably would have been if the Republicans had not been afraid of him; but the candidate was satisfactory to him, at least until Roosevelt had irrevocably committed himself to the nomination, though his patience was sorely tried by Hughes's silence on the war issue through the greater part of the campaign, while Wilson, whom he thoroughly distrusted, could write such plain-spoken words as those to Jeremiah O'Leary.

That pro-German had telegraphed threatening Wilson with the loss of votes, and Wilson replied: "Your telegram received. I would feel deeply mortified to have you or any one like you vote for me. Since you have access to many disloyal citizens and I have not, I will ask you to convey this message to them."

That must have made Roosevelt's heart unwillingly vibrate; it did thrill the people. The public did not know that at that time Wilson was still trying to bring about a "peace without victory," and kept it up until he discovered how Germany was swindling him in the following Winter.

It may seem a contradiction to say that Roosevelt regarded himself as a pioneer and yet always fought for the reform immediately in sight; that, for instance, though he believed in woman suffrage, he told Mrs. Harriet Taylor Upton, Treasurer of the National American Woman Suffrage Association, in 1908, that he would not take the issue up because he did not consider it so pressing as others. But it is precisely "the lunatic fringe" which wants to embody every reform in its platform, and which consequently never makes any headway. That is why Garrison impeded the progress of abolition by linking it up with the Sabbath question, woman suffrage, the abolition of tobacco, and heaven knows how many other reforms which might have been excellent or might not have been, but which certainly repelled votes. Roosevelt frankly told me—told everybody—that he had his eye on votes, not necessarily for himself but for whatever it was that he was trying to push along. He always took the view that intentions which can't be carried out are of no consequence beside votes.

So he was always a pioneer, but not a Cortez; more like a Boone, who always kept in touch with the settlements and never let himself get too far ahead. He was no Pizarro, to disappear in the ocean on a desperate chance; rather he was a James Robertson, who crossed the mountains back home every year from the frontier to make sure that the home folks were still backing his adventure.

When he talked of himself as a pioneer, as he often did to me, he always referred to his pioneer work in 1916 in behalf of preparedness for the war he saw just ahead. It was done in advance of the Republican Convention, and from Chairman Warren G. Harding down to the humblest delegate, except for a handful of Roosevelt men, that blind Convention believed that the Republican Party could win the election by carrying water on both shoulders, most of the water on the German shoulder. The galleries heartily disagreed with them, as they showed when Chauncey M. Depew forgot himself for a moment and got away from the narrow lines laid down for his speech and talked real Americanism. It was only for a minute, but the galleries turned loose with an ear-splitting roar that made Depew happy and turned his face red, though the next moment he was back on the reservation again. The delegates sat stolid, of course; they were busy preparing their own defeat in November, and the sad thing was that they really came to

Chicago with the idea of nominating at any cost a ticket that "would win."

In that matter Roosevelt really was a pioneer, as he had been in so many other cases; but he was more of a pioneer then, because by that time he had come to disregard wholly his own political future. He always disregarded it when it really came down to a matter of duty, but by 1916 he was utterly reckless of it, because he believed, as I know, that his political career had come to an end. When he spoke with a saddened irony about the "heroic mood," he was gibed at again by the men who misunderstood him, or rather hated him, to the end. But he meant, of course, that he had no chance of the nomination unless the country was prepared to defy Germany—for he would not compromise or soft-pedal—and he was absolutely certain that it was not. It was the nation he blamed more than Wilson. He was intensely surprised when General Wood permitted him to make a speech at Plattsburg and the General was reprimanded by the War Department because the speech was alleged to contain an attack on the Administration. He had not mentioned the Administration or President Wilson; but he had said that no preparations had been made for war since Germany began her depredations upon us. He was so engrossed with the shortcomings of the people in this respect that it actually came to him as a thing not to be understood that he should be charged with attacking the Administration when it was chiefly the people he was condemning. There was such a deep difference between the two parties to the controversy that Secretary Baker and, doubtless, the President himself, regarded any attack on the "softness" of the nation as an attack on themselves. And certainly Roosevelt held them fully responsible as far as their power went; but his main quarrel was with that "softness" that he saw universally.

To him Wilson and Baker were no leaders, only followers, and followers where the easy path led. In 1916, at any rate, whatever happened in later years, that is exactly what they were. The nation was impatient to be led, in some direction, but it was not led. It wanted to hear a voice, whatever the voice should say, but it heard none. In the dead silence of 1915, when everybody was striving heroically to obey Wilson's impossible injunction to be "neutral in thought as well as in act," Roosevelt sounded his first bugle call. That morning there came into my office one of the bitterest anti-Roosevelt men I knew—George MacAdam, afterward author of a life of Pershing and other well-known works. "By George," he said, reluctantly but explosively, "it's good to hear a bass voice in politics again!"

A great deal of unintelligent stuff was written at the time about Wilson's success in putting Germany in the wrong by his two years of note-writing, and about how fortunate it was we had him in the White House instead of the rough-riding Roosevelt. But one of the clearest-headed of English observers, E. T. Raymond, wrote in London after Roosevelt's death: "The late Mr. Roosevelt could not, with Mr. Wilson's patient skill, have stripped Germany's case of one fallacy after another, as one must peel an artichoke, till no shred of it remained. But Mr. Roosevelt would not have tried; he knew from the first, on instinct, that Germany had no case; he smelt across the Atlantic the smoke of Louvain and the taint of civilian carnage, and that was enough."

When Wilson became a Presidential candidate his speeches fascinated and exasperated Roosevelt. He studied them with increasing fascination and exasperation. "He can't get away from the academic manner," he said to me one day, laying down the paper in which he had been reading Wilson's latest speech. "And that is why he doesn't get under the skin of the people. His manner is still that of the college professor lecturing his class." The Colonel assumed the detached and impersonal manner of a college professor and beat the air oracularly with his finger. "Is the platform of the Democratic Party a program? No, it is not a program. What, then, is it? It is an abstract expression of discontent. Discontent with what? Discontent with prevailing conditions. What are those prevailing conditions? And when you have finished reading his speech you can almost hear him say, 'Mr. Jones, you may repeat in your own language what I have said and apply the principle thus laid down.'"

Wilson, by the way, was just as much interested in Roosevelt's speeches. He studied them with the same interest and with an admiration Roosevelt did not feel for him; and, I think, so far as the matter of constructing campaign speeches was concerned, each had the right idea about the other. One day in that same campaign, when I was taking lunch with Wilson, he cross-questioned me at great length about Roosevelt's speeches, and seemed all the time to be mentally contrasting his own methods with Roosevelt's, and not at all to his own advantage. I had already had occasion to notice that he distrusted his ability to "get under the skin of the people," as Roosevelt had said. "And you say he dictates his speeches in advance?" he said enviously. "I wish I could do that. But it's no use; I've tried it over and over again, and I can't do it." It was a fact that Roosevelt dictated his speeches in advance, but it was for the purpose chiefly of clarifying the arrangement of his ideas. He never committed them to memory; but his memory was so photographic that when he came to speak the language he had dictated was before his eyes. That would have been impossible for Wilson.

One day in 1915 I was lunching with the Roosevelt family at Sagamore Hill. Nicholas Longworth and Alice his wife were there. The conversation was proceeding along lines too tame for Alice, and, glancing at me with a now-watch-for-the-fireworks sort of look, she turned to her father and said:

"I see Mr. Wilson has sent another note to Germany."

It had the desired effect. "Did you notice what its serial number was?" inquired the Colonel, with that sibilant deliberation he employed in such cases. "I fear I have lost track, myself; but I incline to think it is Number 11,765, Series B."

Then he turned to me. "Suppose, Charley," he said, "that after Fort Sumter was fired on Lincoln had embarked on a series of notes to Jefferson Davis, just as logically perfect, just as irrefragable, just as stupendously reasonable, as those of Wilson. In sixty days the white heat of indignation over the firing on the flag would have disappeared; so would the virtual unanimity of the people; and when at last he was forced into war with the South, he would have found behind him an unprepared, irresolute, divided nation. Instead, he instantly called for volunteers, and the white flame of patriotism had no chance to die out; it deepened.

"Wilson had just such a moment when the *Lusitania* was sunk. For that moment the nation was ready to follow a leader. He opened his really admirable series of notes—they are admirable, considered just as specimens of correct reasoning—and the country cooled off. He will have a hard job warming it up again, as he will have to do. When the time comes and he, like Lincoln, is forced into war, he may find behind him an unprepared, divided, irresolute nation. If he does, it will be his own fault; or rather, it will be the fault of the people who elected him. I don't suppose it will really be his, for he can't help it."

A year later I was reminded of this conversation by something Doctor Nicholas Murray Butler, President of

Columbia University, said. Doctor Butler knew Wilson well, long before he entered politics. He and I were discussing the President's characteristics, and Doctor Butler said:

"The other day a lady said to me, 'Just what sort of man is Mr. Wilson?' I said, 'He is this sort of man. Suppose you and Mr. Wilson were well acquainted. Suppose he—as he would be quite justified in doing—should write you a letter proposing marriage and should mail the letter at ten A. M. He would then dismiss the matter from his mind. If I should meet him later in the day and say, 'I should think you'd like to marry Miss ——,' he would look surprised and say, 'Why, I have married her. I married her at ten o'clock this morning. The incident is closed.' "

One of the "Cabinet," as Roosevelt used sometimes to call the reporters who rode herd on him at Oyster Bay and who were in his continuing confidence, was John J. Leary, of *The New York World.* I knew Leary very well, but he did not come to Oyster Bay until after I had ceased to be a correspondent and had become an editor, though I saw him when I used to go out to Sagamore Hill to visit the Colonel. After Roosevelt's death he published *Talks with T. R.,* a most admirable book and simply essential to any one who wants to know Roosevelt; for it reports the things he used to say privately on public affairs during the years Leary was with him, and shows his mind as no description could. In one of these "Talks," when Wilson was about to leave for Europe to join the Peace Conference at Versailles, Roosevelt compared the President to a tenderfoot with money playing poker with professional gamblers. The only difference was that Wilson was playing with "other folks' chips."

"If my poker terms are bad," he continued, according to Leary, "the other members of the Charley Thompson

Finger Club will correct me. They (the European diplomats at the Peace Conference) will play with Mr. Wilson. They will give him a grand time, and he will, unless I am greatly mistaken, give them promises the American people will not endorse. There will be delay and confusion, and in the end the thing will have to be done right."

To him Bryan was a lightweight intellectually and somewhat humorous as a character. I shall never forget how once, having blundered into a comparison between him and Bryan, I was transfixed with that ironical stare which he assumed for the purpose of squelching people, as he slowly answered, after a still more annihilating pause: "I am a different breed of cattle from Bryan."

CHAPTER XIII

ROOSEVELT MEETS MANKIND

THERE have been many attempts to account for Roosevelt's way with men. I do not account for it, but I will try to give a picture of it from which any reader can draw his own conclusions. The best way to do it is to run over some of the times when he met men face to face on one of his campaign trips, that of 1912. That was the one in which he could most nearly be himself. "Damned if I know how he does it," said Colonel Lyon, of Texas, after marveling for a week. "He doesn't have to make a speech; in fact, half the time he doesn't make one. He says, 'Friends, I'm glad to see you,' and they go off and vote for him."

This trip lasted a month. It was the nearest thing to a real swing around the circle ever seen. That phrase was first applied to President Johnson's progress, but Johnson only went as far as Cleveland. It is applied to every considerable political journey. But Roosevelt's was almost literally a circular swing. He left New York, went up into New England, crossed the Middle West, went through the Mountain States to the Pacific, down the Coast to the Southwest, through the South to the Gulf, and back up the Atlantic Coast to New York again. It was as much a circle as the shape of the United States permits.

In the State Fair Grounds, half-way between Minneapolis and St. Paul, he had an audience of twenty-five thousand. Talking to that many people is a pretty hard job, especially when they are not massed in front of you, but distributed to your right, your left, behind you, and in front. The Colonel managed it by making his speech in sections. He would talk first to the left-hand crowd, then to the right, then to the back, and then to the center. This kept him running around the platform, while each crowd which he temporarily deserted yelled for him to come back.

The first time he quit the left-hand audience to speak to those on the right, the left-hand crowd shouted, "Come back! talk to us!" The Colonel turned, shot his under jaw out at the shouters and cried, "Square deal!" They laughed and applauded, and remained silent, not hearing a word he said, while for many minutes he talked to the crowd on the right. After a while the left-handers again called to him to come back, and the Colonel stopped in the middle of a sentence to call out to them, "I've made a solemn engagement with these people to talk to them for five minutes. After that I'll come to the other side of the platform." And after the five minutes were up, he said with an engaging grin to the right-handers, "Now, friends, let me go over there for a minute," and ran like a squirrel over to the left-hand side, where he was greeted with a rapturous shriek.

"Come back!" shouted the right-hand side, after he had talked to the other group for a few minutes. He dropped the sentence he was uttering, turned toward them and said sternly, "Look here! That's not a square deal!" The right-handers applauded him, cried, "Go ahead," and sank into silence.

This happened half a dozen times. Once as he turned from the right and ran down the platform to the left, a thousand voices from the back shouted, "Talk to us. There's a lot of us over here." Roosevelt stopped in his rush to the left, surveyed the crowd at the back, and recognized the justice of their complaint. He turned suddenly around, walked over to them, and said, standing under a tree freighted with boys and men on every branch, one or two of whom dangled their feet not more than twelve inches over his head, "I'm willing to do anything except go into a hurdle race. I like you all, but I don't know how to divide myself." But he did speak to the back crowd, while the tree branches above him almost broke with the audience that loomed over his head.

The insistent demands from all sides that he should speak to each finally led him to say, "Friends, this is the only time I ever wished that I could face two ways at once—or even five ways at once, but I'd have to be built like a starfish to do it." As he went from right to left for the seventh time a voice in front shouted, "Talk to the center." He hesitated a moment, then turned to the right and left with a debonair wave of the hand, and said, "The center complains that I have been playing both ends against the middle."

Toward the close of this quadruple speech an old Grand Army man fainted. He was standing directly in front of the Colonel, who had just made one of his sweeps from right to left and was in the middle of a sentence. He leaned down and caught the old man as he was falling. In a jiffy he had lifted him up to the platform, laid him down, and summoned Doctor Terrell, his physician, who administered restoratives, while the Colonel went right on with his speech from the middle of the sentence he had been uttering.

I wondered how far his sense of the dramatic extended, and if he was not a little bit awed by the consciousness that a single man could draw out such immense multitudes as lined the way from St. Paul to Minneapolis, with so many of them looking upon him as a sort of John the Baptist. To me it seemed enough to have awed even the most light-minded of men. At one point in his speech at the Fair

Grounds, an old farmer standing near the platform reached over the edge of the stand and touched the Colonel's foot, and then drew back, perfectly satisfied. He had touched the hem of the garment of Moses.

The cow country turned out to greet, not a Presidential candidate, but an old friend. The folks East who called out, "Hello, Teddy," said it in a half-jocular way. But I noticed that the Montana folks said it just as you would say, "Hello, John," to an old and intimate friend who was coming back after an absence of several years. In each of these Montana crowds there were always one or two men who had known the Colonel in his ranching days back in 1883. Each of these men had become famous in his own little community as the man who worked with Roosevelt, and had told stories of cow-punching with the Colonel until every neighbor felt that he too knew "Teddy," and consequently every man, woman and small boy at each wayside stop had the same kindly personal interest in Roosevelt that was felt by the one man in the community who had ridden with him years ago.

The same influence was noticeable in the Colonel's own manner. He did not exactly make speeches to these people, he just chatted with them. Everything he said to them was in a gossipy, friendly, intimate sort of way. It wasn't even a monologue, for the cow-punchers talked whenever they felt like it. Neither men nor women felt the least hesitancy about breaking into his talks with reminders of the old days on the Little Missouri, when Roosevelt was running the Northwest Cross Ranch, near Medora, and the Colonel always joined in and discussed these occurrences in a neighborly sort of way. The Northwest Cross Ranch was in what is now North Dakota, but the Dakota pioneers had been moving west so that there were really more of the Colonel's old friends in Montana than in the Dakotas.

The first stop was at Miles City at seven-fifteen A. M. The Colonel emerged from his car blinking and rubbing his eyes.

"The rest of my worthless party," he said with a grin, "is asleep. I wish I had them on the round-up and could hear the cook say, 'All set!' That would wake them up."

The cow-punchers fairly yelled with joy. Roosevelt started to denounce Amalgamated Copper—he was now in Amalgamated's own home—when one of the punchers broke in. The Colonel took a close look at the man and asked, "Who are you?"

"George Myers," said the cowman.

"Do you remember the other George Myers—Little George?" asked Roosevelt, who had now forgotten all about Amalgamated Copper.

"You bet!" replied the puncher.

"Well, he was one of my men down in Chicago that they could not buy," said the Colonel.

Little George Myers was one of Roosevelt's four ranchmen in 1883, and all four of them were delegates to the Republican Convention which stole the elected Roosevelt delegations, presented them to Taft, split the Republican Party and elected Woodrow Wilson. But the four ranchmen all voted against the machine and for Roosevelt.

And then the Colonel went on talking about the part Amalgamated Copper had played in the Chicago burglary.

The wayside crowds were typically American. There is, I had always held, no such thing as a "typically American" crowd, but I had to make an exception in Montana. Indians were present in every audience, and children were numerous. The children took as large a part in the joint debates between Roosevelt and his audiences as did their elders. Pretty girls on horseback, riding astride,—which was not so common then in the East,—galloped after the train at each station, and kept up with it for long distances. At one short stop an old man reached up just as the train was pulling out and said, "I am for Teddy Roosevelt and Eugene V. Debs."

"Thanks," said the Colonel, "but he's not running on the same ticket with me." Then he went into the car chuckling and said, "Just fancy Debs's feelings if he could hear that."

At Rosebud, a drunken man kept interrupting the proceedings until the big Sheriff of Rosebud County pounced upon him and dragged him out of the crowd.

"Much obliged to you, Sheriff," called the Colonel. "I have been a deputy Sheriff myself."

"I know you have," said the Sheriff. "Don't you remember me? I am Big Joe Smith."

"Why, sure," exclaimed the Colonel jubilantly. "You were with me when I was a deputy Sheriff at Medora." Then he and Big Joe exchanged reminiscences to the heartfelt delight of the crowd.

At Huntley the cow-punchers rode around the car while Roosevelt was talking. The crowd was dense, and it seemed miraculous that the men could weave in and out on horseback in that mass of humanity. But the people seemed sure of the riders' skill and nobody even took the trouble to move as the cowmen plunged and cavorted among them. At Big Timber he contemplated a crowd that jammed the railroad tracks and described himself as "a middling old settler," and a roar of happiness went up at the announcement. "I was here," he added, "at the end of the buffalo days. Things have changed since then." Here he interrupted himself to point to the cow-punchers astride their horses on the outskirts of the crowd and say: "I have been on the hurricane deck of a broncho myself." At Columbus he remarked that he was glad he had lived in the West before becoming President. "It is a good thing," he explained, "to have a President who knows an irrigation ditch from a dry farm, and who knows alfalfa. I was always," he digressed, "in the short grass country, and I worked among the cows."

This bit of local color set the crowd wild.

At Big Timber he was explaining that his new party intended to give every man a fair show, but that it had no idea that legislation could make everybody equally rich or equally successful.

"I know some men," he said, "that you could give the best rifle in the world to, and after one of them got the rifle I could beat him with a club. At the same time you want to give a good man a good rifle."

This was what you might call metaphor of a local sort, and the riflemen present applauded gustily.

The stop at Blackfoot, Idaho, was more wild-Western than anything in Montana. The town is in the heart of the Indian country, and many Bannocks and Shoshones live in the town, and have pretty homes. Roosevelt's automobile was escorted to the Fair Grounds by Indians, cowboys, and girls astride fleet horses. Before his speech had got very far along he said, "This talk that I was a dictator came chiefly from Wall Street."

"That's where they need one," replied a plump and pretty woman. The Colonel agreed to this, and was going on with his speech when she called out, "You don't know me, Colonel, but I'm Otto Raphael's sister."

"You are?" cried the Colonel joyously. "Then you're the sister of one of the best policemen I ever put on the New York police force. Do you live here?"

"Yes," she said, "I live at Idaho Falls."

"Well, that's fine," said the Colonel. "Look here," he went on, addressing the crowd, "I'll tell you how I came to put her brother on the force. I happened to notice one day an account of a very gallant rescue of women and children from a burning building by a young fellow named Otto Raphael. I was trying to get good men on the force wherever I could find them, and I said, 'That fellow must be the right sort.' I hunted him up and found him at the Bowery Branch of the Y. M. C. A., though he is a Jew by faith. I found him a husky lad, but not as good looking as his sister," and Otto's sister blushed and laughed, and the crowd cheered. "And he turned out to be a number one policeman. I think the only time he was ever disappointed in me was at the time of the Spanish War. He wanted to join my regiment, but, fine policeman as he was, he did not know one end of a horse from the other."

The lusty Westerners roared hilariously at this, and even the Indians relaxed a little.

"I think," conceded the Colonel, "he had a general idea that a horse didn't have horns."

In Los Angeles, when he appeared on the platform at the Temple, while every throat was trying to tear itself apart, a bent old negro mammy with a crutch insisted on making her way to the Colonel and speaking to him. Some of the local committeemen tried to turn her away, but the Colonel caught sight of her, and beckoned her forward with a kindly smile. The committeemen fell back, and the old woman hobbled up to Roosevelt, grasped his hand, and talked to him for half a minute. The Colonel detailed a couple of the leading citizens of Los Angeles to see that she got safely off the platform and through the crush, and then turned to face again the waiting and frantic crowd.

On a campaign tour the itinerary is in the hands of the National Committee, which orders the candidate to stop at places where votes can be made. It picks out these places before he starts and makes changes by telegraph; the candidate is its slave. Every hour has to be conserved. But on one occasion Roosevelt's train spent precious time by stopping where not a vote was to be made. The National Committee may have torn its hair, back in Washington, but the Colonel had his way.

The stop was made in the course of a through flight of five hundred seventy-eight miles, from Phœnix, Arizona, to Albuquerque, New Mexico. Only one other stop equally short was made on this run, which was taken at high speed. The stop I am writing of was at the Indian pueblo of Laguna, New Mexico. A pueblo is a village of adobe houses, built one on top of another, and they look as though they were rocks or small buttes pierced with windows and doors. The Indians flocked around the car as the Colonel came out of it. The full-bloods were traditionally stolid, but the half-breeds were more demonstrative. Many of the Indians were attired in the clothes of civilization—some of the girls and women in up-to-date garments—but the larger number wore the Indian garb. There were squaws in red shawls and short blue skirts, carrying little papooses, and some with baskets of fruit on their heads. Some of the half-breed girls were unusually pretty. They made an engaging picture, with the fortlike pueblo houses as a background and the sandy, cactus-covered, mesquite-surrounded country broiling in the hot New Mexican sun.

The reception Roosevelt got from these Indians was the result of a little idea which originated in the fertile brain of that ingenious gentleman Colonel Cecil Lyon, of Texas. Indians are not much up on politics, and most of them didn't know that a Presidential campaign was under way. Colonel Lyon decided that it would be a waste of time and telegraph tolls to explain to the pueblos of Laguna the political situation and the meaning of the term Bull Moose, so he simply wired ahead to Laguna that the Great White Father was coming for a visit.

Just as Roosevelt was beginning his speech Richard J.

Cummins, the Progressive Party's moving-picture man, started up the track with his machine. Roosevelt's quick eye detected on the outskirts of the crowd a lot of squaws so picturesque that they would make an ideal subject. "Movie, Movie," he shouted, that being, as I have explained, Cummins's nickname among the party. Cummins turned, and the Colonel, pointing to the squaws, shouted, "Over there." Cummins saw the point and ran toward the squaws. They, somewhat alarmed, began to back out of the range of his strange-looking machine. Seeing this, Roosevelt called out, "You've got to get it going quick, Movie, or you're done."

Cummins succeeded in convincing the squaws that there was no danger, and they came back in a scared sort of way. Cummins took aim and was about to fire when the Colonel shouted, "You've got two bully ones over there, Movie. There, that one with the papoose." Cummins took them in and Roosevelt started on his speech.

"At one time," he said, "I had a Pueblo Indian on my ranch, and he came from New Mexico. He worked on the round-up, and was a number one roper and rider." Here Cummins coaxed several especially bashful squaws into the center of the crowd where he could get a good line on them.

"Bully for you," cried the Colonel. "Movie's a diplomat. I'm going to make him Ambassador at the Court of St. James."

Here somebody introduced to the Colonel, Frank Simons, a tall dignified Indian, as the Governor of the pueblo. He stood just before the car platform with arms folded, listening with immovable gravity to what the Colonel said.

"I've always taken a particular interest in you Indians," said the Colonel; "you Indians who live in the pueblos."

"Thank you," said the Governor, with a grave inclination of his head.

"I've done everything I could to preserve your rights and see that you were not oppressed," continued the Colonel, "and I hope to see you all made American citizens."

"Thank you," said Simons, with the same slow, dignified inclination. The Colonel saw he had an unusual person to deal with. He bent over and said, "Where did you go to school?"

"Carlisle," said the Indian briefly.

"We had a Carlisle boy at the Olympic games," said the Colonel, "and he cleaned up everything. I'm glad to see you with the Moose here in New Mexico," he went on, pointing to several Indians wearing little German silver bull moose. "Here in New Mexico, you know, you generally see the antelope and the coyote. [Laughter by the half-breeds and a faint approach to a smile by the full-bloods.] Well, that Carlisle boy ran better than a coyote with a torch in his mouth."

This time even the full-bloods laughed. "A coyote with a torch in his mouth" is Indian slang and is a term designed to convey the idea of great speed. This indication of familiarity with Indian phrases made the biggest hit yet, but the Colonel went further and improved on it.

"Do you use the sign language here?" he asked the Chief.

"Not much," responded Simons.

"Well," said the Colonel, "when I lived up north among the Mandans and Sioux we used to have the sign language, and I used to talk with them. Have you got the blacktail deer here in the mountains?"

"No," said the Chief. Somehow he managed to utter a single word in such a way that it seemed as though he had uttered a long sentence.

"Well," said the Colonel, "our sign up north for the ordinary deer used to be this," wiggling his fingers, "but the blacktail deer we would make this sign for," wiggling them in a different way. "For the beaver we'd make this sign." He hit the back of his hand a quick slap and then dived his hand suddenly down before him. "The beaver drops his tail and goes down, you know," he explained.

The Indians were delighted.

"You don't know these signs?" asked the Colonel.

"No," responded the Chief.

"We had the same sign for a Pawnee and a wolf," went on the Colonel. "Two fingers raised like this over a bush," illustrating. "That meant the ears of the wolf, you know. For the Comanche we had this," making a quick, serpentine movement of his hand. "That represented a snake. For the Sioux the sign was cutting the throat," drawing his fingers across it.

"Yes," said the Chief, moved to unwonted loquacity, "I've seen that in the Sioux."

"In our regiment," said the Colonel, "we had about fifty Indians, mostly Pawnees, but we had Cherokees and Chickasaws, too."

As the train was about to start the Colonel distributed several of the little German silver bull moose to the Indian children. As the train rushed on, trying to make amends for its divagation at the pueblo town, he appeared refreshed. You would have thought these voteless Indians would give him the Electoral College, by the care he expended on them. The National Committee, meanwhile, was turning down the applications of places like Chicago, on the ground that Roosevelt couldn't spare the time to stop there. I meant, when I got back East, to take a look at O. K. Davis, the Secretary of the Committee and strategist of the itinerary, and see if his hair had turned white over that stop at

Laguna, but I forgot it. Davis displayed such ingenuity in mapping out the route that it sometimes drove us to mutiny. The third time he ordered us back to Kansas, a State which Colonel Lyon held in abhorrence because of its puritanical views, Lyon was bitter. "I'm going to send Davis a telegram," he said, "saying, 'You seem to have confused a Presidential trip with a monastic retreat.'" Jack Pratt, however, evolved a long political explanation for our spending so much time in Kansas. "That's probably Davis's reason," he concluded. "Shucks," said Lyon morosely; "nothing is reason enough for coming to Kansas. Davis," he continued, "must be an awful good newspaper man. I say that because everybody is good for something, and as a deviser of itineraries he's simply terrible."

A little later we passed a place where the train ran around the town and backed on two or three tracks. We were on the Frisco, and Lyon had already remarked with cynicism, "Frisco brakemen make the best sailors in the United States navy, because they never get seasick." When we began to revolve rapidly around this Kansas town even the optimistic Doctor Terrell revolted. "There is more backing and twisting on this road than I ever saw before," he complained. "Easily explained," said Lyon, who was still embittered. "This train is naturally trying to get out of Kansas, and doesn't know how to do it."

If you desire an idea of the way in which Roosevelt's admirers admired him, you may get it from the fact that by the time he reached Oklahoma on the way back the single suit of clothes which he brought with him had been nearly wrecked by the frenzied crowds. The right side of his coat was torn from the armpit down on the inside by a woman admirer in the crowd at Joplin, Missouri. When we headed for McAlester, Oklahoma, the left side showed the same kind of tear, caused by a male admirer at Tulsa, "who," as the Colonel put it, "wanted to show that he approved of me." At several points efforts were actually made to tear off pieces of his coat as souvenirs, and in Oklahoma he was obliged to telegraph ahead for a new hat. After doing so he came into the press car and told us about it, and then went on:

"Did you ever hear the story about the Confederate soldier who was plowing his weary way through mud a foot or two deep? Every time he drew his foot out of the slough there was a deep sucking sound. It took him half a minute to move a step, and his knapsack got heavier and heavier every second; and he hadn't had anything to eat for a day and a half. Just then General Polk came riding along, and said, 'Hurry up there, what's the matter with you?' The soldier looked up at the General with a gaze of mingled wrath and misery, and said, 'Well, if I ever love another country, damn ME!' That's the way I feel," continued the Colonel, ruefully, going back into his own car.

Long before this he had been moved to misgiving about that single suit. For the greater part of a month he had quite literally lived in the car. Of course, ranging all over the country, he hit every variety of climate; when he arrived at Denver it was snowing and when he struck Phœnix it was one hundred and six in the shade. The climate of Phœnix is lovely and dry, and no matter how hot it is you never notice it, if you take it easy; but stump speaking is hard work, and although everybody else was comparatively cool the ex-President's coat began to look more and more like a lake the longer he talked. He was still about fifteen days from home. When he got back to the car he took the coat off, looked at the watery map of Arizona which the temperature had traced on it, and, turning to me, said ruefully: "When I get back to Oyster Bay the only thing I can do with this coat is to burn it."

He met with his first hostile reception in Atlanta. Atlanta did not intend to give him one. The feeling there was of friendship, rather more so than even in Little Rock, because Roosevelt's mother was a Georgian and that counts heavily in a Southern State. But I have already remarked on Roosevelt's habit of waiting until he got into sin's home town before he lambasted sin; a practise utterly foreign to the conception of the pitiful vote-hunter, who will save his denunciations of prohibition until he gets into a wet town or of tariff reform until he gets into Pennsylvania. In this campaign he had been going through Northern and Republican States, mostly, so he had attacked the Republican Party and said little about the Democratic. Now that he was in the Solid South he let the Republicans alone and turned his vocabulary on the Democrats.

The Atlanta audience quickly turned from smiling and friendly interest into black rage. The storm of howls and hisses would not die down or even moderate, and it seemed as if the speech was at an end; that he would have to give it up and leave the platform. The noise, in fact, grew louder instead of diminishing. Suddenly the Colonel sprang up on a table. The movement was so unexpected and unexplainable that the uproar faltered and gradually died away; everybody wanted to know what he was going to do next. He waited until he could be heard, and then said, beaming amiably, "I got up here so that you can all see me clearly." After that it was difficult to keep up to a very high pitch of reprobation, and he was allowed to finish his speech.

CHAPTER XIV

CHARACTERISTICALLY, HE GOES TO MARQUETTE

In 1913 Roosevelt astonished the country, and at first scandalized it a little, by bringing a libel suit against an editor who had accused him of being a drunkard and a man of evil conversation. The tone of the comment was that he was cheapening himself by descending to discuss such a charge in court; that it was undignified, unworthy of the great office he had filled. The ex-President trying to punish an obscure editor for a single, isolated campaign canard! Why, it was making a mountain out of a molehill.

They were wrong about it. As he afterward wrote, in summing the matter up, in *The Outlook:* "Any man familiar with public life realizes the foul gossip which ripples just under the surface about almost every public man, and especially about every President. It is only occasionally printed in reputable papers and set forth in explicit form; but it is hinted at in the press and set forth with circumstantial mendacity in private; and if left unrefuted until after the man's death it lasts as a stain which it is then too late to remove. From Lincoln and Garfield to Cleveland and McKinley this gossip has circulated and still circulates. In the case of Mr. Cleveland, for instance, it took the form of accusing him of actions so atrocious that even to think of them makes one feel indignant, and in this case I know personally that there was not the smallest shadow of foundation for the charges. Yet it is such an unpleasant task to call the slanderers to account that any man tends to shrink from it."

I do not know why he said "from Lincoln and Garfield." He could have started earlier. When I went to live in Washington negroes were pointed out to me on the streets, with the information, "That man belongs to the —— family. You know, the illegitimate descendants of George Washington." After I had lived there a while I became accustomed to hearing this sort of remark about every President, sometimes with meticulous details, such as that President Arthur's mistress was the daughter of a certain Supreme Court Justice; that President Harrison had suffered a heart attack and nearly died in a house of prostitution, and so on. In New York, on a great civic occasion, an intelligent and honorable reporter said to me, "Mayor Gaynor, you know, reviewed the parade; and Jack So-and-So tells me that as each regiment passed by the Mayor took a flask out of his pocket and tilted it up and took a drink." I looked at him with utter astonishment; I thought he was joking, but he actually believed the total impossibility he was narrating.

President Wilson's friendship for Mrs. Peck was made the handle for great numbers of utterly impossible stories, all scandalous, and all related on the authority of somebody "in a position to know." I do not know how many times I was confidentially and mysteriously assured, always on "irreproachable authority," that Justice Brandeis got his appointment to the Supreme Court as a reward for his services in stealing or buying Wilson's letters to Mrs. Peck. One day Cleveland H. Dodge, calling on Colonel Edward M. House, said, "I've just learned that I paid Mrs. Peck one hundred and twenty-five thousand dollars for her letters." "When were you informed of that?" asked House. "This morning," replied Dodge. "I beat you," said House; "I learned the day before yesterday that I paid her one hundred and fifty thousand dollars."

When, in 1912, Roosevelt's special train stopped at Butte, one of the party, Angus McSween, of *The Philadelphia North American,* stepped into a hotel lobby and got into conversation with a stranger, a prosperous and benevolent-looking man. "Roosevelt's drinking like a fish," said this man, who looked like a bank president. "I was just talking to one of the reporters who are going around with him, and he tells me that he has just had an interview with Roosevelt fifteen minutes long, and that in those fifteen minutes Roosevelt drank fourteen highballs." The man was lying, of course, and had no idea that McSween was himself one of the reporters.

"Did you tell him he was a liar, Angus?" I asked.

"What was the use?" said McSween. "He would only have made it twenty highballs the next time he told the story, and said that I was the reporter who told him." This man was one of the "unimpeachable authorities" from whom these slanders spring.

In that same campaign I made the western tour with Woodrow Wilson. In Denver the Press Club gave a dinner to Wilson and his party, and entertained us sumptuously. My neighbor at the dinner, a refined and pleasant Denver gentleman, thinking to say something that a member of the Wilson party would like to hear, said smilingly to me: "This is rather different from last month. Roosevelt was here then, and we intended to give him the same sort of entertainment. But Roosevelt got so drunk he could not come and had to be carried to bed at the Brown Palace Hotel, where he fell into a drunken sleep and could hardly be roused to go to the Auditorium and make his speech."

"How strange," I said. "I was here with him that night, and he seemed sober when we left the car I went with him to the Brown Palace, where he talked with us for a while before going into his dining-room. When he came out I went with him to the Auditorium, where he made a fine speech. Somehow I didn't notice the things you saw; they all escaped me."

The conversation languished.

While I was with Roosevelt I wrote from Los Angeles a private letter in which I said:

"The campaign they are making against the Colonel here is a dastardly outrage. A concerted effort is being made throughout the West to paint him as a drunkard, despite the fact that he drinks almost nothing at any time and is now absolutely on the water wagon.

"The limit was reached by *The Los Angeles Times,* the paper which was dynamited (I am now inclined to think very properly dynamited) by the McNamara brothers. In Portland the Colonel lost a birthday present given him by his wife, a book. You know how fond he is of his wife, and this seriously disturbed him. He told McGrath and Martin, his secretaries, to drop everything else and recover the book, and at frequent intervals, as the train time drew near, he would send for George Roosevelt and anxiously inquire about it.

"That was what happened. Here are the headlines in *The Los Angeles Times:*

MAD SCENE IS ENACTED

Teddy Raves and Gnashes Teeth.

Creates a Panic in Portland Over the Loss of a Book.

Name of Woman Mentioned in Connection with Raid of His Room.

Hosts of Candidate Unable to Account for His Disgraceful Conduct.

"The article speaks of his 'maudlin conduct,' and says that when he found a book he wanted to read was missing 'he flew into a maniacal rage. "Find me that book," he yelled to his secretary. "I want it now." The Colonel paced the room like a caged beast while he waited for the volume, in the meantime demanding over and over again that the book be produced.' Etc., etc. Wouldn't it jar you? The Socialists in Portland distributed copies of an obscene and filthy pamphlet, not fit to be touched with the tongs, and were very anxious to have us print some of it. My old acquaintance Anthony Comstock would confiscate the whole edition of any paper that printed it in full, but aside from that there is no reporter in the party so low-down as to touch it anyway."

It will be observed that *The Los Angeles Times* skated close to the verge of safety from the libel law, but was safe. Nowhere did it directly charge Roosevelt with drunkenness, and nowhere did it mention liquor, only the effects of liquor; which effects, it might be argued in court, are often produced by other causes. As for the horrible insinuation about a "woman," in court the paper could say, with injured innocence, "Why, it was Mrs. Roosevelt we meant, of course. Wasn't her name mentioned in connection with the book?" The filthy innuendo in the word "Raid," too, could be made to appear perfectly innocent.

After many years of experience at first hand with this universal and inexplicable quirk in human nature, by which honest and truthful men become obscene liars the moment the name of a public man is mentioned; after running down, as a newspaper man, an infinite number of circumstantial slanders told "on unimpeachable authority," and never finding one such story to be true, I have adopted an invariable rule for myself in all such cases. Whenever I hear any scandalous story whatever about a public man I instantly say, without any inquiry whatever, "That is false," and dismiss it from my mind. It may happen, once in a hundred times (though it never has yet), that I am mistaken and the story is true; but the chances are so much against it as not to be worth taking.

When George H. Newett, editor of *Iron Ore,* a paper published in Ishpeming on the Upper Peninsula of Michigan, wrote in his publication that Roosevelt was a person who "gets drunk frequently, and all his intimates know this," he penned the words in sheer lightness of heart. He did not know that Roosevelt had instructed all the Bull Moose leaders to keep a sharp lookout on the newspapers and send him anything that might get published. For a long time the hunt was unproductive. No slander was ever so universally spread without getting into print. Once there was momentary joy at headquarters; a paper in Salina, Kansas, published the libel. Roosevelt's hopes rose. But on inquiry it turned out that the Kansas paper was owned by ex-Senator J. R. Burton. Roosevelt, while President, had pounced on Burton for shady practises, forced him out of the Senate and ruined his political career. If now he sued Burton for damages he would be charged with hounding the fellow.

One evening in Atlanta, about two weeks before Newett slung his boomerang, a reporter for an Atlanta paper came in to ask him what he had to say about a charge of drunkenness made by a campaign publication of the Prohibition Party. The Colonel, without irritation, gave the reporter a list of all the drinks he had taken that he could remember. After the reporter had gone the Colonel said regretfully to the rest of us, "I hoped he had brought me that charge made in some responsible paper. This little campaign paper in Indiana has no assets; but the moment a responsible paper, with money enough to pay a damage verdict, makes that charge, I'm going to settle this thing once for all."

So in about a fortnight, while he and some friends were dining in a Chicago hotel, Oscar King Davis, who had been looking over his mail, jubilantly waved a letter. "Congratulations, Colonel," he cried; "I think we've got them now! I think a responsible paper has called you a drunkard!"

"Good!" shouted the Colonel, and gave orders that instant inquiry be made about the financial responsibility of *Iron Ore*.

The trial was held in Marquette, the county-seat of Marquette County; a fine little city on the shore of Lake Superior. Newett's counsel included two noted Eastern lawyers, one of whom was called the best cross-examiner in Ohio. Cross-examination was all the defense ever had a chance to show their skill with, and the result even of that was unhappy, since no cross-examination could trip up truthful witnesses and the only effect was to emphasize their original testimony.

Fortunately, Newett's charge had set no boundaries in time, so that Roosevelt could account for every year of his life. He came as near as he could to giving a complete list of all the drinks he had ever taken. He produced such a staggering array of witnesses from Cabinet officers and doctors to Secret Service men and barbers that as soon as he completed his evidence, Newett withdrew his charges, retracted and apologized, and threw up his defense. Greatly to the discontent of his lawyer, James H. Pound, Roosevelt immediately rose and said that his only object in bringing the suit had been to drag out the slander and crush it, and so he would ask only nominal damages—in Michigan, six cents. "I have achieved my purpose," he concluded, "and I am content."

As he uttered the last sentence he lifted his hand above his head and clenched his fist.

Judge Flannigan instantly ordered a recess of fifteen minutes and the whole audience rose as one man—or woman, for the women were in the majority—and surged against the barriers that separated the counsel and participants from the general crowd. Everybody was trying to get near enough to the Colonel to shake his hand, or, failing that, to call out some joyful word that he would hear. He was in the center of a struggling mass that nearly tore him apart and kept him swishing about like a chip on a billow. Emlen Roosevelt was the first to get to him with a congratulation, and the rest descended upon him like an avalanche. "We put it through, by George!" the Colonel said, trying to make two hands do duty for the octopus arrangement that was clearly needed.

When the court reconvened the Judge directed the jury to return a verdict for the plaintiff, and then the court adjourned. The rush on the Colonel was repeated, and all the women who could not get through the crowd waved their handkerchiefs from the rear ranks. When, at five o'clock, he went to the station to take the train home, he encountered another crowd, including many of the leading men of Marquette County. Automobile parties had come up and were waiting for him, and the Colonel went over to each to shake gloved hands and raise his soft black hat.

There was no cheering; in fact it wasn't at all like a crowd assembled to applaud a popular man. It was like a lot of friends seeing another friend off. Everybody stood around with a happy smile and total strangers chatted in a neighborly fashion and exchanged cards. Instead of cheering or giving the strange incoherent jubilances of campaign times, such as the invariable "You're all right, Teddy," the people wore the aspect of persons who had come down to the station to wish good luck to a neighbor starting out on a journey.

After the trial he published an editorial about it in *The Outlook,* of which he was contributing editor. In it, enumerating the multifarious classes of witnesses who had flocked tumultuously from all over the country to testify for him, (of course he did not put it that way, but it was the remarkable fact), from army friends like General Leonard Wood to business associates like Doctor Lyman Abbott, he included "the correspondents of the various newspapers—Gilson Gardner, Curtis, Charley Thompson, O. K. Davis—who had been in close touch with me both in the Presidency and throughout my campaign trips, and on many or all public occasions ever since."

He wrote that this impressive outpouring of witnesses included both his intimate friends and those who, while friendly, followed him about in the discharge of their professional duties, and continued: "This latter group included especially the newspaper men. They owed me nothing. So far as there had been any favor shown on either side, it had been shown by them to me. I had merely treated them fairly and courteously. They had nothing to gain by testifying for me, and in two or three instances I was uneasy at their doing so, because I feared that they might be damaged thereby. But they came forward eagerly, and because of the training they had had in accurate observation and statement, they made invaluable witnesses."

He purposely wrote "in two or three instances" so as to make it general, but he meant me; in fact, he had indicated that uneasiness more than once before we left Marquette. What he meant was that *The New York Times,* by which I was then employed, had warmly opposed him for thirty years (as he had once remarked, in a speech answering one of its attacks, "*The New York Times* is opposing me with a fervor of spirit that makes hydrophobia seem calm"), and might not be expected to be enthusiastic over my action. That impression was general, both then and whenever I wrote something which gave him the best of it. But it did that newspaper an injustice. As I left *The*

New York Times years ago, it is a pleasure to be able to say that under the presidency of Adolph Ochs it made no requirement of its writers except that they should comport themselves like honorable men. That was the surest road to his approval, and the only important one.

One of the witnesses to Roosevelt's constant sobriety was his young cousin, Philip J. Roosevelt. On cross-examination one of the editor's counsel asked him if the Colonel did not keep a regular collection of liquors at Sagamore Hill, and the young fellow replied, "He keeps a gentleman's cellar." The phrase made a great hit in Marquette, and became a proverb over night. A day or two later, as we were coming out of the court-room, Philip's foot slipped.

"Look out, Phil," said the Colonel, catching him by the arm. "If you tumble, every one will say that you've just come from a gentleman's cellar."

That reminds me of something which has no relation whatever to the subject I am writing about at the moment. Nearly forty witnesses gave evidence for Roosevelt, including some of the most eminent men in the country; one of them being Admiral Dewey, who sent a deposition. Though the Judge directed a verdict for Roosevelt, I found by inquiring that the jury had meant to return that verdict anyway, and I asked one juryman, a teamster from Negaunee, which one of that great array of eminences had produced the greatest impression on the jury. He replied promptly that it was ex-Secretary of the Interior James R. Garfield. I asked him who else, if anybody, had greatly impressed them, and he replied, "Mr. Riis, Judge Blair, and young Philip Roosevelt."

CHAPTER XV

TO SAVE THE NATION'S SOUL

DURING the World War I was writing editorials for *The New York Times* and doing all I could to influence public opinion favorably toward maintaining the traditional American policy. Since the word Americanism is claimed by both sides, I must explain that I do not mean the traditional American policy by which we submitted to insults and outrages on the high seas in Jefferson's Administration; I mean the traditional American policy by which we refused to submit to them, in Madison's Administration. Colonel Roosevelt was the great leader of those who believed in maintaining that attitude; and, since Madison was not the best exponent of it, it might better be called the attitude of Lincoln in 1861, and the attitude which McKinley was dragooned into taking in 1898 after the *Maine* was blown up.

The Wilson Administration, which began with the impossible injunction on all Americans to be neutral "in thought" as well as in act, which emitted the profound absurdity that with Germany's ambition to dominate the whole world we had "no concern," and which proposed to end the war by a "peace without victory" that would enable Germany to repair her mistake of 1914 and resume her conquests later in a shrewder manner, ended by discovering in three years that the war was one "to make the world safe for democracy" and that we must enter it without delay.

During the three years in which it had not yet made this discovery it refused to prepare for the possibility that we might be drawn into the conflict. Colonel Roosevelt was the leader of those in both parties who believed this refusal might have terrible results.

These two things—the maintenance of the traditional American attitude of Madison, Lincoln and McKinley, and the preparation in any case for an event that might happen without warning without our doing anything to bring it about—were the issues to which Colonel Roosevelt devoted the last years of his life; and he called them "the issues of preparedness and Americanism."

Because I was doing what I could to support these principles, and because of our friendship, I consulted with him very often during those years. Sometimes I asked to see him, and sometimes he sent for me; particularly on one occasion, when he was trying to get the President to let him raise a division and go to the front. He asked me to meet him at luncheon at a hotel in New York, and there he told me all his hopes, plans and intentions. They are well enough known now, and I refer to this meeting only because one of the things he said bore on a falsity still believed by most people—that he, with hardly any military experience, wanted to lead untrained troops to sacrifice in Europe to gratify his own love of the limelight.

"They say it would be criminal to put a politician, with only one short military incident in his record, in such a post," he said, "and it would be. I have no idea whatever of doing anything so silly and wicked. I propose to raise a division, and I can do it. In command of that division there should be, and would be, a Major-General appointed from the regular army. Under him there would be Brigadier-Generals. No one should be, or would be, appointed to one of those Brigadierships except officers who had been demonstrated to be fit for the command of a brigade. At the close of the Spanish War, when I was Colonel of the Rough Riders, I was designated for such a command; and the end of the war was all that prevented me from getting it. I am still recorded as an officer fitted to command a brigade. Therefore my desire is that, after I have raised the division, I should get one of the brigades; and I should insist that I be ranked at the foot of the list of the Brigadiers in that division."

He really did not understand why Wilson should shy at such a proposal. In some ways Roosevelt, strange as it sounds, was a little blind to his own unique excellences; he did not, in this case anyhow, understand that, even if he entered the division as a Corporal, the limelight would pass the Major-General by and strike the last company in the last regiment to find him; that it mattered nothing for the MacGregor to be seated beneath his inferiors, because where MacGregor sits, there is the head of the table. But Wilson understood it very well, and so did Baker and Pershing. Wilson and Baker, criticized for making the Colonel stay at home, shifted the onus to Pershing; what could they do if the commanding General didn't want such a Brigadier? If Pershing had enthusiastically welcomed that diversion of the limelight to a Brigadier, his recommendation to accept Roosevelt would of course have been submissively endorsed by Wilson. This not being the age of faith, people are ready to believe anything; and perhaps some will even believe that.

Most of my visits had nothing to do with anything I was writing. Once, for instance, I went to Sagamore Hill to propose to him—on behalf of certain public-spirited gentlemen—a platform which, if it proved satisfactory to him, an attempt would be made to get the Republican Party to adopt at its next Convention, then near. The idea was to bring about a unity of purpose and policy in the face of German and pacifist aggression. At this time he was still the head of the Progressive Party, but its end was in sight, and there was a movement on foot to have the Republicans nominate him.

Though the newspapers and the Old Guard politicians were much exercised over this boom, it did not mislead him. He knew he could not be nominated, and his concern was not with the nomination but with keeping America from losing her soul. At this time, the early part of 1916, the Republican nomination was very much in doubt, with Hughes leading, and with a number of other booms, including those for Theodore E. Burton, John W. Weeks, Albert B. Cummins and Charles W. Fairbanks. There were early booms for Elihu Root, and Governor McCall, of Massachusetts, but they flattened out before the Convention met.

In these talks of ours he always told me that his only fight was for "Americanism and preparedness," and that the Conventions were the battle-ground. The Progressive Party was going to hold its Convention at the same time with the Republicans, and he intended, if the Republicans crawfished before Germany, to continue the bolt of 1912 and defeat the party in November. But he would not be the Progressive candidate himself; the candidate would be Hiram Johnson.

"The Progressives," he remarked grimly, "want me to run on their ticket instead of Johnson, but they will have to show me, good and hard. I bore the burden in 1912, I have borne the burden for preparedness, and somebody else should do his bit."

"That Republican Convention," I observed, "is going to be pretty bum."

"I know it is," he said rather gloomily. "Most of them are going there with no patriotism, no feeling of love for their country, nothing but a desire to nominate somebody, anybody, who can be elected."

"Why is the Old Guard talking about nominating Burton or McCall?" I asked.

"The Old Guard is up in the air," he replied. "It is in a state of confusion, and doesn't know what it wants. Burton and McCall would be utterly unsatisfactory to us, because their records on preparedness are very bad.

"As for the financial people, they believe everything is coming their way, and Davison (Henry P. Davison, of J. Pierpont Morgan and Company) thinks that if it is necessary to spend twenty millions it can be done with satisfactory results." (I knew that his information was accurate; George W. Perkins was even then in communication with the Wall Street people to find out, on Roosevelt's behalf, what their attitude would be and what they thought.)

"The financiers," Roosevelt went on, "have an idea just now that they can put Root over. Such men as Davison, for instance. I have always found that financiers don't know anything outside of business [a remark he had made to me in the White House just ten years before]. They are able men in the money-making way, but it stops there. They can't understand politics. Now, Mark Hanna has become a myth with Davison. He and a lot of others firmly believe that Hanna bought the election of 1896. He didn't. Politicians know that money is very useful up to a certain point, but after that it's like pouring more powder into a gun. Besides, most of Hanna's money was used, not in vote-getting, but in the most real campaign of education that was ever made in this country; the overcoming and upsetting of Coin's Financial School.

"They want Root because he agrees with them and they know where he stands. If they can't have him, then, as

Davison says, 'We want a blank sheet of paper on which we can write.' And if they can't have either, they will be fairly well satisfied with Wilson. He hasn't recommended any new legislation against them or pushed any trust prosecution for a year and a half, and they think the demand for it—and Wilson, they think, only did that sort of thing because he believed the people wanted it—is ended. They understand politics so little that they can't be made to see that there will be a reaction as soon as the war is over, and a new demand."

(He was mistaken about that. But this was not because the financiers were better judges than he; he was perfectly right about their almost incredible childishness whenever it comes to any question of politics.)

"But," he continued, "Murray Crane and those fellows don't want Wilson, though they did in 1912. They don't want to lose their Governors and Senators again as they did in 1912, and to have the Democrats get the offices. The original idea was for a tariff campaign, which is why they put Harding forward; but the frost he got at the Hamilton Club showed them it couldn't be done. [Harding's boom got such a bad reception that he had to wait four years.]

"The trouble with Hughes, from their standpoint, is that nobody knows what he will do. [With regard to business, he meant; that was all that interested the Old Guard; they were not interested in preparedness and Americanism, the only things for which Roosevelt cared.] Many of the Old Guard would feel safer with me than with him. It is a little different from what it was four years ago. Then, you know, they didn't want to win the election, they only wanted to beat me for the nomination. They had to steal the Convention to do it. This year they won't have to steal it, because they have it. They will have, I estimate, seven hundred out of the nine hundred eighty-five delegates.

There are some of them who would prefer me to Hughes, because, they say, 'He understands politics; if we got in back of him he would play fair. If we accepted his ideas, he would let us have the Post Offices.' But about Hughes nobody knows. The day after he was elected he might discover that the great issue of the hour was the abolition," said the Colonel, falsetto, "of horse-racing by constitutional amendment."

I asked him what was the best he hoped for in the way of candidates, and he replied, "Leonard Wood or Hadley."

"Is Hadley all right on preparedness?" I asked in some surprise.

"Hadley," he answered in his slowly final way, "is all right on preparedness.

"But if that Convention does its worst, we will go ahead and nominate Hiram Johnson. What would be the use of throwing away all we fought for in 1912 just to put in the Presidency a man as bad as Wilson? And a man as bad as Wilson will be worse than Wilson.

"They actually think they can get me to support Root. I am going to stand by the men who stood by me. [He meant the Progressives; he knew that as a party they were done for, but he intended to save as much as possible of the things they had fought for.] With what grace could I go on the stump and face the men who were driven out of the Republican Party by the crooked work at the Convention of 1912, and ask them to support for President the head devil of the whole thing? How could I face them and say, 'The emergency is so great that I must ask you to forget the burglary of 1912 and put this unconvicted felon in the White House?' It would be too difficult.

"The Republicans ought not to insist on our swallowing such a nomination. It is precisely as if we should insist on their accepting Hiram Johnson. Neither party, neither the

Republicans nor the Progressives, should insist on extremes." At this time Johnson was more distasteful to the Old Guard Republicans than any one else except La Follette; but in addition he had been the most extreme of the Roosevelt men at Chicago in 1912, when the party split; the most radical figure of their camp as Root was the most radical figure of the other.

As Roosevelt finished that sentence, John McGrath, his secretary, came in the room and said, "Perkins is on the telephone." The Colonel stepped out, and I heard enough of his end of the conversation to be aware that George Perkins was reporting a conversation he had just had with some power in Wall Street; and I had no earthly doubt that it was Davison. Presently I heard the Colonel say, in that way he had of using each syllable as a separate sentence:

"What was that he said? That Root is an excellent man and would make a fine candidate? Tell him, George, from me, that Hiram Johnson is an excellent man and would make a fine candidate. Yes, George, that's all I want you to tell him. Good-by."

Then he came back, and we began talking about Hughes. He was willing to take Hughes, provided he could find out where Hughes stood. He would, of course, hold out for Wood or Hadley until Hughes was nominated, but would then support him as the candidate—if he only knew that Hughes was all right on preparedness and Americanism. "But," he said, "men come to me and tell me they know just how Hughes stands, and that his views are identical with mine. Then other men, equally authoritatively, tell me that his views are identical with Wilson's. I don't know what to believe.

"We've got to have somebody who stands for something, and I'm not the only one who feels that way. There is a widespread longing for a *man*. You'd hardly believe it," he said, with a grin, "but I have actually received offers of support from a few Germans. Their idea is that, at bottom, it is better even for them to have a man in the White House; they will at least know what to expect and where they stand, and they don't now. Charley, Wilson has done more to emasculate American manhood and weaken its fiber than any one else I can think of. He is a dangerous man for the country, for he is a man of brains, and he debauches men of brains. Bryan and Henry Ford only debauch fools."

I repeated this sentence the next day to Charles R. Miller, the editor of *The New York Times,* and he said, "Do you suppose the Colonel realizes that Wilson represents the average American of to-day, the fat and comfortable American who wants to stay fat and comfortable and does not like to work his mind too hard or to hear disagreeable news?" Under Miller's editorship *The Times* was Wilson's most powerful newspaper supporter except *The World;* and it was interesting to hear his real appraisal of Wilson and of the kind of citizen he represented. There was no inconsistency, however, for Miller was doing all he could to steady Wilson's blindfold wanderings among the issues of the war and thereby to serve the true interests of his country; and ultimately, after Bernstorff had reluctantly presented to Wilson the proof that Germany had been playing with him all along, Miller's course was vindicated, though he must have despaired at times. I never, however, heard him speak what was in his mind so frankly as he did in this comment on what Roosevelt said.

In the course of this talk the Colonel dictated a few letters to a stenographer. One of them was to a man who wanted to know why Roosevelt was so stiff in calling Germany to account, when he didn't call England to account for interfering with our mails. His reply was to this effect:

"Because England has held up our mails and Germany has murdered our people. If a man tried to rape your daughter, and at the same time another trespassed on your land, which would you attend to first? Wouldn't you first try to make the man stop raping your daughter, and after that wouldn't you turn around and make the other man stop trespassing on your land?"

"I'd call England to account," the Colonel remarked, to me, as the stenographer went out. "If I were President I would make Germany stop murdering our people. As soon as I had got her to obey international law I would say to England, 'Now you see we have made Germany stop her violations of the law; you must stop it too.' But I wouldn't send a lot of notes, I would not embark on any diplomatic correspondence without an end. I would send our mail over on war-ships. If there were not enough war-ships, I would send our mail over on merchant vessels convoyed by war-ships."

He asked me if I had met the newspaper men who were assigned to "cover" Oyster Bay. He said, "They're an unusually fine crowd this year. I call them my Cabinet. All of them are all right. You remember Jack Slaght, of *The World?* He has been against me for years, but now he is the head of my Cabinet." The Colonel always took the greatest joy in the way in which newspaper men came to Oyster Bay dead set against him and then "absorbed the Oyster Bay atmosphere," as he used to put it. "I'd like you to meet them. Suppose you go into the room where they are waiting for me, and I'll be in in a moment."

I went into the room, which was dark—for it was now twilight, we had been talking so long—and there rose up dim figures all over it. "Hello, Charley; haven't seen you since we sat in that tent at Gettysburg in the storm." "By George, I don't think I've seen you since the Bryan days in Lincoln, Nebraska." "Remember what you said to me down in Georgia after the Leo Frank lynching?" "Haven't seen you since we were up in Canada after Harry Thaw escaped from Matteawan," and so on. Then the Colonel came in and "held a meeting of the Cabinet," as he said, and stemmed the flood of reminiscence.

In the course of the "meeting" somebody asked him about the latest newspaper report, which was that he had called Hughes "a Baptist hypocrite."

"Isn't that ridiculous?" asked the Colonel patiently. "Isn't it likely? I'd be just as likely to call him a Baptist hypocrite as he would be to call me a Dutch Reformed dinosaur. By the way, that's a pretty good sentence; you can print that.

"Here's a funny thing," producing a letter. "When I was Governor there was a fool named Asa Bird Gardiner who was District Attorney, in New York County. He was a member of the Colonial Dames, or the Daughters of the Revolution, or some such organization, and mentioned that fact a good many times every day. The city and county governments were interfering with John McCullagh in his work as Superintendent of Elections. I threatened to remove the Mayor and the District Attorney if they didn't stop. The Mayor, who was Van Wyck, stopped, but Gardiner wouldn't, being a fool; so I removed him. To-day he writes me a letter saying that he is for me for President, on the ground of Americanism." The Colonel chortled.

The Colonel accompanied me to the door and stood there a while talking about Hughes, and he was deeply aggrieved at that candidate's silence. "It is nothing short of infamous," he said, "for a man to steal into the nomination by presenting himself as 'a blank sheet of paper.'"

"Suppose Hughes is nominated and turns out to be all right on Americanism?" I asked.

"If Hughes is nominated and turns out to be all right on Americanism, I and the rest will support him. With how good a grace, with how much enthusiasm, I can't tell. He is making it very hard for us." He seemed full of forebodings.

To avoid annoying breaks in the narrative, I have combined in what I have just written things which actually were said in more than one conversation. Of the other things that were said I made no notes at the time, and decline to rely on my memory. No man's memory is reliable after a few years. I publish them here because I think they show what was really in Roosevelt's mind in his political maneuvers in the early months of 1916, which were so vastly misunderstood at the time and are not understood even yet. He pulled every political string he could get hold of to control those Conventions, but not for his own advantage; solely for the sake of his country.

His description of Elihu Root as an "unconvicted felon" referred to the larceny of the Roosevelt delegations at Chicago in 1912, which were stolen and presented to Taft by the Old Guard. I think he probably forgave Penrose and most of the others, though I never heard him say so; but he had expected nothing from them. Root, however, had been his friend and was the man he really wanted for President in 1908 when he had to turn to the more feasible job of giving the nomination to Taft. And, as he spoke thus to me of Root, I suddenly remembered a day, a year before, when Nicholas Longworth, his wife and I were driving from Sagamore Hill to New York in their car. Alice Longworth had been moved to a recollection of the time when her father's term as President was ending, and when his friends gathered around the White House table for a farewell luncheon.

"It was a pathetic scene," she said, and I saw by her

eyes she meant something else. "The saddest person there was Elihu Root."

"He was much affected?" I inquired.

"Affected is not the word," said Alice Longworth and her eyes danced. "He was overcome."

"In what way did he manifest this grief of his?" I asked.

"Elihu," said Alice Longworth, "displayed the depth of his emotion by weeping in his wine-glass."

And then she lay back in the car and laughed a long, melodious and rollicking laugh at the memory; nor did she regain her composure until Nicholas had sped the car past at least two hamlets.

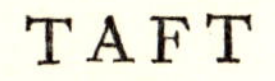

TAFT

CHAPTER XVI

MR. MALAPROP

"We have two Tafts, dear,
Two, and yet the same."
—ROBERT BUCHANAN, sixty years later.

IF WE hadn't, there would be no amiable Chief Justice expanding under the soft glow of universal public approval; there would be only the blundering politician who was hurled out of office by the greatest revolt his party had ever known, one that must have comforted the ghosts of Harrison and Blaine. The queer thing is that all his life Taft had wanted to be a Judge, not a politician; he had wanted to do what he could do, not what he couldn't. Well, circumstances, in the form of Republican votes, as he himself would say, for he has a fine sense of humor and is honest with himself, decided that his ambition should be fulfilled at last, and there he is on the bench. If ever, on dull days, he hankers secretly for the fleshpots of politics, then he blunders again, for in politics Taft was ever all thumbs.

Taft the Blunderer! It seems a strange title for a President; and it is not a correct title for the Chief Justice. It is only true of Taft the politician, the honest greenhorn at the poker table, and it tells the story of that politician's fall. A fall from which a splendid Judge rose to add honor to the seat of Marshall and Taney. The popular notion that a Supreme Court Justice is a passionless dummy, or a machine uttering finalities with as little feeling as the Delphic Oracle showed in handing down decisions, is all wrong. A highly human man who goes on the bench does not shed his humanness with his sack coat, or put on deity with his gown. The only great failure in the Supreme Court's history was caused by its humanness. That was when Justice Wayne, considering the case of an obscure negro named Dred Scott, had visions of himself as a beneficent god showering peace on an endangered and distraught land, and so went visiting the houses of his fellow-Justices to point out to them the path of glory. He was, as it took a civil war to prove, a little mistaken about his place on Sinai; but a well-regulated mind will love him for it.

And if the Supreme Court does not freeze beneficent patriotism, as Justice Wayne and the Justices who listened to him in his travels to their houses proved, it does not freeze other warm human attributes, such as righteous anger. The unwritten history of Judges would tell of many a fist pounded on the table, including the Taft fist, which struck a table on the other side of which sat Medill McCormick, of Chicago. It was not pounded in his judicial capacity; the fist belonged only to a President. It was pounded in release of the emotions aroused in the President's breast by McCormick's warning that if he did not back water in his support of the Payne-Aldrich tariff, the West would bolt, saddle him with a Democratic Congress, and defeat him for reelection. The fist was accompanied by a voice carrying to the McCormick ear an outraged defiance and laden with cuss-words. McCormick took his hat and his departure to the Middle West to spread the incendiary news among the already mutinous Progressives; and a year later the House of Representatives was voting so Democratic that it became difficult to find a Republican there. Two years later the Republican voters of the West were carrying out McCormick's threat at the polls, and Taft was reading the unsatisfactory news that, running for reelection, he had succeeded in carrying the States of Utah and Vermont. The men whose wrath McCormick had waved in Taft's face that day no longer even called themselves Republicans; they described themselves as Bull Moosers and voted for Roosevelt. And McCormick was on his way to a Senatorship.

Taft never wanted to be a politician, but in Ohio one can hardly help it. Politics was thrust upon him, both as an Ohio boy and as the son of a man so deeply immersed in politics as to be himself a Cabinet officer, Judge Alphonso Taft. (He held, by the way, the same Cabinet post in Grant's Cabinet that son William was to hold in Roosevelt's—Secretary of War.) Young William was mixing involuntarily in politics before he came of age, and even encountered the majesty of the law for dealing pugilistically with a hostile partisan who made unseemly remarks about Judge Alphonso. Pleased by this apparent indication of an aptitude for Ohio politics, the Judge interrogated the youth concerning his ambitions, and found to his sorrow that they inclined not toward politics, the natural vent for youthful Ohio energies, but rather toward the law. Some minor Judgeships therefore came his way in due course, but in Ohio a Judgeship is ever intricately mixed with politics, and so the two Tafts in one just naturally couldn't help running along together.

But Taft, unlike so many Ohio Judges, had as little to do with politics as he could help, and never learned enough about the distasteful subject to hurt him; or to help him, as his later career was to prove. He won so good a name on the bench that he was sent out to the Philippines, which we had just subdued and which were still seething. He governed wisely; his duties in those "still vexed" islands were quasi-judicial, or at any rate not at all political in the American sense, and he came home with enhanced fame and became Secretary of War. In that office he increased his fame by doing just what the President, Roosevelt by name, wanted him to do. It is curious that both Roosevelt and Wilson used to require their Cabinets to do not what the Cabinets wanted, but what the Presidents wanted; and that Roosevelt's Cabinet used to find great joy in doing it—even such dissimilar characters as John Hay and James Wilson—whereas almost all the members of Wilson's Cabinet made mouths over it and largely resigned, from Garrison and Bryan to Lansing and son-in-law McAdoo. It wasn't because Wilson wanted them to do anything disgraceful, either. If Roosevelt had asked them they would probably have done it.

Hitherto Taft's progress had been one of uninterrupted and shining success. Then Roosevelt forced him into the Presidency against the wish of the party, which wanted Roosevelt himself; and he was not a successful President. It is strange to recall that he was bitterly hated at the end of his term, though he was the same honest and kindly and patriotic and right-thinking man he had been in so many other offices and was to be as Chief Justice. In reviewing his history it is customary to dwell significantly on the fact that in 1912 he carried only two States, the most politically insignificant states in the normally Republican column, except Rhode Island. Considering that the American public was off on one of its periodical and unreasoning jaunts of hate that Autumn, I regard this as something of an achievement, and should be disposed to compliment Utah and Vermont if it were not that the Mormon machine pulled Utah through and that it's a capital offense to vote a third party ticket in Vermont. Otherwise Taft would not have carried anything. People used language about Taft which they would have been ashamed to use about Gyp the Blood.

This general hatred of Taft, which seems so queer a thing when we look back upon it, and which was nowhere so strong as in his own party, is largely attributable to the fact that, in politics, "he can not ope his mouth but out there flies a blunder." Often his blunders in those days were not blunders per se, but only blunders for a President. A President is not merely an executive. He must also be a judge of men—and of words; oh, most emphatically, of words.

The first and perhaps the worst exhibition of his supernatural skill in saying the wrong thing occurred when he was Secretary of War. As he got off a train a reporter asked him what would be the outcome of the unemployment situation, then a frightfully tender one with the labor men because of the hard times and what was unjustly called the "Roosevelt panic" of 1907. Mechanically Taft answered, as anybody but a President-designate or a President might have answered, "God knows!" All he meant, of course, was that William H. Taft did not know; but in print it seemed to show a heartless indifference, the callous contempt of the Dives class for the Lazarus class. It flew all over the United States, was reiterated and embroidered and twisted, and became the text for a thousand indignant speeches and a rallying cry for demagogues. Long afterward labor men were still calling him "God-Knows Taft." Any one else could have said it without raising a ripple; probably hundreds of people did unthinkingly say it. But it was one of the things a President, or a near President, just must *not* say.

He never could learn this difference between a President and a private person. He was for the Payne-Aldrich tariff bill of 1909. This was awkward enough, since the bill was opposed by that wing of the party which was going to be in control of the party in the next Congressional and Presidential elections, or else wreck it. But that was not enough for President Taft. The bill was not regarded with favor anywhere west of Pittsburgh, and the warmth with which it was hated in Illinois rose to heat in Iowa and to the boiling-point in Michigan and Wisconsin. Minnesota was far beyond the boiling-point; it had reached that height assigned by Holy Writ to the place where "the worm dieth not and the fire is not quenched." Speaking in favor of the bill was one of the few things for which a man might legally be lynched in Minnesota. So, of course, that was the place which Taft picked out as a likely place in which to eulogize it. It was good nature, that omnipresent good nature which is Taft's most endearing trait, which led him to the choice. One of the Republican leaders, Jim Tawney, of Winona, was Chairman of the Appropriations Committee, one of the "two great committees" of the House, and was a great favorite in Washington. The upsurge of the West against the Payne-Aldrich bill threatened the Old Guard Republicans with defeat, and Jim was especially nervous—with good cause, for in the next election Winona retired him to private life so pointedly that he never entered politics again.

So, when the House leaders asked the President to do Jim a good turn by going to his home town and saying a few well-chosen words showing that the West and Winona had misjudged the Payne-Aldrich bill, Taft light-heartedly promised, haled himself forth to that Waterloo, Winona, and made the speech. The reaction throughout Winona, Minnesota, the Northwest, the Middle West, the Far West and the United States came in the form of a reverberating roar. The Rocky Mountains stood on their heads, the Great Lakes turned inside out, and the Sierras danced like the hills of Scripture. Even the House leaders and the always purblind Aldrich saw that something must be done, and they affrightedly advised the President to say something that would calm the mountains down and restore the Mississippi to its bed. Taft hurriedly said it, and what do you think he said? What might have been expected. He said he had "dashed off the Winona speech hastily between stations!"

Now, you or I might say that, but the President of the United States is supposed to think thunderously, and his utterances are reckoned as revelations of God. Wilson loosed his "too proud to fight" aphorism before he became aware of that fact. "Makes up his speeches between stations, does he?" yelled the infuriated populace. "Is that the sort of President we've got?" And it took a magnifying glass to find the Republican minority in the next House of Representatives, and to find Taft's electoral vote in the next Presidential election.

When Roosevelt started after his scalp in 1912, Taft at first refused to take the stump against him. He had not even been very much set on the nomination in the beginning. But his quarrel with Roosevelt was at its height. The ex-President was the head of the Republican faction which was assailing the Taft Administration and Taft himself. He finally completed the sum of his misdeeds by announcing "My hat is in the ring," and declaring that he himself was out for the nomination as the opponent of Taft and all Taft stood for. Hitherto the only avowed candidate of the Progressives had been Senator Robert M. La Follette, but Roosevelt was so obviously the right man and La Follette so evidently the wrong one that most of the Progressives had been importuning Roosevelt to take the nomination himself, and at last he yielded. This final act of hostility roused the blood of all the conservatives, even of the easy-going President himself. Those around him urged him to take the stump. Roosevelt was already stumping those States which held Presidential primaries and vigorously attacking conservatism, reaction, standpattism and Taft. No President had ever stumped in a primary campaign; it was undreamed of until then. In fact, Presidents did not even take the stump after they had been renominated. It would have been charged that they were lowering the dignity of the office; and it was seldom that even a man who was not President, but had been named for the office, took the stump. Horace Greeley, William J. Bryan, and to a limited and circumscribed extent Blaine and Taft himself in 1908 had been the only exceptions.

When Taft finally did decide to go out on the stump in the primaries his slow wrath had been kindled and was burning high. In the course of a confidential chat with him in the White House I spoke about the contest on which he was about to enter in the primaries, and Taft said, looking reflectively out of the window and without any heat, "Whether I win or lose is not the important thing. But," he added with sudden vigor, and as he turned from the window to me his blue eyes suddenly began to blaze, "I am in this fight to perform a great public duty—the duty of keeping Theodore Roosevelt out of the White House."

He set his lips grimly and looked steadily at me with bitter eyes which had grown dark and stormy. This was the feeling that had led him to overcome his reluctance to violate precedent by going into a party primary as a factional candidate—he, the President of the whole people, Democrats as well as Republicans. Whatever personal feeling he had, as the consequence of Roosevelt's appearance as the opposition candidate and because of the break in their friendship long before, was obliterated by his belief that Roosevelt had become a dangerous radical and revolutionist and that the safety of the country demanded his exclusion from power by any means. At least Taft convinced himself that that was his motive. After this and some other conversations on the subject I had no doubt of that. I knew he did not believe he was the choice of the party, but he thought the party had gone mad, and that it would be a patriotic act to hold it by the throat until reason returned. He might sacrifice himself in doing so; he certainly would sacrifice the good opinion of those who valued the dignity of the Presidential office, but his duty, he thought he saw, was plain. Nor was he at all concerned over the fact (which he knew, even then) that through him a minority of the party was endeavoring to thwart the will of the majority. The majority, he convinced himself, had fallen under the spell of an artful and dangerous demagogue, and if left to itself would wreck not only the party but perhaps the country. He knows better now. Passion, especially party passion and above all factional passion, warps men's minds unbelievably for the time.

One day about a month before the Convention I called at the White House to talk to him not about politics but about a matter of executive administration. I had no intention of bringing up politics, but it was too much in his mind, and, after telling me what I wanted to know, he said in a slow and solemn manner:

"Thompson, I expect to be nominated for President, and I want to be. So that I can keep Theodore Roosevelt from wrecking the Republican Party."

"Seems to me he's got pretty far along with that already," I remarked unsympathetically.

"That isn't what I mean," said the President, still with the same measured gravity. "I don't mean wrecking it in an election. I mean warping it away from its purpose and changing its character. I mean changing it to a radical party from a party of moderate liberalism."

The people knew nothing of Taft's mistaken but honest

conviction, expressed in these conversations, that he was trying, at whatever cost to himself, to save the party and the country. All they saw was that, apparently in desperation at the prospect of losing his job, Taft was dragging the Presidency in the dust of a personal row. Taft felt that he ought to make some explanation of his course in breaking the precedent set by every President from Washington to Roosevelt and appealing to mass meetings for votes. Even in his long list of luckless experiments in the art of expression, this one shines out as a pearl of great price. "Even a rat will fight when driven into a corner," he said gloomily—and thus vanished the last lingering chance he had of getting a look-in in the Presidential primary States. All the Republican States voted for Roosevelt, save only that gnarled State where La Follette reigned supreme and gnashed his teeth at both Taft and Roosevelt impartially.

In all the explanations of the break between Taft and Roosevelt, I have seen no mention of the devastating effect of one short sentence. Roosevelt had made Taft President. The Convention wanted to renominate Roosevelt himself, and so did the party. For a year before the Convention was held Roosevelt was busy strangling the Roosevelters. Whenever he heard that a State boss, such as John G. Capers, of South Carolina, or Cecil A. Lyon, of Texas, was going to bring a Roosevelt delegation to the Convention, he would summon that misguided chieftain to the White House and say, in effect, "Let your delegation be for Taft, Cassio, or never more be officer of mine!" It was a bound and gagged Convention, with Roosevelt's friend, Henry Cabot Lodge, running it. Lodge was at one end of a telegraph wire; the other end was in the White House. At Lodge's end of it was William J. Lee, the fastest sender the Western Union had. Through him Lodge let Roosevelt know all that was going on as instantaneously as if he had been in the convention hall. The moment Lodge told Roosevelt that there was any danger the stampeders would put him over, Roosevelt was to flash an unconditional refusal of the nomination, for Lodge to read.

But Lodge didn't need it; the man was able to cope with any emergency. He was the most Napoleonic Chairman I ever saw at a Convention; a combination of Bismarck, Machiavelli, Peter the Great and John L. Sullivan. The galleries were packed with Roosevelt rooters captained by ex-Senator Jonathan Bourne. The delegates, rounded up, roped and branded by Roosevelt for Taft, were sullen, hostile and uneasy, and might take fire if the galleries touched a match. Sulkiest of all was the Texas delegation. Its boss, Colonel Cecil Lyon, had returned home from Washington sadly months before, saying, "It's all off, boys; the big chief won't let us vote for him, and we've got to vote for Taft." It had taken Lyon many hard, toilsome months to whip them into line, though he was absolute master of Texas. Now he sat glumly on the platform, looking dourly at his muttering henchmen down below as he and they took their medicine.

An orator mentioned Roosevelt's name. The Bourne-filled galleries let loose an ear-splitting screech, and unfurled a picture of the President. As they rose by the thousands, yelling and roaring, Lyon's eyes flashed. Forgetting what he was there for, he sprang up, waved his big sombrero, and shouted for Roosevelt. The grouch of the Texans was succeeded by unbelieving joy; turned in a second from stone images to men thanking God, they jumped on their chairs and howled like Indians. The sight recalled Lyon to his senses; he waved his hand at them, shrieking "Down! Down!" and the faithful delegation sank dejectedly into its seats. The stampede was foiled. The danger was over for the time.

There came a tempestuous renewal when the balloting began. It was the last and best chance for a stampede, and the rooters raised such a clamor that one could not hear his neighbor shout in that long din. Lee was waiting at his key twenty feet away, but instead of flashing the news to Roosevelt that magnificent Chairman, Lodge, took the extraordinary, unprecedented course of calling the roll unheard. The roar was so great that nobody could hear a word, so Lodge stepped to the front of the platform and beckoned in turn to the chairman of each delegation. That delegate would step up to the platform and hand the vote of his State to the clerk, who would record it, and then make way for another chairman. The delirious galleries went on yelling, never noticing what was being done, and the watching reporters expected that when they did stop their clamor they would find Taft had been nominated without their knowledge. It did amount to that, for when the noise subsided Taft had a majority of votes already recorded for him.

Roosevelt had thus forced Taft on the party leaders for a year and crushed opposition, and then he had jammed Taft down the Convention's throat at the finish. But he did not stop there. He intended to stand aside and let Taft run the campaign, but things came up that Taft could not handle. He went on the stump, but the nation's eyes were still turned toward the White House and its ears still inattentive to any new voice. Inevitably he found hurdles in his way, hurdles that had to be jumped by a rough rider, and he was no rough rider. Whenever such a hurdle showed up the rough rider was at hand; he issued from the White House with gun and lasso.

For instance, Hearst suddenly produced his disastrous revelation of the Standard Oil Company's pay-roll of Senators. One of them was Senator Foraker, who was in the forefront of Republican leaders. This was a situation Taft was never meant to cope with. It was, however, pie for Roosevelt. The President met it by issuing a blast reading Foraker out of the party, thereby extinguishing his career. But the Democrats still expected to make capital out of the exposure, and Taft knew no way to prevent them. Roosevelt did, though. He demanded that Bryan, Taft's opponent, should explain why Governor Haskell, of Oklahoma, who was also on Hearst's Standard Oil list, was running Bryan's campaign as one of the two chief officers of the Democratic National Committee. Bryan had to meet the issue, and he met it by forcing Haskell out; but the Democratic guns were spiked, and the Hearst exposures had no political effect except the ruin of Foraker, which was a tremendous event in those days, and of Haskell, who was only beginning his national career and did not count for so much. Their effect in another direction was permanent. They put an end to the pleasant corporation practise of putting the Senate on the pay-roll.

So, throughout the campaign, Roosevelt watched over Taft like a hen over her chickens, always on the alert and never missing a trick. After the election Roosevelt expected a word of thanks. He got it, in this form: "I owe a great deal to you, Theodore, and I want to take this opportunity of saying so." Proper expression by Roosevelt. "Yes," continued Taft, "in thinking over the whole campaign, I am bound to say that I owe my election more to you than to anybody else, *except my brother Charley.*"

I do not mean to say that this astonishing remark alone was what made Roosevelt go off to the Potomac meadows and bite his teeth till the blood came, but it opened abysmal gulfs. He saw the next four years in a flash, and the happenings of the next few months, in which Brother Charley and the others at Taft's ear turned their thumbs down on all Roosevelt's friends, surprised him no whit. He went to Africa disillusioned and unhappy, having seen the beginnings, and when he reappeared from the jungle it was to meet Gifford Pinchot, who had hurried across the ocean to be the first to tell him all the things that had befallen himself, Garfield, Loeb, and all the rest of the Rooseveltians. Roosevelt, who at that time still did not want to be nominated again, responded vigorously by announcing that he was a strong supporter of Governor Hughes. The rest is history. Taft was surprised, hurt and grieved. He could not see what he had done to break the friendship of a man whom he highly esteemed and, in his way, loved. Nor did he know that, human nature being what it is, nine men out of ten would have done exactly what Roosevelt did, though it may be a regrettable fact.

This gives a measure of Taft's inability to judge how his remarks would sound to a hearer, but it was in a private conversation. Now, for four years, his conversations were to be with the people of the United States, and he was to demonstrate the same quality in public that he had often shown in private; and now the effect was to be calamitous, for he was talking to millions who did not know him and would make no allowances.

The political reconciliation between Taft and Roosevelt staged by the Hughes managers at the Union League Club in 1916 was so far from being the real thing that the public found it hard to swallow. But the reconciliation behind the scenes later on was entirely real. It began with one of those letters Taft always wrote, frank, open-hearted and warm. It was just after Roosevelt's first serious illness, in 1918, and was a letter expressing joy over his recovery. How it affected Roosevelt can be guessed from the fact that it was the first letter of congratulation the invalid answered. There were other letters, an accidental meeting in Chicago, and when Roosevelt came to make his key-note speech in the Fall campaign he submitted the manuscript to Taft for criticism. All the changes Taft suggested were incorporated. The reconciliation was complete. It had been helped along by friends who repeated to each the kind things said about him by the other.

One of these is recorded by Jack Leary in *Talks with T. R.* Governor Harding told it to Roosevelt, who enjoyed it hugely, liked it better than any of the others, and repeated it with gusto to the Old Guard at Oyster Bay. Taft had been talking to the Governor (not Warren Harding, but the Iowa man) about the Wilson Administration, and said, "When I see the way things are going at Washington it makes my blood boil, but when I think how much madder they must make T. R., I feel better." After Harding laughed at this, Taft spoke more seriously, calling Roosevelt "the one man in the country best capable of handling the situation, denied any part in it, and compelled to sit in the bleachers and see the ball booted all over the lot." When the Colonel heard this typical Taft story, he said, "Taft is not much better off"; and he went on to tell of the great things Taft could do if Wilson should give him a chance, say in Paris or London or Rome, or Washington itself.

CHAPTER XVII

THE TONGUE IS A LITTLE MEMBER

WHAT was the reason for Taft's verbal ineptitude? It came from his frank and unstudied naturalness. He always said what he thought without the slightest regard for how it would sound or read. He was the only man I ever met in politics who had this childlike frankness. It was no equipment for a politician; would indeed have been no equipment for a business man. It was not so much that Taft did not care what people thought as that he was too much a child of nature to calculate on it. Premeditation is indispensable when a politician says anything; but Taft never premeditated. He didn't know how. With the brain of a man, the big brain of a remarkably able man, he had the innocent candor in speech of a boy under ten.

As for the effect of words on himself, he never thought of that at all; and I am not speaking now of his public utterances only. Nor, for that matter, of their effect on others. When he was Secretary of War the reporters, about eight in number, whose duty it was to "cover" the War Department for the morning papers used to visit him daily at the close of business and question him about the day's events. He was always jolly and hail-fellow-well-met, and we had no suspicion that he had not the faintest idea which paper each man represented. No suspicion, until one day Colonel W. R. Nelson, the famous proprietor of the *Kansas City Star,* came to Washington on public business and had a conversation with Taft. In the course of the talk he spoke of Dick Lindsay and Taft looked blank and said:

"Lindsay? Dick Lindsay? Who's he?"

"Why," said Colonel Nelson, dumfounded, "he's my Washington correspondent. I understand from him that he comes in to see you every day. Don't you know him?"

"Never heard the name," said Taft innocently.

There was a painful interview that evening between Nelson and his Washington representative. Lindsay finally convinced the Colonel that he really was not soldiering on the job and did see Taft every day, and Nelson returned to Kansas City with his opinion of Lindsay again at par, but with his opinion of Taft somewhat lowered. The thing was all the harder for Nelson to understand because Lindsay was the sort of man anybody would notice even in a crowd; a large, fine-looking fellow with a remarkable face. The next day, when we trooped into Taft's office, Lindsay walked directly over to him, put his fists down on Taft's desk, bent over him, and said:

"Take a good look at me, will you, Mr. Secretary? I want you to be able to remember what I look like, so that the next time you talk to my boss you will be able to describe me. I'm Lindsay, of the *Kansas City Star!*"

Taft pounded his fists on the arms of his chair and roared with joy. The incident passed, and still we had no idea that Taft did not know who any of us were—except that he now knew who the *Kansas City Star* man was. But about a week later the *Pittsburgh Dispatch* correspondent told me that the Secretary had asked him who *The New York Times* man was. That afternoon, when we entered his office, I said:

"Mr. Secretary, Mr. Heiss tells me that you asked him yesterday who *The New York Times* man was, and that he replied, 'He is a short man with a fragmentary mustache and a catarrhal voice.' I don't impugn the accuracy of the description. On the contrary, I hope you'll commit it to memory, so that you can recite it if Mr. Adolph Ochs ever asks you, as Colonel Nelson did, if you know his Washington correspondent."

It took Taft probably two minutes to stop laughing. But after that it did seep into his mind that to say, "I never heard his name," was not quite the surest way to make a reporter solid with his boss; and he found out our names and papers and remembered them. I tell this story because it so thoroughly illustrates his naive inability to judge the sound of words in private conversation, as well as in public utterances. We all came rapidly to entertain a great affection for Taft; and before long we became aware of this characteristic of his, of the harm it might do him now that he was beginning to be talked of for President, and of how unfortunate it was he did not have somebody who could protect him from his language.

One day, at this stage of the game, when we made our daily visit, we inquired about a matter of considerable importance which he had taken up with President Roosevelt. Taft answered with his usual abounding frankness. He and the President didn't agree about it, and the President had overriden him; he still thought he was right and couldn't understand why Roosevelt didn't think so too. He believed Roosevelt would change his mind. He was not in the least put out about it, he was simply firing off his mind as if he had been talking to his wife behind closed doors. He had not the smallest notion how it would look in print, or the explosive consequences it would have; how it would not only raise Cain with Roosevelt's Administration, but perhaps make it difficult for him to stay in the Cabinet or run for President. Yet, before the eyes of every man in the room but himself, there rose the picture of the head-lines certain to come in the morning: "Roosevelt Splits with Taft! Serious Division in Administration! Secretary Stubbornly Holds Out! Interviews with Leading Democratic Senators on Sudden Upheaval in Cabinet."

There was a moment's pause. Taft sat beaming, wait ing for the next question, wholly unconscious of the bomb he had touched off. He was safe enough in the hands of most of us; but the Hearst representative would assuredly print it under streamer head-lines in bold face type on the front page. Taft was not talking in confidence, and he could not be accused of taking any unfair advantage.

"Mr. Secretary," said Arthur Wallace Dunn, of the Associated Press, speaking in a resolute and significant manner, "what you have just said is not said under the injunction of secrecy. Therefore, unless you do enjoin secrecy upon us, we shall most certainly print it. But we feel it our duty to warn you that if we do it will have the most unpleasant consequences to President Roosevelt, and the most disastrous consequences to yourself. We strongly advise you to place the injunction of secrecy upon us. Do I speak for all of you, gentlemen?"

We all said he did. The Hearst man, looking as if he could bite Dunn's head off, hesitated and finally nodded ungraciously.

"It's up to you, Mr. Secretary," said Dunn. "Do you place the injunction of secrecy on us, or shall we print it?"

Taft had been the picture of astonishment, and now he looked alarmed. He nodded hastily and vigorously. "Certainly—you're right," he said hurriedly; "the injunction of secrecy is laid on all of you, and you will please regard it as confidential."

As we went out, after asking him about the rest of the day's business, the Hearst man said sadly, "Dunn, why do you hate a good story so intensely?"

It was only in politics Taft blundered. Outside that field he was a different person. The incidents just narrated may seem to contradict that statement. But in private a man may have this inability to see the words he says, and still not be blundering. A blunder is a harmful mistake. Taft's private mistakes were not harmful. His public mistakes were, because the chance words of a public man are material things, as material as a charge of dynamite. They may be harmful to himself, his party, his country, or the world. Taft's hapless adventures in the use of words harmed only himself and the Republican Party (which badly needed a drubbing), whereas Wilson's far fewer blunders had their effect on the United States, on Europe, and on remote communities not yet heard from. Taft's blunders are mainly forgotten. Wilson's will never cease to reverberate until the Resurrection morn.

It was only in politics that Taft the Blunderer blundered. I emphasize this, because unless the distinction is drawn, what I have said will give the impression that he was a chump, which is absurd. He had a keen and powerful mind, and displayed it in all matters wherein he was at home. In political management he was certainly not at home; in politics he groped his way, foggy and bewildered, through an endless maze. He was not the only proof of Roosevelt's lack of judgment in picking men; Roosevelt's fondness for his friends often made him insert the right peg in the wrong hole. Taft at the beginning felt that he was not a born President, and by no means wanted the office. From 1905 onward Roosevelt kept urging him to be a candidate and telling him that he, Roosevelt, could put him over. Taft shrank from it. As early as November, 1904, about four days after Roosevelt's election, he sent for Milton McRae to come to Washington, and when the Ohio publisher arrived Roosevelt told him Taft was slated to be his successor and that he wanted McRae to go back to Ohio and start the Taft boom in the Scripps-McRae newspapers immediately. McRae obeyed, but Taft was cold to the idea. He told McRae he could not imagine himself as a President and did not believe there was anything in it. He was seemingly full of forebodings.

But Roosevelt kept incessantly at him, little dreaming that he was starting something which would bring about a rupture in their friendship and smash the Republican Party. (I do not mean by this that their rupture broke the Republican Party, but Taft's Administration did, by infuriating the progressive element to a point where they would have voted for a Democrat rather than Taft. Roosevelt's Bull Moose nomination saved them from having to make that choice.) Whenever Roosevelt would press it on him, Taft would reply, uneasily but with much good sense, "It's good of you, Theodore, but I'd rather be a Judge." In that sentence he showed that he correctly judged his own limitations and his own excellences. Roosevelt, with all his intuition, could never understand that Taft knew himself better than he did, and never took warning. At last Taft began to think that after all Roosevelt might be right and he might have the makings of a good President. His family kept urging it upon him, and finally, though Roosevelt had practically given up hope of inducing him to run and was willing to give him the Judgeship he wanted, he surprised and delighted his friend by saying that he had given up his judicial ambitions and would take the Presidency. If Taft had not been over-persuaded the history of the next years would have been very different.

On the bench Taft was not merely a good Judge, but he was a progressive and far-seeing man. His judgment there was strong, broad and long in range. For instance, he became one of the principal leaders, if not the foremost leader, in the cause of law reform, a great question which is not spectacular enough to interest the public as it should, but which would interest them if they realized how profoundly it affects their own lives, from the highest to the humblest. What is more remarkable, Taft out of office was a man of good political judgment. In office he lost his bearings, but as a spectator on the side-lines he was capable of shrewd, just and penetrating observations. He had no egotism and never, in judging political events from the side-lines, was misled by vanity or self-appreciation.

A couple of months after he left the White House, following on his overwhelming defeat in 1912, I was sitting with him at his home in New Haven, where the ex-President was giving lectures at Yale. Naturally the talk turned on the last campaign, with its bitter animosities and ungoverned violence. There was at that time the usual slight reaction that comes when the nation sobers down—a reaction at least in the tone of newspaper comments—and many papers were saying that Taft was getting popular again. I mentioned this, and said, "I suppose you've seen that sort of comment."

"Yes, I've seen a lot of it," he said, ruminating. "Well," he added quizzically, looking shrewdly at me and pulling the ears of the adjacent dog, "you may have noticed that nearly three million five hundred thousand Republicans voted for me, even though I did run third in the race. Now, Thompson, whenever I read the gratifying news that there is a visible reaction in my favor, I have a strong suspicion, I know not whence it comes, that the visible reactor is simply one of those upright and intelligent three million five hundred thousand." And, releasing the dog's ears, he patted its head and softly roared his rollicking laugh. He was quite right and I had nothing to say. I tell this not because it illustrates the fact that Taft was a good loser and a good sport, but because it shows the sanity and levelheadedness of his political criticism—when he was out of the cast himself and viewing the drama from his stage box.

Another striking difference between Taft the bewildered politician and Taft the able critic is that his public utterances were couched in a stodgy and soggy style, whereas he was witty and humorous in conversation, with a gift of phrase and much acuteness. He could compress a page of sound criticism in a witty sentence. After he left the Presidency Alden March, then Sunday Editor of *The New York Times,* asked me to introduce him to Taft, who was then in New York visiting his brother Henry. March wanted to contract with him for a series of articles of five thousand words each on public questions. I took him to Henry Taft's and introduced him to the ex-President. When March broached his plan, Taft considered it dubiously and began to shake his head. He said he didn't think he would be able to get the time every week. "If you haven't time to write five thousand words," broke in March eagerly, "I would be satisfied with two thousand." Taft threw up his hands and let out his gigantic laugh. "Oh, Lord!" he cried, "I might possibly find the time to write five thousand words, but where in the world would I ever get time to write two thousand?" There is a world of sagacity in that; it sums up in an epigram much of the philosophy of authorship.

He was a shrewd and practical observer of events, and after he retired from the Presidency he got great enjoyment out of watching the wheels go round in the old machine of which he had once been the engineer. "Oh, Thompson, you don't know how much fun it is," he once exclaimed, "to sit back here and watch the playing of the game down there in Washington, without any responsibility of my own. I am watching it with all the dispassionate interest of a man up a tree." This was only a couple of months after he turned the White House over to Wilson. He talked about the men he and I had known in the Senate, and said: "I never saw the Senate in such a low state as it is to-day, did you?"

"Well," I replied, "it surely doesn't much resemble the Senate I found when I first went to Washington."

"Oh, no," he said, "there was a solidity and strength about it that is all gone now."

"Do you think that was why Spooner got out?" I asked. (Spooner, of Wisconsin, was one of the five men who governed the Senate, and pretty much the United States, along with the Speaker of the House, in the old days, and a man of great ability.) "He gave as a reason that he wanted to make some money before he died, but I thought another reason was that he had ceased to feel at home; the Senate was growing strange to him."

Taft nodded. "Yes, it was a reason," he said, "but the controlling reason was that Spooner hadn't any stomach for a fight, and La Follette had. La Follette was coming to the top in Wisconsin, and Spooner had to fight or quit. He was a man to run away from a fight, and in this case he did. He left the field open to La Follette, for there was no one else in Wisconsin who could fight him, and so he came to dominate the State without a scrap. Then, too, Spooner did want to make some money for his family.

"I can't help admiring La Follette," he went on. "He hates me worse than the devil hates holy water. But I can't help admiring him. He isn't a gentleman, of course, he's a cad. And has no desire to be a gentleman; but it is impossible to withhold admiration from a man who is so direct and indefatigable a fighter for what he believes to be right. He can't be swerved or side-tracked; he sees exactly what he wants to accomplish, and having made up his mind nothing can weaken him or distract him. He is an indomitable man.

"For that matter, I haven't got anything against most of those insurgents, though they don't love me. There's Bristow. He is always just as close to a keyhole as a man can get and see through it with both eyes at once, and he's as narrow as a toothpick; but he's honest and sincere and means to do his duty as he sees it.

"But as for Senator X——, he's a hypocrite. He's always talking about virtue and morality, and it would be better if somebody else did that. I haven't any use for him. One day, about a year before the National Convention, he was trying to give me the impression that he was supporting me. Butter wouldn't melt in his mouth. I stood it for a while and then said:

" 'X——, I happen to know that you're trying to get your state away from me.'

"He got indignant and said I would find myself mistaken. I said, 'X——, I know you're trying to take your State away from me, but I don't mind that. What I do object to is your thinking me such a damned fool that I don't know it.' He arose, stuck one hand in the breast of his frockcoat oratorically—you know that gesture of his—and said, 'I demand one hour to prove to you that you are wrong.' "

I did know the gesture. X—— used it not only on the platform, but in private conversation, in the most theatrical manner.

"Did you give him the hour?" I asked.

"I should say not," said Taft emphatically. X—— became a Bull Moose leader a few months after this talk and did all he could both then and afterward to defeat Taft.

A year later he recurred to this topic of the low estate of the Senate. But as most of the men he mentioned are still alive and some of them in the Senate, I will quote only one of the things he said. I quote it as an illustration of Taft's ability at thumbnail summaries:

"You take Blank," he said. "He sizes up away ahead of most of them and has become, by reason of the falling-off in the Senate's character, one of its best men; and yet what is Blank? A graduate of the lobby who, now that he is in the Senate, tries to act like a statesman, but is no more a statesman than when he was nothing but a lobbyist; and, though a Senator, he is a lobbyist still."

The complete characterizer, as Franklin P. Adams would say.

CHAPTER XVIII

EX-PRESIDENT TAFT

When Taft left the White House he could have had his choice of any one of a number of lucrative law partnerships, but he thought it over and decided that it would not be right for him to practise law. That struck me as leaning over backward in the matter of scruple, so I asked him how he figured it out. He said it was because he had appointed so many Federal Judges. On the Supreme Court he appointed a majority of the Justices, six out of nine, and he appointed about forty-five per cent. of the District and Circuit Judges.

"So, you see," he explained, "it wouldn't be fair to the courts and it would put me in a questionable position to go around and argue cases in these courts, where undoubtedly I would be offered employment for the very reason that I had made those appointments. No, the active practise of law is barred to me."

But that, of course, did not prevent him from responding to invitations to furnish opinions in cases where they were desired by some lawyer. That kind of work involved no objectionable relations. Aside from this he had to give up the law entirely; and he accepted an invitation to deliver lectures at Yale, with the understanding that it would flower into a professorship. He would have made a wonderful professor; he invited me to attend one of his lectures, and it was worth while to see his way with the boys, and the response he got out of them.

"Hello, Thompson, old man!" he roared when I came into his room at the Taft Hotel in New Haven—Taft always roared in preference to just talking; he roared rapturously and happily. "What does *The New York Times* mean by letting you off for a day? Don't they know it's dangerous?"

"Probably the circulation will fall off heavily tomorrow," I replied, sitting down, "but I wanted to see what a college professor looks like."

"You won't be able to find out by looking at me," he said. "Not till next Fall. I'm not a college professor yet. I take the Kent chair at Yale then, but now I'm just delivering a course of university lectures."

I went to the lecture, and found he was very popular with the students, who applauded wildly when he came in and also applauded whenever he gave them the slightest excuse. As he afterward told me, no man could have had a more appreciative audience. They were alive with interest in everything he said. And it wasn't because he was an ex-President; he was full of vim and clearness itself, and could make his subject as interesting as a story. I had asked him the subject of his lecture course, and he had replied, "We the People." As I didn't know what he meant, he reminded me that those were the first three words in the Constitution, and said people who used the phrase didn't know what it meant or what it should be made to mean; and his lectures were for the purpose of telling them.

"I want to show them," he said, "not only the importance of keeping the old Constitution, but how to keep it."

And he explained that he was hewing to the old idea of representative government as distinguished from what he called "hair-trigger government." That day his subject was the making of nominations, and he showed the young men the difference between the convention system and the direct primary. He told them that one of the bad features of the direct primary was that men of "wealth, activity and little modesty" had a better chance than men of small means. This was fifteen years before the yahoo brand of Senators were to split the welkin over the money-splashing election of Frank L. Smith in Illinois and William S. Vare in Pennsylvania, and on the way the nation was to endure a similar uproar over the largesse of Truman H. Newberry in Michigan. The yahoo Senators never admit, though they know, that such scandals are the certain and inevitable outcome of the direct primary. They do not admit it because the words "direct primary" are a fetish, just as is the word "prohibition" in connection with the Volstead law—a statute which has nothing to do with prohibition, and which would be rightly understood if it were entitled, as it should be, "An Act to foster the sale and consumption of intoxicating liquor and increase the earnings of dealers in it."

"The direct primary," Taft went on, "reduces the probability that the office will seek the man; it puts a premium on the man seeking the office." Then he put down his notes and said, "I wonder if I dare tell a story about that matter of the office seeking the man." The students indicated gleefully that he might dare, and he plunged ahead:

"In Kentucky, not long ago, the Republicans, after years of fruitless effort, finally elected a Governor, William O. Bradley. There came down from the mountains a gentleman riding his horse, who announced that he would like to have an office, and they told him that he would have to establish his qualifications, because under the Republican régime the office was going to seek the man.

"He put up at a hotel in Frankfort for a while, and

then his funds got low and he went to a boarding-house, and then to a second-class boarding house, and then to a free-lunch place, and then his funds gave out altogether and he started for home. As he passed the Capital Hotel on his old mare some of the men who knew him called out to him to know what he was going to do.

"He reined in and looked at them. 'Well,' he says, 'my friends, I'm goin' home. I heerd tell a good deal about the office seekin' the man, an' I came down here to be convenient. I hain't seen no office seekin' any man yit, but if you see any office that seems to be lookin' for a man you jist holler out that you've seen old Jim Robinson on his old mare Jinny goin' down the Versailles Turnpike, an' he was goin' damn slow!' "

The students received this with such enthusiasm that a little later he enriched their fund of information with another, this time a personal, experience. He was explaining the abuses of the primary, and in particular the way in which, in many States, members of one party vote in the primaries of the other, and of the various attempts by law to circumvent this sort of thing. That reminded him of something, and he laid down his manuscript and took off his glasses. The students by this time knew what that meant, and they leaned forward eagerly.

"It's now thirty-three years since I went into politics," he said. "I roomed in a ward where there were some respectable people and some not so respectable—the old Fifth Ward in Cincinnati. It was constantly represented in Republican Conventions by a patriot named Martin Muldoon. He was a provident man, in the sense that he never attended a convention that he didn't make something out of it, and there were two or three of us reformers who decided to try to beat Martin.

"So we sent around circulars and visited the voters and

stirred up as much excitement as we could among a rather lethargic 'better element,' and then we went to the polls. The gentleman who assisted me was named Aaron Ferris. He was a very solemn and earnest individual. We agreed that he should be one of the judges and I should act as challenger. In those days," he explained, "I was more formidable than I am now, and we had to consider the weight and appearance of a man who acted as challenger in the old Fifth Ward."

The students laughed uproariously and the ex-President grinned.

"The first man who came up," he went on, "was a Democrat named James Flanagan, and he proposed to vote for Martin—just as Martin always used to go over to the Democratic primaries and vote for him. So I challenged his vote. Aaron, with his utmost solemnity and in a deep voice, said, 'James Flanagan, hold up your hand!'

"Flanagan looked puzzled and a little frightened, and said, 'What's that fur?' 'In order that you may swear in your vote!' thundered Aaron. Flanagan put up his hand, in a tentative sort of way. Aaron went on in a deepening voice: 'You—solemnly—swear—in the presence—of—Almighty—God—as you shall answer to Him at the last day of judgment——'

"Before he could say any more Flanagan backed off and said, 'To hell with the vote!' and then——"

But what happened next nobody ever knew. Taft was still talking, but the rest of that anecdote was lost in the storm of laughter. Yes, I think if he had stayed on as a college professor he would have been one of those professors who become legends.

A few weeks after this I went to New Haven to see if I could get an interview on what, for courtesy, may be called Wilson's Mexican policy. I was sure I couldn't, but an optimistic editor thought I could. Wilson had just lifted the embargo on the sale of arms to the Villistas, and he thought the ex-President might be moved to speech. I went to New Haven and found him rubbing the ears of a weird-looking poodle with kinky white hair. He was addressing the object as Carus'.

"Is his name Caruso?" I inquired.

"His baptismal name," said the ex-President shamefacedly, "is Carol. No, not Carlo—Carol. But I think Carus' is more appropriate, don't you?"

I said it was more distinguished, and broached my mission. As I had expected, he refused. "You know how I feel about that Mexican business, Thompson," he said, "and you know that if I made any comments on Wilson's policy they would be unfavorable. That would be unpatriotic. His hands are full of prickly foreign affairs, and no one should embarrass him by criticism just now. Come out and take a walk."

As we strolled through the New Haven streets in the twilight, he elaborated. "Wilson," he said, "is entitled to what I didn't get—freedom from criticism in his foreign policy." I told him he had talked pretty freely about Wilson's Philippine policy, and he said, "That's different. That's a domestic question. And besides, I'm an expert on Philippine affairs, and the country—including the President—has a right to the information I have on that subject. That's a different thing from assailing the President's unmatured foreign policies out loud, where other nations can overhear you.

"Wilson ought to have recognized Huerta in the first place," he continued as we rambled on. "Of course it wouldn't do any good now. It's all very noble and altruistic and angelic to say that you won't shake a blood-stained hand, but where in Mexico, right now, is he going to find any other kind of hand to shake? Huerta shot his enemies, but the revolutionists will do the same. The trouble with this Administration, and I include Bryan as well as Wilson, is its Chautauqua way of dealing with foreign affairs. Chautauqua diplomacy, I call it."

Taft was originally fat, and so much was printed about it that people got the idea he was a sort of Falstaff; they saw "the likeness of a gross fat man." This, however, did him good, because of the reaction wherever he appeared. Everywhere he went, and he was called the "Great American Traveler," he moved to a chorus of murmurs he could not help hearing—"Why, he's not so fat after all!" The idea that there was anything gross about him was dissipated the moment one saw his fine, pale, intellectual, handsome face. Still, the Judge, the Governor-General, the Secretary of War, and the President was fat; the Chief Justice became something else again. For at least sixteen years he sought the secret of banting, and once nearly killed himself in the pursuit. At that time, in bitter disappointment, the future Chief Justice gave up his ambition and allowed himself to swell out like a poisoned pup—if such an expression be not contempt of court. Then he took up the labor again, and finally succeeded.

Not that he ever became a living skeleton. But he did cease to be globular. He continued, naturally, to be a large man, but not so large as in the days when he cabled from Manila to Secretary Root: "Took long horseback ride today; feeling fine," and Root cabled back, "How is the horse?" Taft was very tall and had the right weight to go with his height. The ladies called him "a lovely dancer." He had a light step, graceful movements and a fast stride. In fact, in his post-White House years he became a fine figure of a man.

This being the case, it is remarkable that people kept

on making jokes about his fatness, even after they had seen the man with their own eyes. But probably it isn't remarkable at all. Chesterton has ably exposed the psychological fact that when you go anywhere with the expectation of seeing any particular thing you have heard about, such as a Morocco filled with quaint and picturesque ancient Moors, or empty and deserted churches in France, you will see what you look for even though your eyes are resting on a spick-and-span Moor in European clothes or a French church crowded to the doors. When the great reunion of the Blue and Gray was held on the battle-field of Gettysburg in 1913 to commemorate the fiftieth anniversary of the battle, the editorial prelude was in a strain of gentle pathos. What a sad sight it will be, the editorial writers mused, these white-haired, tottering old men with quavering voices and dim eyes, meeting as friends where half a century ago they met as foes. The reporters who went to Gettysburg took up the strain and tapped the tear-ducts of their readers. Looking over the shoulder of that great reporter, Lindsay Denison, as he tapped out an eloquent and mournful dispatch on the battle-field, I at last protested

"For God's sake, Lindsay," I stormed, "use your eyes! Look out of the door of this tent. See those sturdy old fellows rampaging up Cemetery Ridge. You are half their age and you couldn't keep up with them half a mile. Look at that red-bearded giant swinging by now; hardly a gray hair, and you're writing about the white-haired old totterers. As for those quavering voices you're writing about, weren't you kicking at three o'clock this morning because those old Confederates over on Seminary Ridge, a mile and a half across the valley, were making night hideous with *Dixie* and dancing *Turkey in the Straw* until daylight?"

But Denison refused to look; and he and all the other reporters continued to write about how the poor old men were dropping dead like flies, despite the fact, shown by the statistics of actuaries, that the death rate at the great encampment was less than it would normally have been if the veterans had stayed home. Maybe I would have done the same if I hadn't just been reading Chesterton. And in the same way people continued to gaze on the well-proportioned figure of the later Taft and see Falstaff. And since Error only dies gradually, paragraphers and editorial writers and cartoonists will go on till the end of Time, or of Taft, portraying him as Falstaffian, just as they used to ascribe Roosevelt's misdeeds to the artless exuberance of youth long after he had joined, as he phrased it, the grandfather class.

But for the truth of history it must be recorded, before it is too late, that even in his fattest days Taft was not as other fat men are. He was no Daniel Lambert. On such a question it is unwise to trust one's memory; the years may have idealized Taft's large gracefulness in a tender but unveracious haze. So I will have recourse to something I wrote at the time, the very time when he was popularly believed to be egregious. I exhume it from *Party Leaders of the Time,* written when he was Secretary of War and vainly banting:

"One day an inquisitive reporter asked, 'Mr. Secretary, how much do you weigh?'

" 'I won't tell you,' boomed the Secretary. 'But you know that when somebody asked Speaker Reed that, he replied that no true gentleman would weigh more than two hundred pounds. I have amended that to three hundred pounds.'

"When Secretary Taft speaks, he speaks in a sunshiny roar. When he laughs, the surrounding furniture shakes and rumbles. Yet he is as light on his feet as the frisky Beveridge. You expect to see his horse sag in the middle when Taft mounts, accompanied by his slender, lath-like companion, Colonel Edwards [this was the officer who in the World War became famous as General Clarence Edwards, commander of the New England Division], but Taft sits erect as an arrow and gallops around like a West Point graduate. He walks erectly and sturdily, as little bothered by his great weight as if he were a schoolgirl in a gymnasium. Wherever he goes he takes life with a buoyant breeziness that makes it very difficult for political opponents to feel hard towards him."

As for the legend of Taft the Good-Natured, that legend might be allowed to pass if it were not that the word is used so as to give a false impression. The idea grows that Taft was an easy mark. Now, Harding was an easy mark, but he is not thought of as one because the epithet "good-natured" was never saddled on him. We all have a way of applying one good enough word to a public man and then filing him away and docketing him under that cross-index reference,—which works injustice and is unscientific. The word "strenuous" was Roosevelt's cross-index word, and people actually did get the idea, by much repetition of it, that he was always battling furiously about something, with bared teeth and hissing breath and clenched fists. That he had any other characteristics than strenuousness would have seemed incongruous. So, when I went to see him in Mercy Hospital I wrote in my report to *The New York Times* that "he was the same kindly soul as ever" and had won the affections of the hospital attendants. When I returned to New York I encountered Professor Franklin Matthews, of Columbia, and he began laughing uproariously.

"Do you know what you did?" he exclaimed between bursts of mirth. "You said in your first story from Chicago that Roosevelt was 'the same kindly soul as ever'! Lord, what a break! Imagine Roosevelt being kindly!" And he went oft in another spasm. He had never met Roosevelt. The idea that Roosevelt the Strenuous could have any qualities except the one under which he was labeled and classified in the general mind was to Matthews exquisitely absurd. History knows more than that to-day, and 1928's view of Roosevelt is larger than was that of 1912; for Matthews's idea was the universal one, hard as it is to realize now.

And so Taft the Good-Natured was so much the classification of him that he was supposed to be good-natured and nothing else; what the slang of that day and this calls a "fall guy." He was not; he was too alert minded. The only fall guy who ever was President was Harding.

The truth behind the legend of Taft's good nature was that he was intelligently good-natured. His good nature was of a philosophical sort; it was not of the fatly stupid kind. For example: After his defeat in 1912, people who were introduced to him always told him, by way of cheering him up, "I voted for you." It excited Taft's sense of humor. I spoke of it to him one day, and he replied:

"Whenever any one says that to me, I have an almost uncontrollable desire to say, 'Well, my friend, you are one of a select but small body of citizens whose judgment I heartily concur in and admire.'"

And he laughed in that gentle roar of his. This was not exactly crass good nature. It was humorous sanity. If we are to classify Taft under any phrase, let us adopt that one. It fits him better.

WILSON

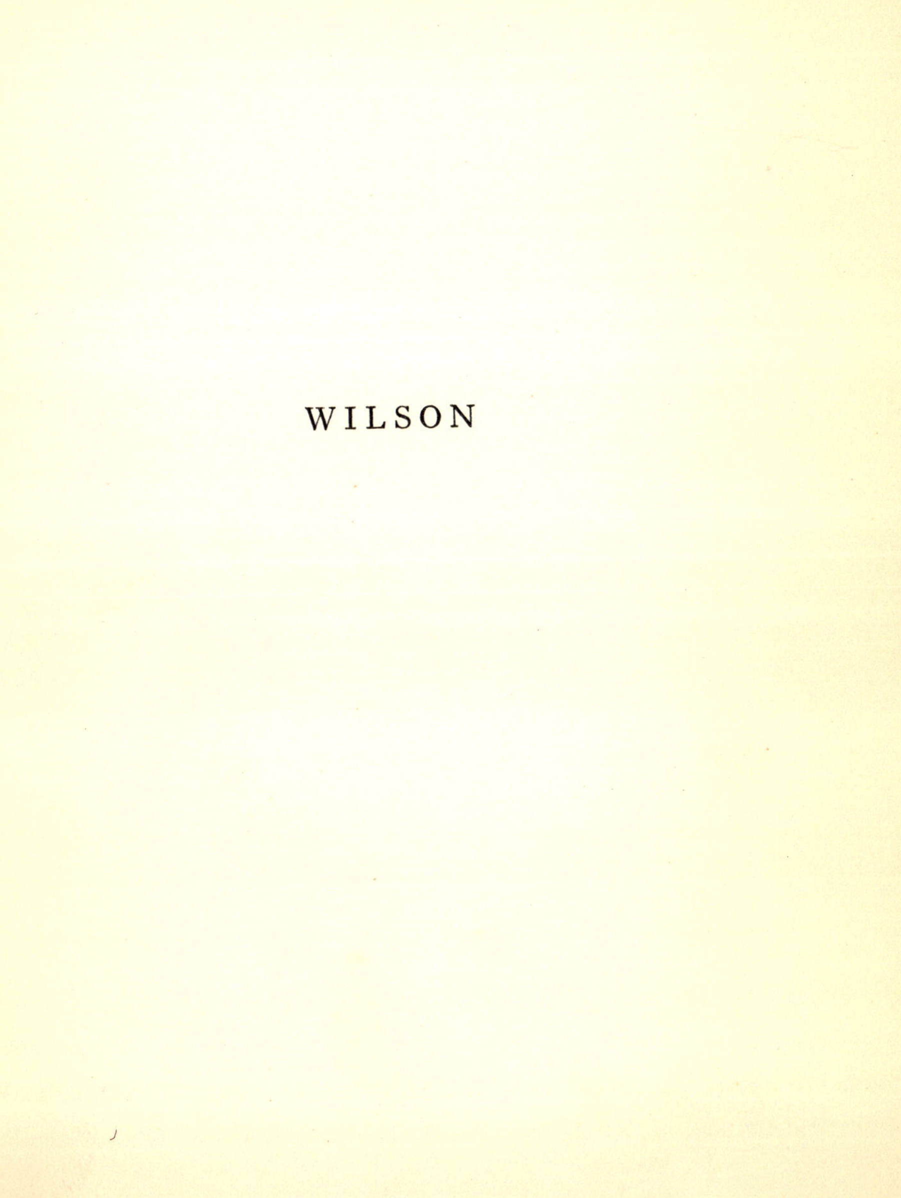

CHAPTER XIX

ALONE AND ALOOF

WILSON not only did not desire advice or guidance, but he did not desire information. When, in the course of the World War, Ambassador Walter Hines Page came to the United States to give the President the inside news of what was going on in England—this was before we entered the war and while Wilson still dreamed that he would be called upon to make peace—he found it impossible to get the President to listen. Every time he sought to bring the subject up Wilson would side-track it and steer the conversation into other channels. Usually he did this by managing to have others present to whom he could address himself on a different topic. At first Page thought this was accident or coincidence. At last he succeeded in getting Wilson alone, seized the opportunity and started to tell the President what he felt it his patriotic duty to let him know. Wilson looked up with a quick gesture, as if he would dismiss the subject, but Page, who by this time realized that there was nothing accidental about the way Wilson had blanketed him, went right ahead. Seeing that there was no way of stopping Page, the President sprang up, stuck his fingers in his ears, and, still holding them there, ran out of the room. Then Page gave it up, and went back to England; and Wilson continued for many months to live in his dream of ending the greatest war in history by negotiating "a peace without victory."

I had observed and been struck by this phase of his character early in our acquaintance, almost from the beginning of it, long before he became President. I therefore expected to see it manifest itself in the White House, which it promptly did. To make my statement accurate, I should modify it by saying that Wilson was willing to receive information, provided the information came from anybody not specially qualified to give it. He seemed to shrink instinctively from having anybody tell him things who was an authority on the subject, an expert on it; it may be that he had an uneasy feeling that they had an ax to grind, were trying to put something over. Though that hardly explains it, either, for I had noticed the same thing at Princeton, Trenton, and elsewhere in his dealings with men who stood on an even footing in that respect. At Princeton, after his election to the Presidency, he did show some desire to profit by the information which political correspondents could give him. At this time Wilson's active political experience was limited to one term in the Governorship of New Jersey, he knew few public men, and his knowledge of national politics was obtained from books. Public men in such a position always avail themselves of the greater knowledge of political reporters; and most public men who have advanced beyond that stage continue to do so, though they have progressed to the point where they know things the reporters do not. They find the information and viewpoint valuable, however, checking it up by their own inside knowledge and discarding what is not of value or is already known to them. Roosevelt, for instance, who knew more about politics than any other man I ever met, never to his death ceased to pick the brains of political reporters and make use of their experience. It is perfectly right and proper, and these writers (who are more than writers, men of experience, themselves on the inside, and possessed of ten times the facts they allow to seep into print) are nearly always ready to furnish the statesman with all they have. Provided, of course, it is not something the telling of which would either violate a confidence or be unfair to the other statesman or statesmen from whom they learned it.

On that point, I should like to say this. Nothing makes a reporter more tired than to hear the repetition of that banal phrase, "I have known scores of newspaper men, have talked freely to them, and have never yet had my confidence betrayed." Many public men repeat this stilted and offensive bromide whenever they make a speech to an audience which includes newspaper men. That famous dining club of Washington correspondents, the Gridiron, got tired of hearing it from the eminences who attended its dinners. So, on one such occasion, the club administered one of its famous snubs to statesmen. Twelve or fifteen Senators, Judges, Governors, Cabinet officers and Representatives had made speeches, and about half of them had used the time-worn phrase. Then the club, which varies speeches by stunts performed by its members, called on one of the Gridironers to submit to an examination to determine whether he really was qualified to be a Washington correspondent or not, conducted by another member. Toward the close of the examination the inquisitor asked, "What of your relations with public men?" He lifted his eyes piously, crossed his thumbs over his stomach and twiddled them, and replied, unctuously and sonorously: "In the course of my experience as a newspaper man I have met hundreds of Assemblymen, State Senators, Governors, Representatives, Senators, Cabinet officers, and Presidents, and on searching my memory faithfully, I can truly say that very few of them have ever betrayed my confidence." For some time after that dinner the ancient phrase went into what Grover Cleveland called "innocuous desuetude."

Wilson, after his election, knew as well as any one else that he could get useful first-hand information from newspaper men about Washington and about national politics and the politicians with whom his lot was soon to be cast for at least four years. He was somewhat handicapped by the fact that the correspondents assigned to stay with him from his election to his inauguration were not, in general, of the first run of political writers, not very experienced, did not know many politicians (in some cases none at all), had no knowledge of politics. This was because the editors, figuring that the most interesting and important political news would come out of Oyster Bay and not Princeton, had assigned their most knowledgeable men to Roosevelt and sent the second run to Princeton. One was a youth of twenty-one who had never done any political reporting in his life. Another was not a reporter at all; he was the private secretary of the man who owned his paper, having been graduated to that post from the place of stenographer, and had done some writing on the side, mostly "greenroom gossip" from the theaters. Another was a copy-reader, taken from his desk to do his first political reporting. Another came from Washington, and on that fact Wilson placed great store; but this man had never done any political or governmental reporting, had never been a Washington correspondent, and was not acquainted either with the correspondents in the press gallery—a place where he was not admitted—or with any public men. His short acquaintance with Washington, to which city he had come briefly from Iowa, was confined to reporting local items of interest to the citizenry for a Washington newspaper office, and he knew as little about the Capitol or the White House as any "realtor" or insurance man in the city.

There were, however, two men of ripe experience. One was Don Martin, then famous among newspaper men as

The New York Herald's political expert. He was the man who for years made *The Herald* (in its heyday) noted for its wizard-like accuracy in predicting, just before an election, how that election would go in every State. He was *The Herald's* general political correspondent, ranging the country from Maine to California, analyzing politics everywhere; and he was on intimate terms with most of the important public men throughout the nation. A few years afterward, as a war correspondent in France, he sacrificed his life to his duty. The other ripened writer, James J Doyle of *The New York Press,* had begun his newspaper career as a labor union specialist, had soon turned to politics, and had spent nearly twenty years among politicians.

So Wilson, having this desire to hear nothing from qualified authorities, never drew on the stores of wisdom that he could have tapped in Martin and Doyle, but sought light from the youth, the private secretary, the copy-reader, and the local reporter. On the latter, because he "came from Washington," Wilson relied for most of what he probably imagined was inside stuff. He was so much impressed with this man that when he became President he appointed him head of the Board of Commissioners for the District of Columbia. This office corresponds loosely to that of Mayor in other cities. Washington is governed by three Commissioners, appointed by the President of the United States, but the President of the board rules and directs it, one of the other members being a sort of assistant mayor looking after special departments, and the third being an engineer officer. It is the only important office which goes to a Washingtonian and is the city's only chance at having an official voice in the management of its affairs. Hence, when the President named this Iowan, Oliver P. Newman, the city for once became vocal; it stormed with rage. Usually the disfranchised city is apathetic and resigned to whatever its rulers may do to it; but this appointment to its municipal headship of an unknown reporter from Iowa, who knew nothing about the city or its needs and who was not even a name to its inhabitants, goaded the town into mutiny. The uproar of indignation lasted a long time, but Wilson was inflexible, and the capital had to submit. Probably he was surprised and could not understand it; was not Newman a "Washington correspondent"? He may have been still more surprised that there was no outcry when he named, as the second Commissioner, Louis Brownlow. The reason was that Brownlow really lived in the city, knew it well, and was a genuine Washington correspondent, knowing Congress and Congressmen like a book; a thing of importance in Washington, whose local affairs are governed by Congress through two committees.

At this point some reader is likely to say shrewdly that I dwell on this because I was piqued over Wilson's failure to consult with me, as well as with Martin and Doyle. Well, the shrewd reader guesses wrong. When I went to Princeton after Wilson's election I knew his ways so well that I had no idea he would ask any of the three for information, and knew that he would be sure to do as he always did throughout his life—turn to somebody not much better informed than himself. I do not have to tell newspaper men that no political correspondent volunteers either advice or information to his political friends and acquaintances or is anxious to give it; when it is given it is because it is sought, and most newspaper men are none too eager to give it even then. My object here as elsewhere in this book is merely to put down the truth, or all of it that will in any way illuminate the events of our recent history and the minds of the men who made that history; and I dwell on Wilson's course in this to illustrate the course he had always pursued and was now to pursue at Washington.

From my knowledge of him I was certain he would pursue it. I went with him from Princeton to Washington and stuck to him through the beginning of his Administration and my certainty was justified. The World War was still undreamed of, and the great question at the outset of Wilson's term was the Mexican Revolution. Madero had just been murdered and Huerta was reaping the harvest of that crime. Then, as ever before and ever since, our relations with Mexico were delicate, and it was the most difficult of tasks to get accurate information about the meaning of events in that country. Wilson, when he became President, knew the problems of his own country only as a student and not at first hand, but he knew nothing at all about Mexico. The retiring President, Taft, who would have been only too glad to place at his disposal his own experiences with that country that Wilson might profit by his errors as well as by his successes, looked on with ever-increasing anxiety and misgiving. As it became more and more evident that Wilson had no policy—for that was what his "watchful waiting," as he called it, amounted to; "watchful waiting" was his way of saying "nothing doing"—the ex-President became more and more disturbed.

Some time in the first six months of Wilson's Administration I made a visit to Taft. He was aflame with eagerness to have me tell him everything I knew about Wilson's plans for Mexico. I skated over the subject as gingerly as I could, but Taft was quick to see that Wilson had no plans at all, that his policy was only that of drift; the Micawber policy of waiting for something to turn up. He was bitterly disappointed, but he had expected it, though he had not had my advantage of knowing this side of Wilson's character. He had suspected it from his close study of the Washington reports. He talked about it during our long walk in the pleasant New Haven evening, and showed his regret that Wilson could not have the advantage of knowing what he, Taft, had been up against. Sometimes he swore artistically and fluently, for Taft had a pretty gift of profanity. It was not at Wilson he swore, but at the mess the United States had got into, and into which, though he only guessed that, it was to get deeper and ever deeper throughout the long and dismal tale of Vera Cruz landings, A B C conferences, punitive expeditions and what-not.

As an American patriot he was alarmed and discouraged, and it was at the situation, not Wilson, he exercised his talent for profanity. He did not, at this stage of the lamentable story, blame Wilson; he attributed it all—with picturesque cuss-words—to the new President's inexperience. I do not think that Taft then had any idea Wilson was temperamentally averse to first-hand authoritative information, and I did not tell him so, though I knew it; he was blue enough over the Mexican mess as it was. I know Taft himself was blamed for not taking strong action as his Administration closed with the revolver shots that slew Madero and Vice-President Suarez echoing across the Rio Grande and in the halls of the American Capitol itself. But Taft should not have been blamed. It was Wilson, not Taft, who was to shape the American policy toward Mexico in view of the abyss into which that country was plunging, and Taft thought it would be unpatriotic of him to throw obstacles in his successor's way by defining a policy of which that successor might not approve—certainly would not have approved, as we know now. All he felt justified in doing was to preserve the status, keep the peace as far as possible, and turn over his accounts to the new head of the Nation for auditing. This he did, and he was wise and right.

I was reluctant to tell him all the ominous signs, and I did not tell him, because I did not wish to prejudice him against Wilson. But at this time, and thereafter, Wilson was demonstrating again and on a national and international scale that phase of his character to which this chapter is devoted. Nobody who was competent to tell him the truth about Mexico could get his ear, could even get to his presence. It soon became a stock joke among the people who came to Washington eager to lay their knowledge of Mexican conditions before him that the only way to get to him was to tell Tumulty that you had never been in Mexico. It is true that they would all have had different view-points, might have told conflicting stories, and some had axes to grind, but McKinley, Roosevelt or Taft would have sifted their varying contributions and strained the approximate truth out of them. Wilson certainly did not distrust his own ability to do that very thing; he never distrusted himself about anything, being more positive he was invariably right than any man I ever saw. It was simply his character to avoid expert authorities; he was acting according to his nature.

In the case of Mexico, his aversion to authorities was increased by another phase of his character, one also displayed often; having made up his mind, he did not want to have it disturbed by upsetting information. Consequently he would not consult our Ambassador to Mexico; he would take no information from Nelson O'Shaughnessy, who remained in Mexico City as our Charge d'Affaires after the Ambassador's return; he would see none of the lesser authorities, American and Mexican, who flocked to Washington in those early months to place their knowledge at his disposal. But, as time went on, he did seek information, and began to send unofficial emissaries of his own into Mexico. They were a curious and unfit lot. They appeared, as a rule, to be selected because they would give him the side of the case that he had already decided to be the right one, and give him the advice he had already given himself. The most entertaining of these emissaries were John Lind and Doctor William Bayard Hale. He always remained as implacable as at first toward official representatives of the United States and toward unofficial persons who were at all posted about the Mexican situation.

Later on, in the vast drama of the World War, he was to continue the same policy. That it did not become the ridiculous and grisly failure that it had been in Mexico was due solely to the tact and sagacity of the emissary he selected, Colonel Edward M. House. He would not hear Page, but he would hear House, and the *Intimate Papers* which that able statesman has published show how delicately and adroitly the unofficial diplomat threaded his way through Wilson's mind. A misstep on his part might have wrought incalculable disaster to this country and to the world. But at last, when House began, however daintily and carefully, to give him the kind of advice he did *not* want, to let him see that his emissary was thinking for himself, a historic friendship ended summarily; out went House.

House was sent to Europe not merely to get information for the Presidential mind, but to negotiate, to inform and advise with the European statesmen. He was a sort of Super-Ambassador, an Ambassador to all Europe, and this though by law our Ambassadors are nominated by the President and the nominations confirmed, after consideration, by the Senate. In fact, in the true and original sense of the word, House was the only real Ambassador this country ever had. Of old a Minister represented his government, but an Ambassador represented the sovereign; he was the King's other self; when the foreign monarch talked with him, in theory that monarch was talking with his brother-King. In that strictly personal sense the United States has never had but one real Ambassador, Edward M. House.

Nevertheless, on a smaller scale John Lind was much such an Ambassador. He too was sent to negotiate, to represent Woodrow Wilson the man, and to deal on that basis with President Huerta. A more unfit person could not have been sent, nor one mentally and constitutionally less capable of understanding Mexicans or treating with them, than this honest Minnesota Scandinavian. Of all the Presidents from Washington to Coolidge there is not one who would have made such a monstrously absurd appointment, except Woodrow Wilson. The nearest thing to it in our history was when the Government clerk, Nicholas P. Trist, negotiated the treaty that ended the Mexican War, but even this is not a parallel. Trist was in the State Department, understood Mexican affairs and the American foreign policy there and in Oregon, and was a politician who was acquainted with national affairs. Even at that, President Polk had misgivings and tried to call him off, but was too late, and Trist carried out his plans to the ultimate satisfaction of the Administration.

Why was Lind sent? Wilson did not know anything about him. His reputation had been gained as Governor of Minnesota, to which office he had been nominated for the purpose of catching the Scandinavian vote. But that reputation, which was good, was confined to the northern part of the Middle West; it had not reached to the Atlantic Coast, and all this had been in the days when Wilson was a college professor and not given to the minute study of faraway local celebrities. Afterward Lind served in Congress; served well enough, but without distinction, save such distinction as attached in those days to any Northern man who could be elected to Congress as a Democrat and serve his term without making a fool of himself. For those were the days of the Democratic nadir, the days when it touched bottom under the shadow of Bryan's first two defeats for the Presidency; when under the picayune "leadership" of that infinitesimal politician, Slim Jim Richardson, of Tennessee, the pitiful Democratic minority had sunk to the level of a squealing litter of pigs hell-bent for the pork-barrel and nothing else; when only the South was Democratic territory, and when, so far as I can remember, not a single Northern Democrat was counted as a man worthy of Republican steel except John J. Fitzgerald, of Brooklyn. In this disorderly, squalling, gluttonous, envy-eaten, unprincipled mob, Lind was distinguished only by the fact that he was respectable and never said anything silly.

Wilson did not know Lind. But Bryan did. Bryan was Secretary of State, and this was a state mission. Lind was long out of Congress, and living in apathetic retirement in Minnesota. The Secretary of State's chief preoccupation was in finding jobs for deserving Democrats—that is, deserving Bryanites. In the North, particularly in the East, the Democrats of light and leading had begun the rush out of the party with Bryan's 1896 nomination, and the stampede had received additions with every subsequent campaign. Deserving Democrats in the North, therefore, much resembled hens' teeth. Lind was a deserving Democrat. He was not a "progressive," but a party man. When the Northern Democrats, in 1896, flocked either to Palmer and Buckner or direct by the through route to McKinley, Lind stayed regular and voted for Bryan; and so he did in 1900 and 1908. Bryan had a long memory for those who had been faithful to him in the dark ages when he had trudged so long through the Dismal Swamp. To reward them was not only his chief pleasure, but his chief concern as a public official.

This Lind mission is worth a great deal of attention because, if studied, it reveals something of Wilson's mind and makes clear much that afterward happened in the World

War. There were a great many jobs that Lind could have taken over with credit, but none of them was in the field of diplomacy, or in any other division of the State Department. He might have been put in charge of a conservation policy; he might even have made an unobjectionable Secretary of the Interior. But Wilson made him a diplomat, an Ambassador, and sent him to as sensitive and ticklish a Latin people as there is on earth. It was not Wilson's intention to send a bull into a china shop, but if he had meant to do so he would have searched long before he found anybody better fitted than John Lind to play the part of bull. It was a more concentrated demonstration of the way his mind worked than any other of his square pegs in round holes: his picking of a pacifist for Secretary of War, of a kindly and well-meaning dub for Secretary of the Navy, of a minor diplomat who lived abroad to represent the Republican Party on the Peace Commission. These occurrences are numerous though scattered, and have to be assembled and marshaled before they can be made to form a picture; but this one appointment of Lind to his delicate and impossible mission, a mission that would have called for a Benjamin Franklin or at least an Edward House, presents in itself the whole of this phase of Wilson's mind.

Nelson O'Shaughnessy's brilliant and observant wife put the case with her admirable felicity. She said that in August, 1913, the curtain had been rolled up, revealing the Mexican stage set for a tragedy. Madero and Suarez had been murdered, Huerta was consolidating his power and civil war was in the offing. Just as the curtain rose on this drama, she said, "There appeared a man of Viking origin, the pale Northman of Romance, with a blue and agreeable eye, causing the dark drama to develop somewhat along the lines of extravaganza." This comedian who so abruptly altered the plot "appeared from the upper left-hand corner of the stage, in shirtsleeves, barking his shins, in their unpressed trouser legs, against the stage settings, and running into several of the dark-skinned characters, already in full action." Nothing could describe better this comic melodrama which was produced before a guffawing international audience and a booing Mexican one. Lind's mission was the simple one of informing Huerta that if he would resign the Presidency, Wilson would see that the Mexican treasury would get a loan of money from the United States to get her out of her financial troubles; if Huerta was obstinate, she could stew in her own juice. In her graphic and searching book, *Intimate Pages of Mexican History,* published in 1920, from which I am quoting, Mrs. O'Shaughnessy comments thus on this proposal, which to Wilson and Bryan seemed so reasonable, so diplomatic: "Now, nations need money obviously, but also quite as obviously the bread of life, which is respect for themselves. The jangle of the thirty pieces of silver that we offered to Mexico and that she did not take will forever ring in the ears of one who opens our history at that page."

Lind, however, was at least a sincere man and tried to do his duty, which is more than can be said for some of the other unofficial observers and negotiators that Wilson preferred to the experts. It was not his fault that he was grotesquely miscast. He shines by contrast with the devious Doctor Hale, another of Wilson's traveling representatives in Mexico. And that individual, later to suffer from unwelcome publicity in the German propaganda investigations in the World War, was Wilson's own selection. Bryan had nothing to do with that.

Wilson made misstep after misstep, dragging the United States with him, until our relations with Mexico were worse than they had been since the time of Maximilian. He sent marines into Vera Cruz, actually believing that the Mexicans would take it tranquilly, and was horrified and distressed when they and the Mexicans shot each other down in the streets. He hastily recalled them. Then came his fruitless A B C conference, and finally the Pershing "punitive expedition" after Villa's raid on Columbus. In that case he supposed the Mexicans, Carranza being now President, would have no objection to our sending a warlike force into their country, and was again horrified and distressed when they began shooting.

The Mexicans are touchy and hard to handle, and more than one of our statesmen has rubbed them the wrong way. Usually, though, they have understood what we were driving at, whether it pleased or enraged them. Wilson is the only one who puzzled and bewildered them. They studied him earnestly—it was a matter of vital importance to them to understand him—and never could make out whether he was coming or going. I never in those days heard it all summed up better in a few words than was done by Barney Gallant after one of his political trips into Mexico. Gallant has been known so long as a figure in New York life that probably few remember his early years, which were spent in international politics. He was one of the Americans who knew Mexico like a book. He had been run out of Mexico by the Diaz tyranny for his connection with the liberal politicians who sought the dictator's overthrow; he had kept up his connections, and whenever he made one of his mysterious forays into that country doors behind which lay information were open to him. From one such adventure he returned after the Pershing expedition. Gallant, I should say for those who know him only in the rôle he has played in New York for the last few years, was a shrewd, sagacious observer—and also impartial and accurate. He was tolerant and comprehensive, saw everything as a whole, and I would bank more heavily on his judgment than that of many a United States Senator. After this post-Pershing return of his, when I was talking to him about what he had found down there, he said:

"There isn't a Mexican who can make Wilson out. They are all trying desperately to understand the policy of the United States, but every time they think they have discovered what it is and are getting ready to act accordingly, something happens to send them up in the air again. From everybody I talked to down there, I got the same answer. To boil it down in a few sentences, what they say is this: 'We give it up. One day he kicks us and the next day he kisses us. If Washington would fight us, we could understand that. If it would help us, we could understand that. If it would let us alone, we could understand that. But to fight us one day, offer help another, and let us alone on a third, that is beyond understanding. Vera Cruz, the Niagara Falls conference, and Pershing are pieces of a puzzle we can't put together. He has simply got us buffaloed.' "

And yet what else could be expected from a President who habitually and instinctively shut his ears to reliable information and took it only from irresponsible fly-by-nights? Ambassador Fletcher could never get to see Wilson except on one occasion, and then it was only a minor matter. As Mrs. O'Shaughnessy put it, speaking of the Mexicans, "Instead of allowing these protoplasmic Democrats to nourish themselves and evolve along their inevitable lines, President Wilson's desire was to see eighty-five per cent. of them turned into fully developed deserving Democrats over night. This being out of nature's way, history testifies that in the pressure these inorganic bits were simply squashed out of any semblance to anything." But this reason is not the only one, for Wilson did not confine his exclusions to apologists for Huerta. He impartially excluded everybody who was informed, pro-Huerta, pro-Madero, pro-Carranza men and neutrals, all alike, provided they knew anything about Mexico. After the assassination of Madero and the inauguration of Wilson (which followed immediately), Edward I. Bell, long a resident of Mexico City and the editor of a newspaper there, a friend and confidant of the murdered President, came post-haste from Mexico to Washington to put Wilson in possession of all his information. He cooled his heels on the White House door-step for weeks, and departed raging. In fact, more Maderistas than Huertistas were turned away "with all their music in them," for they were more numerous in Washington.

This book is not a history, and I need not pursue this branch of the subject further. It is a selective book, and its design is to group such things, large or small, as will tend to a clearer understanding of events. I have written enough to show the inadequacy of the current explanation of Wilson—that he was a self-centered egotist who "bore no brother near the throne." I shall have something to say about that, too; what I mean here is that that explanation alone does not cover the case of Wilson's aversion to advice and information. Whether he was egotistical or not, his ego had nothing to do with that; it was something else; it was a mental twist, a constitutional infirmity, which closed the anteroom of his mind to unwelcome visitors. The two traits, granting for the moment that egotism was the other, were distinct.

CHAPTER XX

THE SILENCES OF WOODROW WILSON

IN AN earlier chapter I have quoted the appraisal of Roosevelt's personal following by Edward Raymond Thompson. The essayist added, "Mr. Wilson does not inspire that warm personal loyalty. He is respected by all, feared by some, perhaps disliked by not a few. But, while no man speaks more about the people, none could well have fewer points of contact with the people. Louis XI was hardly narrower in his circle of confidants."

This is true, and yet there were those who were willing and anxious to love Wilson; nor was there anything repellent about him. He was, in fact, a winning man. But I never found more than one who succeeded in loving him, and that was the warm-hearted Irishman with the oceanlike capacity for affection, Joe Tumulty.

"The strongest man upon earth is he who stands most alone," says Ibsen. It is a generalization, and a generalization is a statement of truth made so broadly as to make no allowance for qualifications or modifications. Unfortunately it is a human habit to pounce enthusiastically upon generalizations and adopt them as rules of life. A generalization is true only if you expand it into an unliterary length and breadth, but then it ceases to be a generalization. A generalization is also an unrecognized figure of speech—that is, it conveys its meaning by saying something else. Thus you could get Ibsen's truth by enlarging it to read as follows: While in this world it is impossible to rely on one's self entirely and there is no such thing, literally, as self-reliance, still it is a fact that a man who can keep himself to a considerable extent independent of others is generally better off than one who can not. But that is unliterary and verbose, and Ibsen wanted to be epigrammatic; and no epigram ever contains the whole truth.

In Wilson's case he did not deliberately plan his aloofness; he was "most alone," as Ibsen says, because he couldn't help it; it was his nature. He believed in obeying his nature. He acted on Polonius's "To thine own self be true." This is invariably quoted as if Polonius had been moralizing about virtue. It never occurs to the quoters that if a man's "own self" is anti-social, for instance, he would be untrue to it if he forced himself into a different mold.

I think Wilson may, in early life, have recognized his natural solitariness and tried to amend it. But he found he was trying to change his "own self," and that he would do better if he let that self ride. He certainly did know himself, in this matter if in no other. After he was elected President the nation began to study him with eager and nervous interest, to get some clue to the kind of President who had emerged from the Roosevelt-Taft mêlée of 1912. For, hard as it is to realize, Wilson was an unknown quantity. He had become President not because the people preferred him to Taft and Roosevelt,—they did not know anything about him,—but because they preferred any Democrat to any Republican and wanted to punish the Republican Party. Whoever had been named by the Democrats at Baltimore, the result would have been the same. It was mighty fortunate for the country that he got the nomination instead of the man whom a majority of the delegates wanted to name, Champ Clark. The mind falters at the thought of the World War coming with President Clark physically in the White House and William Randolph Hearst spiritually and dominantly animating it. Providence watches over the American people even when it is on a spree, as it was in 1912, and this time Providence came in the unusual shape of William J. Bryan. Whether any one knows it or not, Bryan's real claim to the gratitude of posterity, not in the United States alone, is that because of him Hearst was not the ruler of the United States when Germany crossed the Belgian frontier. And it was no fluke; it was precisely to keep Hearst out of the White House that Bryan stopped the nomination of Clark. Of course he did not know anything about the momentous events ahead, but he knew what kind of President Clark would be and was determined to prevent it at all risks; for he did not know any more about Wilson than the rest of the country did. And he realized that whoever was nominated at Baltimore, whether Clark, Wilson, Harmon, Underwood, or anybody else, would be elected by about the same majority as any other would be.

The country was too intent on its revenge on the Republican Party to care much about Wilson, but when the spanking was over and it had leisure to think of the coming four years there was no satisfying its curiosity about what manner of man this was whom it had drawn out of the conjurer's hat. It generally gets a pretty fair idea, in the time that elapses between the November election and the March inauguration; but as the months went on it became evident that Wilson was as much an enigma as he had been before Baltimore. The reason was plain enough to us at Princeton; it was to be found in this solitariness and aloofness of his. The public had no clear idea of him because he could not give it one. Charles Phillips's line, "Grand, gloomy and peculiar, he sat the throne a sceptered hermit, wrapped in the solitude of his own originality," did not precisely fit him, because he was not grand or gloomy, but its flavor of desolate solitude brought it before my mind in those Princeton days whenever I considered the country's growing wonder about him.

In the last chapter I mentioned, among the reporters whose duty it was in those post-election months to live with him at Princeton, two men of long political experience, Don Martin and James J. Doyle. Martin, Doyle and I used to discuss Wilson's inability to put himself over—that may sound odd now, in view of the thorough way in which he did become visible later, but I am writing about 1912 and 1913—and what a handicap it was going to be to him, especially when he should begin his Administration in the face of a puzzled and critical Nation. We all liked Wilson and were anxious to have the country like and understand him. Our conclusion, erroneous as it turned out, was that Wilson's invisibility was caused by his inexperience, by his failure to grasp the urgent necessity of becoming visible as all other statesmen did. Many things were traceable to Wilson's inexperience, but not that; and so we were speedily to find out.

Anyhow, we told him how other public men established contact with the people through those reporters who attended them daily—not by giving interviews, but by enabling these reporters to interpret their ideas and purposes, without quotation marks, to the people. We told him the importance of making himself clear to those who had elected him, and placed our services at his command, in the same way in which reporters performing this duty always do place them; though never, except in the case of that unlucky misfit candidate for President, Alton B. Parker, have I ever known it to be necessary to tell the public man about it. It always went without saying. I say Parker was the only exception, although Doyle, Martin and I supposed

Wilson to be another. We were mistaken; he knew all about it, and his reason was far removed from the one we had ascribed, inexperience.

He was considerably moved. His face flushed, as it always did in such moments; he felt and looked grateful, and he manifested it in a way that surprised me, and touched me too. For the first time he took us into his heart in what he said. Before that he had been merely the gay and witty companion; now he was deeply earnest and self-revelatory.

"I appreciate this more than I can tell you," he said, speaking with warm impetuosity—for let no man persuade you that Wilson was a cold man; he was warmth itself, and now he was talking in a pell-mell rush of words. "Every word you say is true, and I know it. Don't you suppose I know my own handicaps? I'd do what you advise if I could. I know how other men do—all of them. I have heard how excellently Colonel Roosevelt succeeds in making himself intelligible by following the very course you advise, and often I have wished that I could do it. If I could I would. I've even tried to. But it's not my nature. If I undertook to do it, I'd make a failure of it. I'll have to let the others follow that road while I follow mine, and do things as I have to do them and not as, I realize, it would be better to do them. I haven't a doubt that I will suffer a good deal of damage by my inability to reconstruct myself, but I know my own limitations."

Then he looked at us appealingly, and, throwing his arms out in a wide gesture, said with winning impulsiveness:

"I'd do it if I could. But *I can't make myself over.*"

On that last sentence he laid tremendous emphasis. It was plain to me not only that he had thought out this thoroughly, but that he had studied himself in every detail of his character and planned his life so as to make not only his assets but his liabilities useful to him. For once he had opened that inaccessible soul of his and let us gaze into it. Later, when I read of his telling the National Press Club in Washington, "I have a single-track mind," that conversation in Princeton seemed to have an echo.

The most intimate friend of Wilson and his whole family, at the time of his first election, was Dudley Field Malone. If Wilson was really fond of anybody, concerning which I had some doubts since I never saw the slightest indication of it, it was Dudley Malone. When he went campaigning he took Dudley along, somewhat in the same capacity as that of Cecil Lyon on Roosevelt's train—that of chum to the candidate. At home, in Princeton, Malone had the run of the house. Mrs. Wilson and the Wilson daughters all loved him,—Dudley was the most lovable fellow in the world, anyhow,—and the President-elect beamed on him whenever he saw him, which was often. He used to run over to Princeton and spend his week-ends with the Wilsons, and was just like one of the family.

Malone had done yeoman service for Wilson in the campaign; he was a first-rate stump-speaker who could sway crowds, and not only was he in demand when Wilson was resting, but he would "spell" the Governor on his trips. In short, he was Wilson's right-hand man. And Malone, now that Wilson was surely going to be President, wanted to be Collector of the Port of New York.

One day I was sitting alone in a room at the State Capitol in Trenton when the door opened and Joseph P. Tumulty came in. Tumulty was Governor Wilson's secretary and nearer to intimacy with him than any one else at that time, not excepting Colonel House. "Charley," said Tumulty, "I've got something to show you." He took out a letter and covered it with his hand, so that I could read only a paragraph. It was from a woman, and it reminded

Tumulty how anxious she and her daughters were that Dudley Malone should be appointed Collector of the Port. The paragraph concluded with a request that if Tumulty had been able to find out anything about Dudley's chances for the office, he would write her.

"Who's the letter from, Joe?" I asked idly.

"Mrs. Woodrow Wilson," said Tumulty. He regarded me gravely, to see the effect. The effect was fully up to his expectations.

"Well, I'll be damned!" I finally succeeded in saying. "What did you tell her, Joe?"

"What could I tell her?" said Tumulty. "I don't know any more than she does, and I wouldn't dare ask him."

Tumulty, too, wanted a job. He wanted to be appointed Secretary to the President. His name began to come up in rumors, which finally got so numerous that some of the reporters assigned to "cover" the President-elect considered the advisability of mentioning them in print. They were afraid that if they didn't somebody else would, and they would have to explain to their editors how they came to be beaten on it. But when one of them told Tumulty that a mention of the rumors was contemplated, he was panic-stricken. "Boys, if you love me, don't," he implored; "for God's sake don't print my name at all. Don't admit in print that I exist. If he sees it he'll think I inspired it and he'll appoint somebody else. I know him better than you do. If you actually have to say something about it to hold your positions, say that I haven't the ghost of a show for the job!"

One day *The New York American* printed a report that Malone was going to be appointed Collector, and Malone charged madly aboard the first train to Trenton and arrived there in a frenzy to assure Wilson that he had had nothing to do with the infernal campaign lie. As soon as he had convinced the Governor, he rushed over to our office in the

Capitol, rounded us all up, and delivered the most impassioned oration that even he had ever made.

"You fellows," cried Malone in a fury of entreaty, "are all friends of mine; we've been all over the country together, and I like you and think you like me. Now for the—love—of—God," and here Malone swung his fists convulsively in the air and his face was contorted with anguish, "don't print a line about my being appointed to the Collectorship or any other office from Secretary of State to stenographer. If there's a man here that dislikes Dudley Malone, a man among you that hates him and wants to ruin him for life, let that man print a complimentary paragraph saying that Dudley is a fine man and would make a good Collector of the Port. And now, fellows, about this damn story in *The American*. If you love me, print a story in your papers to-morrow saying that Mr. Malone, when seen to-day, said there was no truth in the report,—he is not a candidate for any office in the gift of the President,—not only has none been tendered him, but no intimation has been given him from any source that he is being considered—Mr. Malone has no intention of giving up his present work.

"And when you've printed that, fellows, will you be kind to a poor down-trodden Irishman and leave my name out altogether?"

Months went by, and one forenoon Wilson sent for Tumulty. The room set apart for the use of the reporters directly faced the Governor's room. I happened to be alone in it. Wilson was sitting at his desk in the straight line of my vision. I saw Tumulty enter the room and go up to the Governor's desk. Wilson raised his head and said a few words. Tumulty listened, bowed, and said something in reply. He then turned and walked slowly out. He was coming directly toward the reporters' room, of course, and as I watched him come there was no expression whatever on his face.

He crossed the hall, walked into my room, and shut the door carefully, so that Wilson could no longer see him. The moment we were alone together his face became a sunburst, and to my intense surprise he danced a jig.

"Charley, I've got it!" he cried. "And me a Pape!"

He meant that all the bigots in the land would descend on Wilson's neck for appointing a Catholic to office; and as a matter of fact they did. The wildest delusions were spread abroad, and the lower-browed firmly believed that the terrible Jesuits reigned in the White House and that the United States had been surreptitiously annexed to the Vatican. It took an unnecessary amount of Wilson's time to cope with frantic delegations which came to the White House to free him from his ultramontane bonds.

Not a word had Wilson said to Tumulty on the subject—or Tumulty to Wilson, of course—until that moment. Then he had informed Tumulty as briefly as possible, and Tumulty had received the news as casually as he could, restraining his real emotions until he was alone with me. Even at that moment any display of joy might have made Wilson reconsider.

I was not at all surprised when I read in David F. Houston's book, *Eight Years With Wilson's Cabinet,* that Wilson never spoke or wrote to him about the Secretaryship of Agriculture and that when he arrived in Washington just before the inauguration he did not know whether he was to be appointed or not. Or to read, in Henry L. Stoddard's *As I Knew Them,* how he found Secretary Lane overjoyed over an important utterance Wilson had just delivered. "Didn't you know he was going to say it?" Stoddard asked. "Not a word of it," replied the Secretary of the Interior. "I haven't seen the President for a month, and don't know when I shall."

One day in that Winter of 1912-13 the tall and stately

form of Congressman Albert S. Burleson, of Texas, filled our vision. He went in to see Wilson and was in conference with him for an hour. He came out wearing his statesman look, and surveyed us with majestic dignity when we thronged around him to find out whether the President-elect had offered him the Postmaster-Generalship or not. The conversation ran as follows:

"Mr. Burleson, can you tell us anything of what the Governor said to you?"

"Gentlemen," with much gravity and deep feeling, "I should like to tell you, but Mr. Wilson has requested me not to. My lips are sealed."

"Was the Cabinet discussed?"

"I can tell you nothing of what transpired."

"Can you give us a tip about who is likely to be Postmaster-General?"

"Gentlemen, I am sure you will respect my position. I can not betray the Governor's confidence."

"Well, do you think Mr. Bryan will be Secretary of State?"

"You must ask the Governor about that. I can say nothing."

"Are you going to be in the Cabinet yourself, Mr. Burleson?"

"Gentleman," with increasing solemnity, "again I say to you that I would gladly speak if I could, but honor forbids. All information about our interview must come from the Governor."

Then he strode slowly away into the corridor. There he ran into Billy Keohan, of *The New York Tribune,* who had not been present at the interview. He grabbed Keohan by the shoulder and drew him into a niche. "Say, Keohan," he whispered, "tell me, for Heaven's sake,—tell me confidentially, I won't reveal to a soul where I got it,—what do you newspaper fellows here know about who's going to be in the Cabinet?"

Subsequently he found out. He was appointed Postmaster-General, sure enough, and was one of those who stuck it out until the end of Wilson's eight years.

Afterward we began to piece together, from the things dropped by visiting statesmen, just what happened at these formidable-looking conferences. Some statesman furtively nursing Cabinet ambitions and looking longingly at Trenton from afar would be electrified by a letter from Wilson inviting him to call. He would boil aboard the first train and curse it for going slow, and sometimes get out and run ahead of the engine for a few miles to get there quicker. Then, when he got to Trenton to accept the Secretaryship of the Treasury or something, the Governor would cross-examine him for three-quarters of an hour, pump him dry, and thank him for his instructive conversation. The statesman would go out deeply mortified. He would think he was the only one who had been treated in that manner, and on the way home would highly resolve that no one should ever know the story of his shame. So, to all inquiries, he would frown mysteriously and say, "Sh! Not a word. My lips are sealed."

Then he would try to extort from some other statesman what Wilson had told that statesman, and Statesman Number Two would frown mysteriously and say, "Sh! Not a word. My lips are sealed." By the time half a dozen statesmen had assumed this pose each began to suspect the others of bluffing; there were mutual confessions, and it became clear that the Sphinx of Trenton had told none of them a single thing.

Wilson, who knew himself thoroughly, was perfectly aware of this phase of his character, equally aware what people said about it, and immovably determined to abate no jot of it. Soon after his election, and when the pilgrimages of statesmen to Trenton were well under way, I inquired whether anybody had asked him for a place in the Cabinet.

"No one has yet committed that indiscretion," he replied grimly.

However, later on, some of those who did not visit Trenton either wrote to him themselves or had their friends write recommending them for office. I mentioned it to him one day.

"Any man who asks me for an office, and any one whose friends ask me to give him an office," he said, "makes it certain that he will not get *any* office."

What is written here about Tumulty and Malone may give some readers the impression that Wilson was cold or ungrateful toward the men who had faithfully served him. That would be a grave mistake. Wilson, though he never said anything about it, was the most appreciative of men toward those who gave him service. He was always observing them, studying them, and making up his mind how to reward them. They never knew it until the time came; never imagined he even noticed what they were doing for him. In the campaign his personal stenographer was a nineteen-year old boy named Charles L. Swem. His stenographer at Trenton was a young man named Warren Johnson. Swem's assistant was an eighteen-year old girl named Salome Tarr. The telegraph operator who handled his dispatches at Princeton was Jack Mendelson. And Tumulty, officially his private secretary, was his political guardian angel. He said nothing to any of them indicating that he was pleased with their work; but as soon as he became President he appointed Mendelson chief telegraph operator in the White House; he appointed Swem to be chief White House stenographer, with Johnson as assistant; and Tumulty became Secretary to the President. As he rose in the world he gathered his personal staff and took them all with him. Inappreciative?

The only one left out was little Salome Tarr, and when she read the news she was bitterly disappointed. Why, when he remembered all the rest, had he forgotten her? She cried her eyes out. He hadn't forgotten her. When the first Cabinet meeting of the new Administration was opened, the new President devoted a large part of it to instructing each Secretary in turn to hunt through his department with a fine-tooth comb and find a nice job for Salome.

Malone did, however, have to suffer a short purgatory for that pleasant little piece in *The American* awarding him the Collectorship of the Port. When Santa Claus Wilson opened his pack, Malone got a tin whistle instead of the nice new pair of skates. He was appointed Third Assistant Secretary of State, which at that time was the last thing any one wanted in the way of a job. That official was only a sort of super-clerk, hidden away in a room where nobody ever came and doing routine duties. It was a graveyard. It might have been called a morgue for unclaimed political cadavers. Malone took his medicine like a man, never whimpered, stuck cheerfully to his unwelcome duties; and after hazing him in this way for a few months, Wilson concluded that he had been punished enough. Without the slightest intimation to Malone of his intention, he suddenly bestowed on him the Collectorship.

CHAPTER XXI

WILSON THE HUMAN BEING

ALONE among the public men of my acquaintance, Wilson was unable to separate his own personality from criticism of himself—favorable or unfavorable criticism. This may seem like a sweeping statement, so I shall have to defend it. No public man, of course, enjoys hostile criticism, or is loftily superior to agreeable criticism. But they all understand the fact that they are continually being subjected to scrutiny and analysis which is not actuated by either love or hatred. Wilson never could get to that point of self-detachment. It is really not a very high point of self-detachment at that; it is only the recognition of an intrusive and inescapable fact. But Wilson could not separate his public acts from his private personality even to the slight extent of realizing that the two things were viewed by others as being separate. His reaction to an adverse criticism was exactly that of a lady who should be told, "Mr. So-and-So thinks you're horrid." His reaction to a favorable criticism was exactly that of a girl who hears, "Mr. This-and-That says you're very pretty." That is, he had precisely the same feeling of wounded self-love in the one case and the same glow of gratified self-esteem in the other. Also, he had the same feeling of involuntary resentment or gratitude that they would have.

One day not long after my study of him began to be close I published an article analyzing certain things he had done and the motives which were evidently behind them.

The article was wholly commendatory. It was written with no feeling of affection for Wilson and no desire to laud him, but simply because it was the truth. As a reporter it was my duty to study him impersonally and analyze him accurately, if I could. In this matter the result of the analysis was altogether to Wilson's credit. That morning he saw me on a railroad train, jumped up from his seat, came down the aisle, and stood beside me with his face beaming with pleasure and gratitude. He was almost extravagant in his expressions.

I was a good deal surprised. It was a new experience, and I could not understand what I had done to be thanked for. I turned it over in my mind without reaching any solution, and finally gave it up. A few days afterward Wilson did something calling for adverse criticism, and of course I wrote an article giving that sort of criticism in full measure. And thought no more about it. But that day I was one of a number of correspondents who had something to see him about, and as we entered the Governor's office at Trenton I noticed that his eye traveled over the group and rested on me with a hurt look. He made us a little speech about his relations with the press, and said that he had found some things that were hard for him to understand.

"For instance," he said, glancing at me, "last Tuesday one of you printed an article praising me, and I was very much touched. I took occasion immediately, the first time I saw him, to thank him and tell him how much I appreciated it. And yet this very man publishes to-day another article in which he criticizes me. This is what I mean by saying that the course of newspaper writers is often beyond my comprehension."

In short, it was impossible for him to get far enough out of himself to look at himself as a subject for impartial criticism, favorable and unfavorable. Criticism of either kind made him automatically divide the critics, for the time at any rate, into friends and enemies. In this case the only thing that puzzled him was that I seemed to him to be both at the same time, and that, as he said, was one of the things that bewildered him about "the course of newspaper writers." I did not explain all this to him, of course; what was the use?

When I say that Wilson was solitary in this respect, I do not wish to be misunderstood as implying that any public man ever receives favorable or unfavorable criticism without any personal feeling at all. That would be contrary to human nature. When John Hay was new as Secretary of State, and when the country knew very little about him and cared less, I came to the conclusion that he was really a statesman and that before long the people would find it out. I based this on the things he was doing, which had not yet attracted notice, and the way he was doing them. So I printed an article setting forth this conviction and the reasons for it. I was then one of the men whose duty it was to "cover" the State Department, which duty included that of visiting the Secretary daily and finding out what information he had to give. That day, when the "seance," as we called it, came to a close, Hay asked me to remain when the others left. His face was grave and his manner sedate; but as the door closed behind the other reporters he changed magically, his eyes glowed with pleasure, his smile seemed to spread over his whole face, and he told me warmly what a help that article had been to him. I did not know it then, but he was nearly discouraged; all that was being printed about him was in the line of misrepresentation and abuse of him as an "English flunkey" who was betraying his country, no one was publishing anything to the contrary, and he was contemplating resigning. He did offer his resignation to McKinley, who refused to accept it. The recognition of his greatness was soon to come, but it had not come yet, and my article was the only one on that line that had appeared.

I was somewhat taken aback, and showed it. In fact, I did say something indicating that I had expected a Secretary of State to be a spirit without body, parts, or passions. (I was new in the Washington field in those days.) He laughed understandingly.

"I know," said Hay. "But just remember this. No matter how far up we get, we never get so far up that we don't want to purr a little when our backs are stroked."

The two incidents may seem alike. The difference, however, is that grateful as Hay was, he never for a moment imagined that I had praised him because I loved him. In fact, the main ingredient in his pleasure was precisely that he knew I had not. It was a pleasant thing for him to find that an impartial critic who neither loved nor disliked him had studied his public course without feeling and had been unable to find anything in it that did not deserve high praise. That was the difference between John Hay and Woodrow Wilson; or rather, it was the difference between Woodrow Wilson and all the other public men of my time.

I have already shown how Roosevelt understood this situation and reacted to it, in his treatment of the unfriendly but honest reporter at Oyster Bay whom I have called "D——." I never saw the least trace in Bryan of this peculiar trait of Wilson, except once in a very slight degree. When he was contemplating resigning as Secretary of State in Wilson's Cabinet, I knew it—not from him—and published an article announcing the fact and telling why he wanted to get out. He was greatly displeased. Meeting *The New York American* correspondent next day, he asked, "Was it Thompson who wrote that article about me?"

"It was," said the correspondent.

"I wouldn't have believed it," said Bryan energetically. "I can't understand it. I thought he was my friend."

But this was the only time I ever heard of Bryan being unable to separate his public acts from his private character. And, as my acquaintance with him lasted many years, this one aberration from his usual habit of mind hardly counts. It is certainly not enough to put him in Wilson's class.

When Wilson first ran for President it was a delightful experience for him, because it was an utter novelty. Every other Presidential candidate I have ever traveled with, except Alton B. Parker in 1904, had reached the nomination after years of practise in meeting the many-headed face to face. Taft was no exception, though you may think he was. Poor Parker, a misfit candidate if ever there was one, did not know anything about even the many-headed of New York State or Ulster and Dutchess Counties, and the hinterland, as he visioned it, was terra incognita. He did not want to go on the stump at all, and thought he could run for President without leaving Esopus. But he was utterly unknown to the country, which grew angry at being required to buy a pig in a poke, and the more the impenetrable candidate wrapped himself in mystery the louder grew the mutterings. Finally William F. Sheehan, who was personally conducting Parker, forced the unwilling and protesting nominee out of his seclusion and propelled him on to the stump.

I never campaigned with such an unhappy candidate as Parker. He was out of his element; he did not understand the crowd and hated the work. It was irksome and distasteful, and besides he was handling unfamiliar tools, not the tools of his trade. Of dealing with that appraising monster that was studying him in a railroad station at Meriden or a jammed hall in Jersey City he knew no more than his own coachman. Being pitchforked into the pell-mell of a campaign, with that incomprehensible multitude before him and the myriad pitfalls he might blunder into, that was no pleasure to Alton B. Parker.

But it was a joy to Woodrow Wilson. It was like taking his first automobile ride or his first dance with a girl. He loved to play on the crowd and watch its reactions, an experience he had never known. When its pulse bounded under his touch he saw it and was as happy as a boy. He did resemble Parker in one thing: he did not believe himself adept at touching the popular heart, and was distrustful of his ability ever to learn. After all those years as a schoolmaster it was natural. So when he found himself doing it he was almost pathetically happy.

One day, when he had been campaigning about a month, he addressed a crowd of excited Democrats in the Middle West. He uttered several sentences that brought him up to his first effective point. The audience cheered, and as the applause was dying down some one yelled, "That was a good one, Woody!"

The Governor's face was suddenly irradiated with joy. His eyes glistened and his lips shook. He plunged impetuously into a speech delivered with such impetuosity, verve and punch that it stormed the crowd, and he went back to his car with his ears ringing from cheers that came from the heart.

When I sat down with him at luncheon in his car his face was still glowing and his eyes still bright. "Did you hear, Mr. Thompson?" he asked with a happy smile. "They called me Woody!"

I knew what was in his mind. He was always contrasting himself with Roosevelt, especially in the matter of influence with the people; always thinking of himself as Roosevelt's inferior in that respect, and always wishing he could become Roosevelt's equal in it, and doubting that he ever could. But now the same kind of men who rapturously hailed Roosevelt as "Teddy" had called him "Woody"!

The campaign of 1912 was well advanced before I joined the Wilson party. Some of the other reporters had been with him before his nomination, and all had been with him for some time. I had first met him years before, at Princeton University when he was its President; but in our conversations at that time there had been nothing to prepare me for Wilson the politician or Wilson the popular orator, and he, as I afterward found, was more aware of that fact than I was. At the first important stop we made he inserted in his speech his point about Alice in Wonderland. It was used to illustrate the fact that all the hullabaloo about progressive legislation and social justice, in which the other side was so vociferous, had never brought the people a step nearer to the mirage. So he told how, after running violently for a long time, Alice remarked with surprise to the Red Queen, "Why, we're just where we were when we started!" and the Red Queen replied, "Of course we are. We would have to run twice as fast to get anywhere else."

The crowd laughed and cheered. I had never heard his application of it, and he told it so well that I did something reporters pride themselves on not doing; I dropped my pencil and laughed uproariously. Glancing up at Wilson, who was waiting for the applause to die down, I was surprised to see that he was not looking at the cheering and laughing audience; he was looking at me, and there was a happy and satisfied smile on his face. I turned to David Lawrence and said, "What's he looking at me for?"

"He was trying that Red Queen joke on you," replied Lawrence. "He wanted to see how it would hit you. It has always gone all right with the audience, but he wanted to see if he could make a hardened reporter laugh, and especially you because you've just come from Roosevelt and have seen him get a rise out of the crowd so many times. He told the rest of us this morning, 'Don't tell Thompson about my Red Queen story; I'm going to spring it on him at Cleveland and I want to watch him.' So we didn't."

In short, he was trying a practical comparison of himself with Roosevelt; an experiment to see how well he stood up with the Colonel in popular appeal. It succeeded beyond his expectations, for the best the overworked and tired reporters ever permitted themselves in the case of even Roosevelt's witty points was an approving smile. Besides that, it was and still is a rather foolish and senseless convention among reporters to pretend a weary callousness they do not always feel.

Every new day was a joy to Wilson in this novel adventure of meeting the people. Everything was so totally different from the life he had lived so long. For the first time, too, he came closely into contact with oratorical campaign flapdoodle about himself, and it utterly charmed his sense of the ridiculous. At times he nearly spilled the beans by guffawing right out in meeting when he heard himself described in terms that an early Christian would have hesitated about applying to St. John the Divine. At a meeting held at Creighton University, Omaha, he was listening decorously while the solemn Nebraska celebrity who was to introduce him detailed his super-eminences; until finally the eulogist unexpectedly described the candidate as "one of the greatest educators of this or any other age." This conservative and judgmatic appraisal hit Wilson's funnybone so hard that he started to let out what would have been a howl of laughter; but he caught himself, shut his mouth with a look of panic, and bit his lips hard to keep down the rebellious merriment that was still clamoring to escape. He glanced furtively at the crowd, and was reassured; not only had they not noticed his emotion, but they were swallowing the orator's guff with open mouths and believing every word of it. Wilson's eyes shone with amusement as he looked them over, the corners of his mouth twitched again, and it was a minute or two before he could get back to the proper frame of mind.

Another thing that greatly tickled the Governor was the popular curiosity about his personality. It may be hard to realize now, but at that time he was wholly unknown to the country, and there was the most insatiable desire to know what he looked like, how he talked, how he acted. Everywhere we went in that campaign we would hear people say, after studying him, "Well, he may be all right, but he ain't good-looking." It finally got to be a stock saying in the party. Wilson, in fact, had a peculiar face, so much so that he was one of the few public men who had almost no doubles; I never saw but one man who looked very much like Wilson, though counterfeit Roosevelts, Tafts, Bryans and so on were numerous. One day, while we were chatting in the car, some one asked Wilson what he thought of somebody else, I forget who.

"Well, he may be all right," said Wilson, "but he ain't good-looking."

That familiar phrase, in his mouth, took everybody aback. He saw it, and smiled that queer, winning smile and said: "So you've heard them say that too, have you?"

"Yes, but we didn't think you had," I replied.

"I've caught it several times as I passed by," said Wilson. "It reminds me of a thing that happened when I was running for Governor. I stopped in front of a billboard that had my picture on it. As I looked at it I became conscious of two working men who had stopped and were staring at me. One of them said to the other, 'Bill, damned if them two ain't enough alike to be twins.'"

Where the idea came from that Wilson was a cold, self-restrained man I never could understand. It may have been because he was called a "schoolmaster" so constantly. He was full of hot blood. He was a jolly fellow, who loved a story and could tell one to admiration. His sense of humor was prehensile. He loved the ridiculous as well as the witty. And it was easier to make him "mad" than any other public man I ever knew; nor could he control his rage easily. He was a swift and lively talker, enjoyed conversation greatly, took a vigorous part in it without ever trying to dominate it, and seemed in love with life in all its manifestations. For all that, people continued to talk of him as a glacial, forbidding, inhuman sort of monstrosity among men.

I was sitting in his campaign car with Roscoe Mitchell, of *The New York World,* on the day William Sulzer was nominated for Governor by the New York Democrats. Wilson was just about to start out on a speaking trip through the West. Sulzer was a rough, uncouth citizen, and decidedly not a gentleman. *The New York Evening Post,* which was supporting Wilson for President, could not stomach so coarse a candidate—this was in the days when *The Post* was the mouthpiece of the silk-stockings—and promptly printed an editorial bolting Sulzer's nomination. Mitchell and I were discussing what effect this would have on Wilson's vote in New York, when he came into our compartment. He was in a genial mood and smiling his bright, odd, infectious smile.

"I see you are in Committee of the Whole on the state of the nation," he said. "What particular world problem is up for solution now?"

"This; have you seen it?" asked Mitchell, handing him the paper. He had not. He read the latest product of the Villard muse with a gathering scowl. His smile fled, and there rose in his face that high flush which with him always indicated that his temper was getting the better of him. When he finished it he threw the paper on the floor, rose and made his way to the door in two steps. As he reached it he turned, with his face like thunder, pointed to the paper on the floor, and said, fairly hissing the words:

"I don't see any use in being so *damned* ladylike."

In the time that intervened between his first election to the Presidency and his inauguration he used to receive every day, in the Governor's office at Trenton, the reporters whose duty it was to "cover" his movements. On one of these occasions it so happened that one of the reporters had just returned from New York, where his friends had entertained him over-well. His condition was not apparent; he happened to be one of those individuals who "don't show it," and no one not well acquainted with him would have suspected that his mind was disorganized. Of course Wilson did not suspect it. As we walked in and took our seats, the President-elect looked up with his quick smile—he was in the best of humors—and said:

"To-day, gentlemen, you can question me on any subject you like, except one. I don't want to answer any questions about who will be in my Cabinet, and I shall be obliged if you will consider that subject barred. Now, with that much understood, fire away."

The victim of over-hospitality had not heard a word. He wore a benevolent smile; his mind was a universe away, somewhere in the seventh heaven, perhaps twanging a harp or cuddling an houri. But he became aware of the momentary pause, and looking up with the same benignant smile, he said cheerily:

"Well, Governor, have you decided yet on who shall be Attorney-General in your Cabinet?"

Instantly that high flush I knew so well rose in Wilson's face. His eyes blazed. He glared furiously at the reporter, who, all unconscious of offense, was regarding him with a look akin to affection. Wilson sat for a moment, and then, unable to control himself, he sprang out of his chair and ran around his desk, obviously seeking to suppress the words that were rushing through his brain. Having completely circumnavigated the desk, he stopped in front of it and cried out excitedly:

"Mr. ——, are you trying to insult me?"

"No, Governor," said the unwitting sinner, amiably; "not at all. Only trying to get the news."

Wilson stared at him, and saw that the man really had no intention of offending him, though he still had not the faintest idea of the state of the case. Finally he growled, "You're taking the wrong way to get it," walked over to his chair and sat down. He got himself enough under control to answer the questions the rest of us asked, though it was plain enough that he was still agitated; and a few days afterward the bibulous inquisitor learned from his superiors that he was at liberty to return to New York. He did not know what the trouble was, for none of us cared to tell him; and his superiors knew nothing except that for some reason he was not persona grata to the President-elect. As for Wilson, he never did learn why he was "insulted."

So much for the "cold," "glacial," "inhuman" Wilson, the man without parts or passions. So much? Well, perhaps to remove so persistent and widespread a misconception it may be well to give one more case to the contrary:

He was spending a month in Bermuda before taking up his duties as President. With him were reporters whom he knew and with whom he was on fine terms; and there were also cameramen from newspapers and photograph concerns, as there always are when Presidents go vacationing. No automobiles were permitted in Bermuda, because they were thought dangerous to the beautiful coral roads which are the little archipelago's glory; and Wilson used to go about the islands on his bicycle. He wore his old clothes and looked pretty tough. He used to do the family marketing and return with provender strapped to the handle-bars of his wheel.

One day he went galumphing to market accompanied by his daughter Jessie, now Mrs. Sayre. She also wore negligent clothes; good enough to be seen in, but hardly the sort of thing you would choose to appear in if you were to be gazed at in a rotogravure section. Besides, they were out riding a long time, and one never looks very spick after a morning on the wheel. Returning to Glencove, as Wilson's cottage was named, they found reporters grouped around the place—and also the cameramen. Wilson got off his bicycle, smiled his ingratiating smile, and said:

"Gentlemen, you can photograph me to your heart's content. I don't care how I look. But I request you not to photograph my daughter. You know how women feel about such things, and I myself would rather not have the ladies of my family made to——"

Before he could finish the sentence, a cad of a photographer aimed his camera at Jessie Wilson and snapped her. Wilson's face turned the color of a strawberry, and the high flush mounted to his eyes. Even his eyes were red. He clenched his fists and rushed on the photographer with the certain intention of punching his head. He had almost reached the ruffian when he remembered how "President Knocks Down Cameraman" would look in a thousand scareheads. He stopped, with his fists still clenched and his eyes still flaming, and cried:

"You're no gentleman! I want to give you the worst thrashing you ever had in your life; and what's more, I'm perfectly able to do it!"

If the fellow had made any reply whatever, every man

who saw Wilson at that moment was convinced that the President-elect would forget all about the Presidency and the scareheads and give an earnest imitation of the head of a nation whipping a cad. Fortunately, he did not. Probably, when Wilson cooled down, he had some uncomfortable moments of anticipation about how the incident would appear in the papers, even as it was. However, he need not have worried. The reporters held a council and decided to write nothing about it except a casual mention, since nothing could be printed that would not give the idea that the President-elect had lost his temper. We had no acquaintance with the photographers, so the rest of this is only hearsay, but I was told that the other cameramen boycotted the creature who had snapped Jessie Wilson; and this is greatly to their credit. A few days later he received a cable message from his home office telling him to take the next boat back to the United States; so Wilson, compelled by his position to forego the usual pleasures of an insulted father, did at least purge the island of the fellow's presence.

CHAPTER XXII

THE VERBAL STRATEGIST

WILSON had what is senselessly called a "jesuitical" mind. The word jesuitical should properly mean "unselfishly and intelligently devoted," or "filled with a passion for service;" that is, if it is understood to have any relation whatever to the Jesuits. However, in its popular meaning, which is as far as possible removed from anything resembling Jesuits, Wilson was a perfect example of it.

For this reason, it was impossible to rely on anything he said. I do not mean he lied. I mean that he took such an intellectual pleasure in stating a thing so as to give an opposite impression to the fact, though he kept strictly to the truth, that one had to be constantly on the alert to keep from being misled. This made things difficult, at first, for political reporters, who encountered in him something they had never met before. Political reporters are accustomed, from their daily experience with public men, to expect perfect frankness. Of course they sometimes meet public men who lie to them. But they never meet one who takes exquisite enjoyment out of telling them the truth in such a way that they are sure, not to be deceived by him, but to deceive themselves. Not expecting it, they were led at first into traps. Learning this oddity of his, they were thereafter on their guard; and whenever he told them anything, they did not accept it without first turning it inside out to see what hidden counter-meaning might lie in it.

For instance, toward the close of his Administration as Governor of New Jersey, the State Senate decided to go to New York and hold a dinner at the Hotel Astor, in honor of President pro tem. Fielder, who was to succeed him in the Governorship. Wilson notified the reporters "covering" him at Princeton that they were to go with him to New York. (When a candidate leaves his home for any reason, he tells the "covering" reporters his intention of going, so that they can arrange to go with him.) On the train, on the way to New York, we went over to him and questioned him about his plans for the day, so that we could map out our program. David Lawrence was spokesman.

"Shall you make a speech at the dinner?" he began.

"No, I don't think I shall," said Wilson.

"Will there be any speeches at all?"

"No, it will be purely informal; just a sitting around and chatting after the dinner is over."

"Do you expect to go anywhere after the dinner is over?"

"No, I do not."

"Then there is really no reason why we should cover the dinner?"

"None at all. It has no political significance."

"And we might just as well write our stories now and turn them into the office in advance, so that we can have the rest of the day to ourselves?"

"Yes. You won't find anything that will interest your readers in anything that will happen at the dinner. It's merely social, and a passing mention of it will be enough."

Leaving the train at New York, he went on up to Colonel House's, as he always did. With our minds entirely at rest, we agreed that we would go to our offices, write our reports, and then take the day off. Each man announced that he was going to get his wife or best girl and take in some show. We agreed that we would all go to Colonel House's about midnight, to make sure that nothing had happened that needed to be added to what we had written, and then separate again for bed.

But Billy Keohan, of *The Tribune,* and I, who dined together at Shanley's, decided that our duty would not be completely done until we had taken one final look at the banquet hall, to assure ourselves that everything was in proper shape. So we walked over to the Astor, and found the Senators nearly all there, but no sign of the Governor. A little uneasy, we hunted up the guest of honor, President Fielder, and considerably astonished him. "Why, he's not coming," said Fielder. "At least, he hasn't been invited." Two or three other Senators confirmed him. Thoroughly disturbed, Keohan went into the dining-room and found that no chair had been placed for the Governor.

By now we were badly scared. All we had turned in was a short announcement that Wilson had come to New York to visit Colonel House, had attended the dinner of the New Jersey Senate, and had then returned to House's to spend the night; and that no political significance was to be attached to his visit. Not only was this story to be proved false in the morning, but for all we knew he might be spending the time holding political conferences, and that might be what he had come for, since he had not come for the dinner. We hurried into a taxicab and over to House's, and found that Wilson was still there. Then we got back into the taxicab and darted to the Waldorf-Astoria, to get hold of Dick Taylor and Joe Murphy, the two Secret Service men who were assigned to watch over his safety. They followed him everywhere, of course; that was their duty, and if they failed in it they would be in a pretty serious predicament with their superiors. They had dined at the

Waldorf, and were now getting ready to go up to House's and accompany Wilson to the dinner. That secretive statesman had even permitted his official protectors to think he was going to the Astor.

They were dumfounded when we told them what we had learned; dumfounded, and scared, and a little angry. We all jumped into their automobile and went to House's, where they went up to his apartment to get the lay of the land. Presently they came down and told us the Governor was going to stay there all the evening. What was more, our apprehensions were justified; he was holding some important conferences. We got the story of these conferences, went to our offices and wrote it, and a long newsy report of the day's political developments took the place of the silly little paragraph about how Wilson had come to New York to attend the Fielder dinner. We tried to get hold of the other men to tell them, but they were all out at theaters, and we couldn't get them until the round-up we had all arranged for House's place at midnight. They did some hard scrambling, but it was too late for their first editions; the best they could do was to get the news Keohan and I told them into the second. So, without any fault of ours, we had beaten them.

Wilson, as always when he had played a little solitaire game of "jesuitism," was highly pleased with himself. He had told us nothing but the strict truth, but had worded it so as to convey an opposite meaning, and whenever he could do this to anybody it greatly invigorated him. Knowing this, I was much amused when some of the cub reporters—we had an unusual lot of cubs with us, for such an assignment—decided that it was incumbent on them to "rebuke" the Governor, as one of them put it, for his misbehavior. (The older reporters, of course, simply grinned over their experience and thought nothing of it; it was all in the day's work and they would watch Wilson's words more carefully in future; but the cubs were very wroth.) Subsequently I asked the youngest cub if they had administered their "rebuke" to Wilson, and he said they had, and that it had been very successful; Wilson had been properly humbled. He saw nothing funny in the scene he described, but I did:

"When Wes and I entered the car the next morning we just gave a barely perceptible nod as we passed the Governor and walked slowly to the end of the car, where we sat down. We did not enter into conversation with him; and it cut him; you could see that. What are you laughing at? But we were determined to let him see what we thought of the way he had acted; perfectly cool, you know, but determined. What are you laughing at? Finally he called out, 'What are your views of the Mexican situation?' We thought that was rather a queer question to ask; sort of foolish, wasn't it? What are you laughing at? I didn't even answer him, but Wes did. Wes said, calmly but with a good deal of quiet firmness, 'We have no information about the Mexican situation except such as we have seen in the morning papers.' He said it just like that. And then, for some reason, I don't know what, the Governor laughed as if he would split, and said, 'Ah, get down from your dignity. Come off your perch.' So then, having shown him what we thought of it, we came over and talked to him. What are you laughing at?"

My first experience of this trait of Wilson's had come to me two years before, when he was President of Princeton University. I was then a feature-writer for *The New York Times*. The Democrats nominated him for Governor of New Jersey, and the Sunday editor told me to write a page about him, giving his slant on public questions and his personal slant as well. I went to Princeton and spent a pleasant afternoon with him. I told him, what was the truth, that such a story would be a help to his campaign. He knew that, and said he would like very much "to have such a feature in a New York paper." But he was not ready then. "Write to me next Saturday," he said, "and I will set a date with you then, if you still want it."

If I still wanted it; I couldn't understand that phrase. But I didn't know Wilson's artistry with words as well then as I afterward came to do, so I dismissed it from my mind as a conventional locution of his. I wrote to him on Saturday, and got back quite an effusive letter saying that when he fixed Saturday he had expected that to be the right day, but now he must ask me to write him the following Saturday, if I then wanted the story as much as ever. He apologized for the delay, which was caused by something he had not foreseen.

When the following Saturday came I picked up the feature section of *The New York Evening Post,* and there was my page story. He had given it to *The Evening Post* feature writer before I visited him. That was what he meant by "if you still want it." He knew very well it would be of no use to me after Saturday. But the story had not been printed, as he expected, on Saturday; it had been held over for the following issue, and that was what he meant by the unforeseen delay. I now understood, too, what he meant by saying he would like to have such a feature "in a New York paper."

He did not do this either because he delighted in trickery or because he had a malevolent pleasure in thwarting others and putting them to inconvenience. He did it because he enjoyed playing with his own skill in the use of words, so as to make them seem to mean one thing when they meant another. If Roosevelt, Bryan, Taft, or any other man I had ever met had been in the same position, he would have said, "Why, I'd like to give you that story, but you're too late. I've already given it to *The Evening Post,* and it will be out Saturday. You couldn't do anything with it now if I gave it to you." Wilson was the only public man I ever met who had this peculiar mental quirk.

CHAPTER XXIII

HIS INTEREST IN THE ODD LITTLE THINGS OF LIFE

NOTHING human was alien to Wilson. He had a burning curiosity about people, and about things. He took the most intense pleasure in finding out about them. I do not mean that he was unusually sympathetic or tender about the human race, but that he was eagerly curious about it. He illustrated what Shakespeare really meant, not what he is supposed to have meant, when he said, "One touch of nature makes the whole world kin." That is always quoted by benevolent and mushy saps, who have a misty notion that Shakespeare was a sort of Edgar Guest or Doctor Frank Crane when he said it; that he was trying, in a Guestian or Cranic manner, to tell us how kindness and heart-throbs make us brothers. He meant nothing of the sort. He meant something so far from it that it might be worth while for these glib quoters to read him, for once, and find out what he did mean.

Wilson had, too, an insatiable lust for the odd things of life; the little, odd things. Not only did every odd little thing interest him, but he wanted to know the reason for it and hunted for the reason, and when he found it filed it mentally away. Once, when he was Governor of New Jersey, he looked with earnest inquisitiveness at the reporters as we filed into his office for our daily "seance," and when we sat down he said with an eager smile:

"Gentlemen, there's something I've wanted to ask you about for a long time. I've observed that every day, when you come in, you all take the same seats; there's never the least variation. Mr. Miller always goes up to the far end of the lounge, Mr. Doyle always stops at the near end, Mr. Thompson and Mr. Martin always take chairs facing me, Mr. Hamer and Mr. Lawrence always sit together, and so on. I've wondered whether it was a ritual or what. It can't be an accident. Is it something subconscious, or is it intentional? And if it's intentional, what's the reason?"

"It's not intentional, and it's not exactly subconscious," said I. "None of us ever thought of it until this moment. As for the reason, did you ever notice, Governor, that when you come in after a shower you always put your umbrella in the same stand, though you've got two stands?"

"Have you seen me do it?" asked Wilson, alive with interest.

"No, but I know you do," I said. "You can't help yourself. And have you noticed that when you go alone to a restaurant you always make unconsciously for one part of the room? And that when you enter a railroad car you always strike for the front or back end of the car, or the middle, whichever is the place you sat in last time?"

Wilson was more engrossed than I had ever seen him. "Then it's habit?" he inquired.

"Yes, it's habit," I replied. "The moment you do anything once, no matter how trivial it is, you have handed it over to what William James called 'the effortless custody of habit.'"

"And that's why I always put my hat in the same place," said Wilson, "and why I——" and he went on recalling the different places where he set his feet, or his clothes, or anything else, and trying his best to find an exception to the rule. He had forgotten all about the Presidency and the errand that brought us there, and when we delicately reminded him of it he came back to earth with a start. "I've learned something," he said. And it seemed incredible that so small a thing should seem to him worthy of even a moment's consideration.

He often said that he had found, by continued observation, that Friday was his lucky day and thirteen his lucky number, and that he guided himself accordingly. I never knew whether he was joking or serious about it. But I have not the least doubt that, whether he believed the superstition or not, he had studied and observed that day and number in all their relations; it was his character to be gluttonous of information about the little odd things of life.

In Bermuda, after his election, he greeted me one day with the delighted look which always apprised me he had just come on some discovery of great unimportance. "We went down to the south shore to-day," he began at once, "my daughters and I. Haven't you been there yet? Well, you surely must go. The water there is of a color you don't see anywhere else, and it's astonishingly beautiful." This was only the proem; now came the news.

"Some one told me," he continued animatedly, "that if you look at a thing with your head on one side, or upside down, in some way it draws what you are looking at together, compresses it, as you may say, so that you get a comprehensive view of all its beauties. My daughters and I tried that down at the south shore to-day; we put our heads sideways and looked at those beautiful waves, and, by George, it's a fact. Try it some time."

Standing on the veranda of Glencove one day before his inauguration as President, he looked reflectively over at the dazzling coral cottages half hidden among the trees—the Bermuda Islands are coral formations, and everything is coral—with an occasional glimpse of a winding coral road of equally dazzling whiteness. "This is the greatest playground in the world," he said suddenly, turning to me. "The moment you get here there isn't a care on your mind; you can't do anything but play, try as you will."

He gazed over the "playground," and for once he looked actually dreamy—the only time he ever did. "This is an unreal country," he said. "It's a land of witchcraft, a fairyland, a land of make-believe. Why, I give you my word, sometimes when I've been down here and have wanted to get my attention on prosaic matters of business I haven't been able to think of them at all until—now I'm speaking the literal truth—I'd close down all the blinds so that I couldn't see Bermuda, and turned on all the electric lights. Then I could imagine myself back in the United States, and get out of fairyland and back to 'realities' by creating what was in fact an unreal and artificial atmosphere. It is the unrealities that are real, here in Bermuda."

With that conversation in mind, it was rather comical to get the papers from the United States and see the general assumption that the President-elect was burning the midnight oil with furrowed brow, wrestling and throwing mighty problems of state. One day, when I called as usual to see him, he sent out word that, instead of meeting him in the living-room, I could find him in his bedroom. The bedroom was only twenty steps from the living-room, but the Governor was too full of the lotus-land atmosphere of Bermuda to take even those twenty steps. So I went in and found him sitting by a bed, which bore obvious signs of having been occupied by a President-elect. Lying idly upon it was Kipling's *Rewards and Fairies*. "You see what I've been doing all the afternoon," said Wilson, rubbing sleepy eyes. No, Bermuda isn't a place to work in; it's the Land of Nod.

Wilson's own playground, Glencove, was located on a little point of land jutting into the harbor parallel with the mainland, so that he had a little bay all to himself in front of his house. It was called Salt Kettle Creek, though it was not a creek but a baby bay. Here the Governor and his family went in bathing. The tiny peninsula was just visible among the trees from the coral road high above it, and was reached by a winding white road down the hill. Wilson stood on his veranda one day with myself and two other reporters watching some boatmen gathering seaweed on the other side of Salt Kettle Creek.

"What are they picking that stuff up for?" asked one unlearned journalist.

"They make fertilizer of it," answered the President-elect. "But I wish," he continued, "that they wouldn't show such discrimination. They pick it up with great care on the other side of the creek, but they leave this side severely alone, and on this side the seaweed perversely collects itself just where we go in bathing."

"What shape would you call Salt Kettle Creek?" asked another, avid for knowledge. "A rounded V?"

"A rounded V," explained Wilson, twinkling, "is a U."

When he got the home papers and read solemn editorials about how he was working out affairs of state in Bermuda and preparing with incredible toil to assume the heavy burden of running the Nation, he was vastly tickled. I called with two other reporters and found him working, with corrugated brows, over a sheet of paper. He turned around and said with frigid dignity, "Gentlemen, you have interrupted me in the preparation of an important state paper." In much confusion, we apologized and started to withdraw. The Governor grinned. "Don't go," he said; "it's important all right, but it's a domestic formula I am drawing up for Mrs. Wilson."

He was working out for her the sort of reception Englishmen expect at an afternoon tea, that she might do the proper thing by the Governor of Bermuda when he arrived at Glencove.

The Governor was Sir George Bullock, K. C. M. G., and he was a Lieutenant-General in the British Army. He was a soldierly looking man with a stiff mustache and a carriage as straight as if he had had a ramrod inside his coat. When he drove over to see the President-elect he sprang lightly up the steps of Glencove and looked around for the front door. Now, Glencove was built in a deceiving sort of way, so that what looked like the side door was really the front. Lieutenant-General Sir George Bullock, K. C. M. G., hunted helplessly around the side of the house and then held a conference with Lady Bullock. She couldn't see a door either. So Sir George left her standing there and traveled around the other side, still looking for a front door, but no house which respects the proprieties wears its front door on the side; it's not done. Then the Lieutenant-General, still leaving Lady Bullock on the front veranda looking helplessly over at the battery of camera fiends at the gate, went down below and tried to force an entrance at the kitchen door. Margaret, the Irish maid, came out, thinking it was the grocery man, and the troubles of the Governor of Bermuda were over.

This contrast between the American President-elect and his British playground obtruded itself at every turn. The American was to govern a nation of a hundred millions. The British Governor ruled a province of nineteen thousand, or about what was then the population of Jamaica, Long Island. Over on the hill beyond Hamilton the British Governor lived in a palace surrounded by immense and splendid grounds guarded by sentries in bright red uniforms who had orders to admit the public only once a week. Across the harbor from Hamilton lived the President-elect in a comfortable little two-story cottage, encompassed by seaweed gatherers and with a perspective of pickaninnies and goats.

The red-coated sentry at Governor Bullock's palace was undergoing experiences which were rapidly revolutionizing his view of life. Hitherto he had had to do only with respectful Britons who stood afar and looked wistfully at the imaginary gates he guarded. But when Governor Wilson went to call on Governor Bullock the astonished soldier found himself the center of a throng of camera artillerists, who inquired his first name, called him by it thereafter, and insisted on his posing for them. Astounded, and then gradually getting into the spirit of the affair, the Briton permitted himself to be "taken" in the wholly unhistorical attitude of holding up the multitude and indignantly refusing them admission (the reporters playing the multitude), meekly accepted their instructions as to how he should stand and how he should hold his gun, and finally retired to his post with an amazed grin.

When Wilson mounted his bicycle and went wheeling about the islands he passed soldiers all the way—soldiers in red, soldiers in khaki. All the time he was Governor of New Jersey and Commander-in-Chief of the New Jersey National Guard he never saw so many soldiers, except on some official occasion, as he saw on the coral streets and roads of his playground.

However, it must not be supposed that the contrast struck the English and colonials as funny. On the contrary, it impressed them—impressed them to such an extent as to ameliorate Bermudian society appreciably. And this was welcome to Sir George Bullock, who was the first of many Governors to play a human part. His immediate predecessor, Lieutentant-General Walter Kitchener, brother of Lord Kitchener of Khartoum, seldom opened the Government House to outsiders, and during his tenure and that of his predecessors there was little social activity with the

Government House as the center. But General Bullock was a social soul, and with the arrival of his wife and daughter, two months before Wilson's, he gave every indication of a desire to loosen up. Then came Wilson, and the General seized his chance.

He seized it directly after his courtesy visit to Wilson, when he invited the Wilson family and his party, the local aristocracy and Americans of prominence, to the Government House. When the plain-clothes denizens of Glencove debouched on the gorgeous grounds where the beauty and fashion of Bermuda awaited them, they encountered a studied informality of dress among their hosts and fellow-guests. At previous affairs in the grounds the Governor had appeared in uniform and afternoon dress had been obligatory. But Wilson had so strongly impressed upon Bullock his desire to be put under as little social stress as possible that the General and his staff went the limit and appeared in civilian costume. Word was disseminated that the guests were to put on as few lugs as possible, and they obeyed the injunction. It was just as well, for Wilson himself showed up in his usual gray business suit and Mrs. Wilson in a plain gown.

When Wilson, without having any such intention, thus broke the ice for Bullock, it started the biggest social season Bermuda had seen in years. Bermuda's society is at once the most aristocratic and the most democratic in the Western Hemisphere. There are families there which arrived before the *Mayflower* landed. One family is descended from a King of England. But members of these old families are "in trade" and suffer no loss of social prestige therefrom; a thing which, in 1912, was not yet the case in England. A year or so before Wilson wore his business suit to the Government House, an English knight and his wife arrived for the season and took a cottage. They were of the hoity-toity kind sometimes, but not commonly, seen among well-born Englishmen. The lady visited a shop in Hamilton and asked to be shown some carpets. An obliging salesman took one down and unrolled it for her. It did not please her, and she directed him to unroll another. He did so, and after four or five unrollings she found the carpet that suited her, ordered it sent home, and took her stately departure.

That evening she attended a reception given at Government House by Sir Walter Kitchener. In one of the men presented to her she recognized the salesman who had sold her the carpet that afternoon. She refused to meet him, froze him through her lorgnette, and said to the aide-de-camp who had introduced him, in a tone for the salesman to hear: "I can not meet my draper in society."

Later she found, to her confusion, that the salesman was not only a member of one of the oldest families in Bermuda, but was also a Royal Councillor. The Royal Council, be it known, is appointed by the King himself, is the Upper House of the Bermuda Parliament, consists of only nine men and is chosen from the social cream of the islands. A Royal Councillor holds a position higher than any other native Bermudian, except the Speaker of the House.

Another illustration. The Speaker of the House of Assembly, and the most important official person in Bermuda under the Governor-General, was, when Wilson was there, Sir Thomas Wadson, a plain-spoken, democratic sort of man with a genial manner and gray side-whiskers. Sir Thomas was the colony's official representative at the coronation of King George. He ran a bicycle shop and advertised it as follows:

ARIEL BICYCLES
For Sale and Hire
Front Street and Queen Street, Hamilton
THOS. J. WADSON.

This was a little too much for even the democratic-aristocratic society of Bermuda, and a faction arose which insisted that since Sir Thomas had been knighted, and since he had become Speaker, and since he had been official envoy at the coronation, he was lowering the dignity of Bermuda by hanging out his sign. "Why not," they argued, "let him nominally retire from business and have his son's name appear in place of his own? His son is his partner, anyway."

Sir Thomas heard these comments, and his reply was pungent and to the point. "Being knighted doesn't change me," he said. "I'm the same Tom Wadson I always was. I don't intend to hide my head in the sand or disguise myself."

Before Wilson had been there long he had to give up bicycle riding and confine his outings to his carriage. This was not the fault of the Bermudians, but of the gentlemanly and ladylike American tourist. Wilson had been to Bermuda more than once, and was well acquainted, but to the Bermudians Mr. Wilson of Princeton and the Chief Magistrate of the United States were two different persons, and they paid him a deference which has no parallel in our own country. There was no attempt on the part of his old acquaintances to intrude on his privacy, and as for Bermudians who were not known to him, they would have been shocked at the idea. So far as they were concerned, he had every opportunity to achieve the object with which he had come to Bermuda—to get a month's solid rest before entering on his strenuous quadrennium. But the great American tourist was not so delicate, and he had to seek seclusion from curiosity seekers so often that he was compelled to give up his program of walks and bicycle rides and go around in a carriage (automobiles were barred by law), and sometimes to shut himself up in Glencove.

In such emergencies he availed himself of a quaint

Bermuda custom known as "hanging out the basket." If you are going to be away for some time, you hang a basket on your front door as a sign that you are not expected back. Visitors take the hint, drop their cards in the basket, and go away. This is not done if you are going to be gone only a few hours, but Wilson, in his extremity, was forced to adopt the practise as a hint of his wishes, though of course nobody really supposed him to be away.

After a few days he began to venture forth cautiously on foot or on his wheel, when he felt pretty sure the omnipresent American tourist was out of range and the roads reasonably clear of everybody but Bermudians. On such occasions he wore an old suit that didn't look any too good, and a gray golf cap. On some of these occasions he went marketing, with a market basket slung over the handle-bar. As he pedaled tranquilly along one day, a Bermudian friend, trudging down the road, waved him a friendly greeting.

"I see you've hung your basket out," said the Bermudian, glancing at the handle-bar. "Are you conveying the idea that you're not at home on the bicycle?"

He never tired of recurring to the fairy glamour of Bermuda. "These houses," said he one day, waving his hand toward the mass of foliage, checked and interspersed with graceful white buildings, "remind me of driven snow." It is a fact that most of them look as if snow had fallen on them in the night, and in those islands of eternal Summer it gives a curious effect. Those coral islands are a never-ending series of pictures each more beautiful than the last. Even the houses are things of beauty, for they are, like everything else, formed of coral.

"Aren't you afraid to go out boating?" asked one of the party, with humorous intent. "You know the waters hereabout swarm with sharks. Suppose you should drop overboard. Aren't there any sharks near Glencove?"

"Yes," said the President-elect confidently, "but they are remarkably intelligent sharks. They know whom to bite."

He finally persuaded Mrs. Wilson to join him in a sail around the harbor; hitherto she had been enjoying Bermuda in the somnolent fashion which is really the true way to enjoy it. She was much interested in seeing, from the water, the assemblage of coral cottages. She saw one in the distance that struck her fancy especially.

"There!" she exclaimed, clapping her hands; "that is the prettiest cottage I've seen since we came to Bermuda. Oh, why didn't we take that one?"

He grinned, but said nothing. The boat sailed closer inshore, while Mrs. Wilson kept her eyes fixed covetously on the cottage. Suddenly she gave an exclamation.

"Why," she cried, "it's Glencove!"

These things look different from the sea to what they do on land.

With that intense interest in the odd little things of life which I have spoken of, it follows that Wilson was simply enchanted with the sayings and doings of the negro boatmen of the islands, who had a character of their own not at all like that of the American negro, Northern or Southern. He used to go out boating, often, for no reason in the world except so that he could hear them talk, or, as he expressed it, "so that I can back them into a corner and make them talk to me instead of my being backed into a corner and having to talk to some one else." He took inexhaustible delight in drawing them out.

Some of these negro boatmen were Chesterfields. One day the President-elect took his wife with him; she usually did not care for rowboats. When they landed he produced the fee and handed it to the old negro, who accepted it and then turned and raised his hat—not to the Governor, but to Mrs. Wilson, and said with an inimitable bow, "Thank you, Madam." Wilson's joy over this incident went beyond expression.

"Are you making up your Cabinet?" asked one of the reporters as his stay in Bermuda neared its close.

"No," said Wilson jubilantly. "That's what constitutes my vacation."

His vacation; well, he had it, but it took constant vigilance. Once in these closing days, as Roscoe Mitchell, of *The World,* and I were approaching Glencove, we saw an American tourist and his wife hovering around the gates. The lady stepped toward us eagerly and asked: "Doesn't he ever come out and sit on his veranda? We've been here all this morning and most of yesterday, but he hasn't come out."

"No, Madam," answered Mitchell. "He used to at first, but he never comes out now."

"Oh, dear, I'm so disappointed," she exclaimed. "We wanted to photograph him on his veranda."

"That, Madam," said Mitchell, raising his hat and passing on, "is the reason why he never sits on his veranda now."

CHAPTER XXIV

IN THE COZY CORNER

Most people believe to this day that Wilson was a man excessively careful in dress. Until he went to Washington he dressed well enough, but had a liking for old clothes and did not care who saw them; in fact, he did not appear to have any thoughts on whether he was scrutinized or not. He was a good deal more careless about dress than any other President, not excluding Jefferson, who is said to have dropped snuff all over his clothes. Jackson is supposed to have been a little reckless in that regard, but the researchers and delvers prove that he was really a dandy.

When Wilson was about to be notified officially of his nomination for Governor of New Jersey, he was sitting on a porch at his Princeton home, dressed in an unpressed, uncreased suit of clothes that he had worn daily for months. Tumulty, who even at that time was taking a paternal interest in his political welfare, came to look him over, and started in dismay. "My God, Mr. Wilson!" he cried, "the Notification Committee will be here in half an hour and you have to get into some decent clothes."

"What's the matter with these?" asked Wilson, glancing down at them in innocent surprise.

"Never mind," Tumulty screamed, "you go up and get Mrs. Wilson to tell you."

Half an hour afterward Tumulty returned, to see Wilson again sitting on the porch, dressed to the minute.

He looked at Tumulty, and smiled his ugly but winning smile. "Satisfied?" he asked.

The Notification Committee arrived and saw a dignified candidate, irreproachably garbed. It reminded me of the story Gustave Koerner tells in his memoirs of Lincoln's notification in 1860. Koerner, Judd and the other members of the little coterie which did for Lincoln what Tumulty did for Wilson arrived to see if he was all right to receive the committee. Upon finding that he had innocently set out whisky for those gentlemen, they voiced a horrified protest, and shunted the too hospitable provision out of the room.

About a week before his election as President in 1912, while Wilson was campaigning, his automobile skidded on a wet road and his head slammed the roof. A little laceration of the scalp was the only damage. This happened toward the end of October. About the middle of November, when he had been elected President, he was promenading the deck of the good ship *Bermudian,* on his way to spend his month's vacation in the vexed islands. He stopped before me to pass the time of day, and as we were chatting Miss Eleanor Wilson, now Mrs. McAdoo, came up, gave one look at him, and uttered a horrified scream. "Father," she cried, "go right into your stateroom and change your tie."

"What's the matter?" asked the President-elect.

"Nothing," she retorted, and her voice was heavy with scorn, "except that it's all over blood!" So it was; it was the same tie he had worn on that October night when he smashed his head against the roof of the automobile. In putting it on that day he had not even taken the trouble to look at it.

In Washington they took him in hand and made him dress according to Hoyle. I wonder if they ever succeeded in making him like it.

Wilson was a great theater-goer, but he never went to improve his mind and was utterly impatient of those earnest souls who look to the drama for a message. He would have been much jarred if any one had asked him what lesson he derived from a show. He went for fun, for recreation. At first he liked musical comedies and vaudeville, but in his later years he centered on vaudeville exclusively. He made it his habit to go every Saturday night. He explained that if a vaudeville act is dull it is over in a few minutes, whereas if you happen on a dull play you have to sit through at least three acts. This may be thought to add a little to the knowledge of Wilson's psychology, since if it is accepted at its face value it betrays a sort of restlessness or nervousness. Still, it does not cover the case, since many people who are restless or nervous can sit through even a dull play without biting pieces out of the furniture.

The truth is that Wilson's explanation did him an injustice; he went to vaudeville not because he couldn't focus his attention on a play, but because he congenitally enjoyed vaudeville. He always did like light stuff. It was only by degrees that he was weaned away from musical comedy. Once Joseph P. Tumulty prevailed on him to go to New York and see Laurette Taylor in *Peg o' My Heart.* It was the kind of play that appeals to the sentimental streak in the blond-haired type of Irishman. I went along. I thought the show was mushy, but there were tears in Tumulty's eyes and a tremble in his voice when he asked what I thought of it. He asked Wilson, too, and Wilson, observing Tumulty's emotion, said something soothing. But that was the last time Tumulty or anybody else got him to see any specimen of the "legitimate."

John Kernell used to tell a story about a negro girl who did not share Wilson's tastes, "but when Mistuh Shakespeare bring his plays to town, mah parents got to chain me to de flo'." Subsequently a popular song, called *When Mr. Shakespeare Comes to Town,* was made out of this sure-fire jest of John's. Wilson never had any use for Mr. Shakespeare, unless in the seclusion of his library. But in his Jersey days, when a musical comedy "came to town," with Lulu Glaser or even Anna Held in it, Tumulty had to chain Mistuh Wilson to de flo'. As he grew older he lost his taste for everything but vaudeville; and after his breakdown in 1919 he would see nothing else. The vaudeville folks knew him and liked him, and gradually those headliners whom he enjoyed the most came to have a footlights-to-box friendship with him. Once, for instance, the stage had to be darkened for a few moments, and in that interval Belle Baker and the Watsons stepped over to his box—he always had the lower right-hand box, at least he did every time I saw him at the theater—and chatted with him while the darkness lasted.

Ex-President Wilson was not as other ex-Presidents. Generally, after Van Buren's time, ex-Presidents, with the exception of Grant, were by the world forgot, unless somebody started a third-term boom. Cleveland was held in honor whenever he happened to be thought of at all, but for all the additional fame he got he might as well have died on March 4, 1897, when he left the White House. Roosevelt was an exception to the rule, as to all rules, but the place he held differed from that which Wilson held in this—that the place he made after he left Washington he made for himself, while the place Wilson came to hold was made without the slightest effort on that statesman's part.

He really continued to live after he retired; he really added new touches to the portrait he had been making of himself for posterity. Nothing like it had been seen in the United States since Andrew Jackson's retirement at the Hermitage. The two retirements differed radically from each other in character, much as they resembled each other superficially; Jackson was the beloved old chieftain, Wilson the prophet and apostle; and during his last years a sort of religiosity increasingly touched his hermitage.

To illustrate, on his birthday in 1920, before this retirement had even begun, there was formed an organization called the Woodrow Wilson Foundation; and on his birthday the following year it launched its plan to raise a fund of one million dollars to endow periodic awards for "meritorious services to democracy, public welfare, liberal thought, or peace through justice." One could hardly imagine the devotion of Old Hickory's followers taking just that form. Then came the project for a "Wilson hour" from noon to one o'clock on his birthday. It was not a success; but the point is that if at times these outgrowths of affection and admiration took a slightly grotesque form, they were of a sort that certainly could not be called out by any other hero. And they testified eloquently, by their character, to the impression Wilson made on his times. They were essentially mortuary tributes, but they began in his lifetime.

Deeply did he touch the popular imagination, where he touched it at all. Where he did not touch it he aroused a bitterness to which the pre-mortuary honors paid him seemed cant and slush. No man, for instance, who honored Theodore Roosevelt over all others could imagine himself offering this kind of tribute or his hero's accepting it. But it is enough to remember that no one in our history ever did or could arouse such feeling and such tributes, and that God fulfills Himself in many ways. There is room in our National Pantheon for widely differing figures; and in the forefront of that Pantheon Woodrow Wilson has been most certainly elected to stand.

HARDING

CHAPTER XXV

BABBITT IN THE WHITE HOUSE

In writing about Warren G. Harding it is customary to emphasize his attractiveness, his charm. It seems to be regarded as the key to his selection by the Senatorial Soviet as the man whom Ahasuerus delighted to honor. It may be a good explanation, since the choice sometimes seems otherwise inexplicable. In private conversation, too, this attractiveness of Harding is always dwelt on. Therefore it seems that there must be something odd and queer about me, for he never attracted me in the least. He even irritated me with his complacency, his banality, his self-satisfaction, and his triumphant and ostentatious mediocrity; he rubbed me the wrong way every time I saw his standardized smile and heard his comfortable good-fellow voice, and finally, though I had not a thing against him personally, I grew to have a feeling of impatience in his presence. When in the early morning hours at Chicago the news was brought to me that the Senatorial clique had decided on his nomination for President, a nomination which I knew was equivalent to an election, I was first astounded and then disgusted.

Yet I should not have been surprised. One of the best informed political observers I knew, Ted Phillips, of Chicago, had told me long before of a secret conference held in Washington in February at which it had been determined to prevent the nomination from going to General Wood and to make sure that the little clique which headed the Republican side of the Senate should dictate the nomination. I had every reason to suppose Phillips's informant was Senator Medill McCormick of Illinois, a trustworthy source of information. He had even told me the tactics which were to be followed—avoidance of declarations for any candidate, fighting to have a majority of the delegates uninstructed, and playing off one leading candidate against another to produce a deadlock which would make the delegates accept any road that led out of the cul-de-sac.

I had seen it all fulfilled to the letter. Friday night had come with the Convention at sea, with the delegates tired and bored, dismayed by their mounting hotel bills, and with no interest in anything but the overpowering desire not to be stuck in Chicago over Sunday. The Senatorial Soviet calculated rightly that the moment had come. Long before Harry M. Daugherty, afterward President Harding's Attorney-General, had told the reporters that the Convention would be deadlocked and that the nomination would be decided on by twelve or thirteen men "at two o'clock in the morning, in a smoke-filled room." He was correct to the last word; he was wrong only in thinking that he would be there. He did not need to be, since the Senatorial Soviet of a dozen men sent for his candidate in person, and notified him that he would be nominated for President that afternoon—for it was, as Daugherty had magically figured, two in the morning.

The little clique then broke up and left the "smoke-filled room" severally—it was Colonel George Harvey's room, in the Hotel Blackstone. One of them, going down in the elevator, encountered George Morris, of *The New York Telegram*. "Anything decided on at your conference upstairs?" inquired Morris, expecting no news but merely going through his routine duty. "Yes," answered Senator

Reed Smoot astoundingly; "we decided on Harding and he will be nominated this afternoon, after we have balloted long enough to give Lowden a run for his money." Morris hit only the curbstones on his flight to the telegraph office, and this is the never-before-told story of how his paper beat the United States on the news of who was to be the next President. Ted Phillips had been right, Medill McCormick had been right, and Harry Daugherty had been a perfect seer. The February conference had not slipped a single cog.

The news was filtering through the weary and discontented Convention when it met at ten-thirty. Everybody was sore and mutinous, but anxious to end it all and get home. Governor Lowden had gone angrily to the Coliseum and personally released his delegates from their pledges to support him. The Senatorial Soviet was so supremely in the saddle that it was preparing to name the Vice-President as well as the President—to name Senator Lenroot, and have an all-Senate ticket. As I know now, they had had this determination in mind when they arrived in Chicago. In this particular they were unexpectedly thwarted, but that story belongs to another chapter.

The delegates went through their task. They jumped the hurdles and went through the hoops held out for them by Smoot, Lodge, Brandegee, Wadsworth, the absent Penrose, ex-Senator Crane, and the rest of the Senatorial Soviet. There was no enthusiasm. They might, to judge from their appearance, have been nominating a ticket doomed to defeat instead of destined to certain victory. The reason was that, for all the talk about his popularity, Harding was the man whom the delegates least wanted. Nobody was for him, not even his own State of Ohio, for he had failed to get a unanimous delegation, though it is almost a rule that that is a prerequisite to getting the nomination for any man. He did not know he was slated, and so little expected the nomination that he had been on the point, twenty-four hours before, of telegraphing the Ohio Secretary of State to put him on the ballot for reelection to the Senate. The time within which he could legally make that notification expired at midnight, and he expostulated with his mentor, Harry Daugherty, when Daugherty told him not to send the telegram. "Why, Harry, it's my last chance," protested Harding; "you don't want me to give up the Senatorship, do you? And I haven't a ghost of a chance at the Presidency." But Daugherty had insisted, and Harding had obeyed him, feeling that he was ending his political career. A few hours later he had been called to "the smoke-filled room" and told that he was the next President.

Having nominated him without enthusiasm, the Convention adjourned without enthusiasm. All the usual wild scenes after a nomination were missing; absent were the crowds, the cheers, the music and the cavorting. The hotel corridors held no impromptu speakers glorying to excited knots of men. In fact, they were empty. At midnight I sat on a lounge in the Congress Hotel, along with a Lowden worker. His hands were plunged deep in his trousers pockets and his chin was sunk dejectedly on his collar-bone. We were alone in the lobby—strange sight on the night of a nomination. Presently there entered, with quick step, a Harding worker. His glance fell on the Lowden man, and he paused.

"Well, what do you think of the outlook now?" he asked.

The Lowden man came to life, or at least his chin returned to its natural position. "The outlook? Well, you fellows have been saying that you could win this year with a yellow dog," he said in a cavernous voice, "and now," here his chin fell again, "and now you've decided to try it."

And yet, for the moment, there was actually apprehension in Chicago, and a Democratic victory was spoken of as a possibility. That was out of the question, for any nomination the Democrats might make was foredoomed to defeat and any Republican candidate would have received as large a popular and electoral majority as Harding, if not larger; but the mere fact that for a few hours Republican politicians could actually fear a Democratic success speaks forcibly of the effect of this "popular" man's nomination. If ever a Convention threw a wet blanket over a rejoicing and hopeful party on the eve of its triumph, the Convention bossed by the Lodge-Smoot-Brandegee-Penrose Senatorial Soviet did just that thing.

Popular! The people of the United States, whose wisdom and judgment it is so common to knock, never yet have gone crazy over any man just because he was a good fellow. For all that is said in derogation of them, they never yet have put a man in the White House because of what he had in the show window. They never voted for Bryan, but they never got tired of voting for Andrew Jackson. And they did not vote for Harding; nor did they vote against Cox. In 1920 they did not vote for anybody; they voted against somebody; and the somebody they voted against was not a candidate; it was Wilson. Poor Cox made a valiant fight, but the battle was over before he put on his armor—two years before. The battle was over in November, 1918, when Wilson appealed to the voters to show their opinion of him by electing a Democratic Congress, and they showed it by electing a Republican one. This was an event in our history, an event of almost major importance, though it is treated only casually by historians. It will loom larger as time goes on. For it was the only case in our history, so far as I remember, which afforded a parallel to the English system of calling for a vote of confidence in the Government at a parliamentary election. The parallel was not exact in this—that in England the Government, if it fails to get the popular ratification of its policy, submits to the verdict and avoids the tremendous avalanche of wrath which fell on Wilson when he set that verdict aside and went his way to new defiances. The people were only angry in 1918, but in 1920, after the cruise to Versailles, the overseas apotheosis, the struggle with the Senate, and the Mrs. Wilson regency, they were furious. Cox, a fine man and far above Harding, suffered the consequences. But it is unfair to say he was beaten, for he was not in the fight; and it is incorrect to say that Harding won. If the Convention had adjourned without nominating anybody the people, in the mood they were in then, would have voted for Republican Presidential electors just the same and let them pick out their own candidate.

On the day Harding was nominated, my old friend Charles R. Miller wrote, "The nomination of Harding, for whose counterpart we must go back to Franklin Pierce if we would seek a President who measures down to his political stature, is the fine and perfect flower of the cowardice and imbecility of the Senatorial cabal that charged itself with the management of the Republican Convention." Nothing in the lapse of eight years betters that accurate statement. And yet the men of the February conference, the men of George Harvey's "smoke-filled room," acted according to their lights. They meant to control the Presidency, and with that aim I know of no better gun for them to point than Harding. They had had a terrible time in Roosevelt's seven years and Wilson's eight, and had not been satisfied with Taft. No Republican candidate in the twentieth century had promised them ease; Taft and Hughes had been forced on them, and in Wilson's reelection they found some consolation, for they had escaped such a President as Hughes would have been. They looked back on the good old days of McKinley, when President and Congress had not been at war. What Alfred Henry Lewis had said, not accurately, of McKinley in 1896 they thought would come true with Harding; in the White House they could "shuffle him and deal him like a deck of cards."

There is a melancholy and comic indication of the way their thoughts were turning. Immediately on Harding's nomination they decreed, as a happy reminder, that the Harding flower should be the red carnation, and all the Harding coterie should wear it in their buttonholes. Before Harding's nomination was two hours old, red carnations were springing up in their coats. Deluded Senators! The point was that the red carnation had been the McKinley emblem, the symbolic assertion by those who wore it, "We are friends of McKinley." He wore one himself, and in Congress his lieutenants, such as General Charles H. Grosvenor, John Dalzell, Joseph G. Cannon and Sereno E. Payne, always appeared wearing this figurative dog-collar. Dreaming happily of those dear dead days beyond recall, they resurrected the carnation, stuck one—literally, I mean, not figuratively—in Harding's buttonhole, and sprouted carnations themselves. Henry Cabot Lodge was wearing one in Chicago half an hour after the nomination.

The bright idea died early in the campaign. The public was in no mood for such infantile gambols. It had loved McKinley, but it did not love Harding, and it never came to do so, never. Everything about McKinley was revived by these mistaken men; it was announced that, as McKinley in 1896 had conducted a "front porch campaign" at his Canton home, so Harding would conduct a "front porch campaign," carnation in buttonhole, at his Marion home. That idea, too, died early; Cox's whirlwind canvass, useless as it proved to be, goaded them into letting Harding take the stump to some extent. None of these babylike tricks had any more effect on the public than, in 1888, had the childish trick of calling Harrison "Young Tippecanoe" after his grandfather and using miniature log cabins and hard cider barrels as campaign emblems. I remembered that campaign and how flat it had fallen, and was not surprised when this fake recrudescence of McKinley went the same way. Yet both Harrison and Harding were elected, or rather Cleveland and Wilson were defeated; the people were grimly intent on a serious purpose both times, and could not be distracted by these flag-wavings and penny-whistle tootings.

So much for Harding's "popularity." When he was elected, the old-time "drummer," long since superseded by the businesslike salesman of to-day, was enthroned. The "genial," the glad-hander, came into his own. The thing was never done by the American people. That type was the last they would have picked, for with all the blurbing about democracy the people earnestly desire that their chosen ones shall not be of their average, but above their average. They crave not a dead level, but leadership. They want to be led, however they may talk; and they are very fond, not of James Buchanans, but of Andrew Jacksons.

As for his personality, I can not recall that anybody was ever passionately fond of Harding. He was merely a man who had no enemies. He had no knobs; he was the same size and smoothness all the way round. Charles R. Miller faithfully described him as "an undistinguished and indistinguishable unit in the ruck of Republican Senators." And during his years in the Senate he came to grate on me more and more, with his perpetual smile and his meaningless geniality. It was not that he was a gabby orator, for Beveridge was that, and Beveridge was a man to reckon with. It was not that he was a machine-made partisan, for Foraker was that, and, quarrel with myself as I would, I had to respect Foraker. It was not that he had no originality, for neither had Bailey, and with all his faults you had to listen to Bailey. There was, however, something about him that made me more and more impatient every time I heard that rotund voice, more and more anxious that he would finish speedily and make way for another.

Therefore it seemed humorous to me when, in the Winter of 1916, the Hamilton Club of Cincinnati launched his Presidential boom. I regarded it as a joke something akin to Henry Ford's candidacy. It evoked no response except a wondering one, and in a short time Harding withdrew his aspirations, so far as 1916 was concerned. But the short-lived boom attracted my attention to him; hitherto I had thought of him only as "an undistinguished and indistinguishable unit" in that "ruck" to which Miller referred. So I looked at him with more scrutiny in June, when he presided over the Convention which nominated Hughes and made a key-note speech. As I studied his schoolboy gestures and listened to his rolling voice, with not one note of sincerity in it or one indication in his words or manner that anything was stirring in his brain, I was suddenly conscious that mere impatience with his presence had given way to a more active feeling, and that I had come in an hour to have a positive distaste for Harding.

There was nothing in the man himself to arouse such a feeling; it was only the incongruity between himself and his pretensions. If I had known him as a traveling salesman, a vaudeville actor, a night club entertainer, or a restaurant keeper, I should have liked him very much, I know, for I have had a strong liking for many men just like Harding who held those positions. But if one of these hash-twirling or ribbon-selling or banjo-playing friends of mine had undertaken the rôle of public teacher and President of the United States, and had tried to instruct me from a "rostrum," I should have felt toward him just as I did toward Harding. "The bungalow mind," ex-President Wilson said once when he was talking of his successor.

However, he was not at all a humbug or a poseur or a fraud. He did not take himself too seriously, and was really surprised to find himself a Presidential candidate. He knew himself pretty well, and neither expected to be President nor very much wished to be. Left to himself, he would not have tried. But for the persistent insistence of Harry M. Daugherty he would not have kept on trying. Often he used to tell Daugherty that he was no statesman and that it was time to stop the nonsense and close the show. Daugherty always told him he was wrong about himself, and at last, as events seemed to confirm everything Daugherty said, he began rather dubiously to believe.

When he entered the Presidency he had been quite convinced. But as time wore on he ceased to enjoy the Presidency. He came to say more and more about how he longed for the good old days in Marion, and these longings got into his speeches. At the time most people who heard them took them for mere graciousnesses to warm the Marion cockles, but they were from the heart. Many a time he did most earnestly wish himself back in Marion. Harding was a simple sort of chap.

Just a day or two before he was nominated, and while Harry Daugherty was insisting that he stay in the race, Mrs. Harding, who was with her husband at the Chicago Convention, said: "I can't see why any one should want to be President. I would rather have him stay in the Senate. I can see only one word written over his head if they make him President, and that word is 'Tragedy.'"

What she had in mind I do not know, but she was right about it.

There was no guile in him; he was actually an easy mark.

One day, talking with his father, I touched on this, and Doctor Harding surprised me by the vigor with which he endorsed that view. "Why," said Harding's father animatedly, "only a little while ago there was a fellow came around here"—the conversation was being held at Marion—"and visited Warren and told him his name was Harding, too, and he came from Virginia; said he had met him there when we were down in the South. He told about what fine hogs he raised. Then he said he had been robbed of his money and railroad ticket, and asked him for ten dollars. Well, you know Warren. He gave this Harding man twenty and said, 'You send me up some of those hogs, and I'll pay for them.' You know how Warren is.

"So one day I said, 'Warren, did you ever hear from that Harding man again?' 'Why, no,' Warren said in a surprised way; 'I haven't.' I asked what he thought of him, and Warren said, 'Do you know, I believe he's a darned faker.' Well, I thought so too. I'd taken the man out riding, but he didn't get any money out of me."

I could believe that. The doctor was as different from son Warren as if they had not been related. I don't mean that the doctor was close-fisted, he was nothing of the kind; but he was a much more keen-sighted man, a more appraising man, than his son.

"Well," Warren's father went on, "a little bit later Judge Scofield over here, who had kept still about it until then, admitted that after leaving Warren the fellow had gone around to him and told him he was a Scofield, and got twenty dollars out of him. That prompted Charley Fisher to come out and say that the man had come over to him and said he was a Fisher, and Charley gave up ten dollars. Oh, yes, Warren took it good-naturedly."

Can't you see the whole prophecy of son Warren's Administration in that? I say prophecy instead of history, for when Doctor Harding told me this story his son was still only a Senator.

I always warmed more to Doctor Harding than to his son, in spite of Warren's genial simplicity. The doctor was a stockily built man with a ruddy face and white mustache and hair, quick in his movements and with a walk that was hard to keep up with; quite different from his son in all respects. He had eyes that peered sharply at you. There was no sign of age about him. Nobody who distinguished between fifty and ninety would think of calling him an old man. I never saw him after his son became President, but I kept hearing of him, and the things I heard showed that he never changed.

A day or two after Harding's nomination in 1920 I bumped into the doctor, at Marion, coming in from a walk. He began talking right away. "I met a jackass in the park just now," he announced. "He didn't know me and I didn't know him. He started talking politics, and he said Warren was a Wall Street man. I said to him: 'I take it you're a Democrat. There are two kinds of Democrats, intelligent men and ignoramuses. I don't know who you are and don't want to, but I've got you placed; you're one of the ignoramuses. I'm not going to talk to you, but it's not because you're a Democrat; it's because you're too ignorant.' Then I walked off."

Yes, I certainly liked the doctor.

The reason why Warren Harding fell for the confidence man was that he was not only unsuspicious, he was also one of the kindest hearted of men. Never was there a man fuller of good feeling. "Every Christmas," Doctor Harding said when once we were discussing this side of his son's character, "I've seen Warren start out with several hundred dollars and go around among the poor. He has given them more than any other man in this town." But everybody in

Marion knew all about that as well as Doctor Harding. In fact, Harding's generosities were so numerous and so constant that in Marion you never heard the same story from any two men; they always had their own stories, all different; and Doctor Harding didn't know a tenth of them. One day he and Billy Bull and I were talking on this very subject, and Billy told things the doctor had never known. Billy was the foreman of Warren Harding's composing-room; he had been there ever since the time, a generation earlier, when Warren bought *The Marion Star* and became its editor, reporter, advertising man and bill collector. He had helped Warren build the desperate little sheet into a prosperous publication with a smart office building, and with a circulation extending to one-third of the city's population. We were talking, not of Harding's kindness to the poor, but of his kindness to everybody, his desire to do gracious little things to make life pleasanter.

"You know, Doctor," Billy said, "you attended my wife when our boy was born; and you know we named him after Mr. Harding." (Harding's employees always called him Mr. Harding, not the Senator.) "But you don't know this. Every time the boy had a birthday a five-dollar gold piece arrived from Mr. Harding. When he got to be twenty-one I was afraid Mr. Harding would keep up the practise, so I went to him and told him he'd better stop because the boy was of age. So he stopped. None of those five-dollar pieces has ever been spent. They have all been kept as souvenirs. There are several other children in this town who have been named after Mr. Harding, but I don't know whether he keeps up the same practise with them."

The doctor was greatly interested. It is not surprising he did not know about it, for neither his son nor Mrs. Harding ever talked about the kindnesses they were constantly doing. Whenever Mrs. Harding heard of a family in need, and she and Warren were always trying to hear of such cases, she would sally forth and buy things for them; and many such families received baskets of food or coal or boxes of clothing without knowing where they came from. Warren's benefactions generally took the form of money.

As for Harding at his office, Billy Bull once told me that whenever a printer came into town with a hard luck story and wanted a job, and got to Harding, the boss would immediately telephone down to Billy to put him to work. "And if I tell Mr. Harding that I can't make room for the man," he added, "Mr. Harding gives him enough money to fix him up and send him out of town."

"He never fired anybody" was a phrase you heard on the lips of all his employees, so it must have been true. When Billy Bull used it I asked him what he meant, and he expounded it. "Once in a while," the foreman said, "in the last thirty years, he has said to me, 'I don't like that man.' But he never fired the man, nor gave me orders to fire him; he always let the man stay on the paper till he went away of his own accord. The result is," said Billy ruefully, "that there are a good many old-timers left.

"When I came here in 1886," he went on, "I was getting one hundred and fifty dollars a month and I came with Mr. Harding for a dollar and a half a week because in the place I held I was learning no trade. He didn't know it, but I had more money in my inside pocket than he was worth altogether." Harding, as I knew, had bought the paper on borrowed money; he was only a boy of nineteen and had just been fired from his first job. "Why, Mr. Harding would often see to it that his employees all got their money on Saturday night, and then go home himself without a cent left.

"He has men in his plant who have been working for him twenty or twenty-seven years. You couldn't drive them away if he cut their salaries down. I never heard him talk cross or speak rough to any man. He has another way of getting what he wants—kindness is his way. That's how I hold my printers; it is by watching him and studying his ways that I learned the trick."

One of the ways Harding, as an editor, used to make friends was by accidentally printing something they didn't like. They would come to *The Star* office with blood in their eyes and go away firm friends of Harding. It was not because he had agreed to print a retraction, which I guess he always did; the offended individual never waited for the retraction to become a Harding fan. Nor could this be laid to a wily use of soft soap; the fact was that Harding really wanted people to be happy, and if a retraction or so would make them feel better, why, it made him all the happier that he was able to do that little thing for them.

Whenever a new desk man came to work at *The Star* office he was required to learn Harding's rules. So were the reporters, but, though "outsiders" don't know this, rules are a good deal more important for desk men than for reporters. I have these rules, but only desire to quote one of them, which bears on the character I am trying to draw:

"If any item comes in that will cast ignominy or reproach on some innocent woman or child, don't wait for somebody to suppress it, but suppress it."

When I first went to Marion I was skeptical about Harding, the newspaper man. I was acquainted with many of these so-called editors who don't know the bow of their ship from the stern. I distinctly remembered, for instance, Elliott F. Shepard, who had money enough to acquire *The New York Evening Mail* and strut around as its "editor."

"What sort of editor would you call Shepard?" I asked a more experienced newspaper man, for that was in the time when I was just getting acquainted with the newspaper business.

"Well," he cautiously replied, "he is an editor in the same sense that Redfield Proctor is a sculptor. Senator Proctor owns a marble quarry, and Colonel Shepard owns a newspaper."

So as soon as I met George E. McCormick, the city editor of *The Star,* I suspiciously asked, "What does Harding do on the paper?"

"He makes up, writes editorials, and writes news," answered McCormick.

"News!" I echoed. "You don't mean that the Senator does reporting?"

"Not now, though he used to, and for a long time was the only reporter on the paper as well as its owner. But of course in his position news comes his way, and whenever he gets it he comes down here and writes it."

"What sort of newspaper man is Harding?" I asked the managing editor, a man whose name I forget now.

"He is," was the prompt reply, "an easy writer, a fine reporter, a good straight printer, the quickest and fastest make-up man I ever saw, can run a linotype, and in the business office he is one of the best buyers I ever knew."

One evening in the Spring of 1920—not long before Harding was nominated for President, as it turned out, and while the pot was boiling in Ohio—State Senator J. R. Hopley, of Bucyrus, came to Marion to see Senator Harding on political business of importance. He couldn't find the Senator in his home, but he learned that whenever Ohio's candidate for the White House could slip away from visitors for a few moments he would generally trek down to *The Star* office and enjoy himself at his old job. Senator Hopley went to *The Star* office, but he did not find Harding in the editorial chair. "I guess he's down in the composing-room," said the dignitary who occupied that throne. Down into the composing-room went Hopley, and there he found a figure he did not at once recognize. Peeled to his shirt, with his sleeves rolled up and his hands and arms smeared with ink, was the next President. Hopley gazed at him in astonishment for a few moments and then stepped up to him. At his approach Harding turned around, laid down a slug, and extended a grimy hand.

"Well," said Hopley, drawing a deep breath, "you are certainly a hell of a United States Senator."

In Marion—and I prefer to think of him there—he was a useful citizen, deservedly the pride of the community. He was in the forefront of the city's progress; he was always looking ahead and planning for it. During the time of his influence there he was the instigator of practically every public improvement. Even in the business sections Marion had planks for pavements; he agitated for paved streets and got them. He campaigned for electric lights and got them. He was the father of Marion's park system. He proposed the creation of three parks at what were then the edges of the town, on the north, east and west. There was a mighty howl against this waste of the people's money, but Harding had the foresight to know that within a few years the city would grow beyond the localities he had designated for the parks, which it did. He also saw, and said, that the trees in those vacant spaces would be cut down and the places themselves be cut up into building lots unless the city took them over before population pressed around them. He kept up his fight until he won it, and won for the city three beautiful parks, named after Garfield, Lincoln and McKinley.

He was just in the right place; living a useful, busy, fruitful life, an asset to the community. The city had a population of less than thirty thousand. A small puddle.

but he was the biggest frog in it. A happy man; a serviceable man, too. Marion was rich in having him.

It was a cruel thing that the Senatorial Soviet did at two o'clock that morning in George Harvey's "smoke-filled room" in the Hotel Blackstone. Whatever Mrs. Harding's forebodings were, she was right.

COOLIDGE

CHAPTER XXVI

THE LAST OF THE YANKEES

THE only reason why Calvin Coolidge was such a mystery to so many twentieth-century Americans lies in the fact that he is a pure Yankee, and that the pure Yankee is an expiring and unfamiliar race. He is not very familiar even in New England, and in his extreme purity he is hardly to be found at all among *Mayflower* descendants. The extreme type of pure Yankee is the mountain Yankee, and Coolidge belongs even to that tribe. You have to know Massachusetts to know Coolidge, but, in this age of Yankee flux, maybe you have to know that last of the Yankees, Coolidge, to know Massachusetts.

New England had not only a personality but a language of its own in the days when John Quincy Adams was not so much a Congressman as an ambassador from the great Yankee nation to a more or less foreign United States. When, in 1927, Coolidge startled the country by saying, "I do not choose to run for President in 1928," the bewildered fumbling of the American intellect over the meaning of the word "choose" showed clearly that the little section of the country which once divided with Virginia the ownership of the United States has shrunk into the same insignificance socially that it suffers from geographically. "I do not choose" means in the Yankee language "I am determined not to," and nothing could more strikingly mark the passing of old America than the fact that the use of the phrase should have aroused any controversy whatever about its meaning. When a Yankee father told his son, "I do not choose you should go fishing to-day," the boy was in no doubt what the old man meant; he knew he would get a spanking if he did. The Yankee language, in distinction from the American language, is founded on understatement and not overstatement. Where an insulted non-Yankee would say, "Stop using that language," an insulted Yankee would say, "I wouldn't talk like that"; but both would mean exactly the same, and the aggressor would have to stop or fight in both cases. It may be that the root idea is Yankee caution, but I think it is Yankee politeness; in Yankeedom it is not good form to say anything extremely when you are talking about yourself. Another view of the genesis of it is suggested by Robert A. Woods in his *The Preparation of Calvin Coolidge.*

> "The typical rural New Englander is sparing of speech so as to avoid exaggeration, or blunder, or outright offense. He seeks the emphasis of understatement. His humor is cool and dry."

In New England itself the Yankee language has almost passed away, and Hosea Biglow would need an interpreter if he came to life in Salem or Taunton; certainly in Fall River or Haverhill. Coolidge often won a dubious election in Massachusetts—or at least gained thousands of votes, according to the estimate of his unromantic and practical campaign lieutenants—by his Yankee twang. It was natural with him, but when he sprang it on the stump men who had not heard it for fifty years came to life and yelled at the sound of that forgotten music.

It was the Yankee who once embodied the American spirit and was incarnated in Uncle Sam, or Brother Jonathan, as folks preferred to call him in that heroic age. The

Uncle Sam of a century ago did not much resemble the Uncle Sam of to-day. Look at the cartoons of him, then and now. To-day Uncle Sam is portrayed as a noble and humorless character, sometimes benevolent of aspect and more often with eyes of blazing wrath, but always dreadfully purposeful. The Brother Jonathan of the old cartoonists and the old fiction (and the old poetry, taking Lowell to witness) was dry, wise, taciturn and cunning. In reality he was at least as purposeful as his present successor, but he let his acts speak for him. (The English cartoonists have worked a similar transformation with John Bull, who, beginning with Bernard Partridge of *Punch,* has become almost as dignified and solemn as Uncle Sam.) The ancient Yankee struck the imagination of foreigners as well as Americans, and if one wants to find the English conception of him the best place to find it is in two of Charles Reade's novels, in the person of that masterly creation, Joshua Fullalove. The American idea of him is best set forth in Mark Twain's Hank Morgan at the court of King Arthur, though Hank (like Hosea Biglow himself) was a little too fond of conversation to be the perfect Yankee.

When you track the vanishing Yankee to his lair you find him shrewd, grave, and internally humorous. Perhaps because he is not always bombinating about efficiency he is superbly efficient. He is far-sighted without indulging in prophecy. He is, in short, just like Calvin Coolidge. Coolidge does not assume the rôle. He was born to it.

Often one finds the Yankee shy, but this is not because he does not entertain a good opinion of himself. Shyness and self-confidence are not incompatible. In this respect, too, Coolidge is a typical mountain Yankee.

The Yankee would never be able to understand the blatant modern go-getter or sympathize with that banal phrase, "So-and-So is a man who does things." His ruling principle was to look ahead as far as possible, calculate the best means to reach his end, and then leave nothing undone to reach it, but not to waste breath talking about it. The Yankee did not brag, did not put up a front, and was instinctively antagonized by any one who did. If there are still those who find Coolidge a mystery, it is probable that they mystify him as much as he does them. He doesn't see anything mysterious in himself. The way he did things in the Presidency was the way he had always done things. He doesn't know any other way.

In the first year of his Presidency the general puzzlement over the strange doings of this extinct type in the White House finally found vent in a nickname for him. The biologists who were seeking to classify him called him Cautious Cal. If they had known anything about the stigmata of that strange race they would have expressed the same idea by merely calling him Yankee Cal.

To one who congratulated him on never having suffered defeat in politics Coolidge replied that he had always been prepared for defeat. That, too, is in the Yankee strain. So is his smileless humor. The fundamental Yankee, when humorously impelled, does not smile; nor even twinkle. Coolidge did not when, at the end of his first term as Governor, he remarked: "So far as I am aware, I have signed every bill which had the backing of the workers, with the exception of the bill to increase the salaries of members of the Legislature." Over the fireplace of the Coolidge home, when he was Lieutenant-Governor, hung this sentiment:

"A wise old owl lived in an oak;
The more he saw the less he spoke.
The less he spoke the more he heard:
Why can't we be like that old bird?"

Probably Coolidge didn't need that reminder. No real Yankee would need it.

Doubtless there still lingers here and there in other parts of the country the original delusion that Coolidge was in some way a sort of Back Bay aristocrat. The fact is that when he began his phenomenal career he was, from the Massachusetts point of view, a carpet-bagger, an outlander. He came from Vermont, and the Sacred Cod is somewhat like Philadelphia and Charleston in regarding everybody as a foreigner whose family has not been resident for at least three generations. It was a handicap, which Coolidge overcame as he overcame all his other handicaps—not by any change in himself but by being himself in such a way as to impress the community with the idea that if it wanted anything done here was the man to do it. They always got that idea very early, no matter what field of activity he entered, and no matter how indifferent to him its other occupants were.

You can trace this by every step in his career. Though he seemed to have no friends, it was from a Democratic district that he won his first election to the General Court of Massachusetts. When it came time to elect him Mayor of Northampton his nomination was by consensus. Similarly, when it came his time to go to the State Senate, it was by general consent. Pretty much the same thing happened when he became President of that body. There was the same inevitability about his promotion to the Lieutenant-Governorship and the Governorship; in every case it went without saying that if Coolidge didn't get it this year it would have to be handed to him next year, because he was the obvious man. Whatever company he was in, it soon became clear to every one that he must take the head of it.

It is a Yankee trait not to answer back, and Coolidge never does. He never replied, for instance, to the charge that he was a reactionary. But his record in the General Court, first as a member and then as presiding officer, was that of a leader and pioneer in social service legislation—yes, and even in labor legislation. He did not talk labor stuff, he only produced. He fought incessantly for a long program of progressivism, prominent in which were the eight-hour law and the bill aimed against government by injunction. It was just because of this long-settled habit of his that the labor leaders, Gompers in particular, reckoned so confidently on his benevolent neutrality or aid when the unionized police of Boston went on strike and left the city at the mercy of the underworld; and reckoned so vainly.

Since it was just because of his part in putting down the police strike that he first attracted national attention, this previous labor record of his may seem inconsistent. His action in that case came just after he had signed the eight-hour law for which he had fought so long. However, there is no inconsistency. Samuel Gompers, relying blissfully on the eight-hour Governor to lend a hand to the "down-trod," telegraphed him urging him to uphold the rights of the strikers, and got his answer in one of those swinging, crashing sentences so characteristic of Coolidge:

"There is no right to strike against the public safety by anybody, anywhere, any time."

In 1923, the year before Coolidge's unanimous nomination for President, a monthly review with a notably high forehead published a series of twelve articles dealing with twelve gentlemen whom the lightning might strike. Coolidge was not one of them. It was a most instructive series, including studies of such likely candidates as Senator George H. Moses, Senator Medill McCormick and Senator Hiram Johnson. Fortunately, it was concluded before the day when the Convention met and couldn't think of anybody but Coolidge.

There was no contest for the Presidency after his nomination in 1924. John W. Davis, the Democratic candidate, thought there was, and was encouraged by the Intellectuals, who were against Coolidge to a man. Just before the election they had convinced themselves that Coolidge hadn't a chance. Mr. Davis had raged up and down the land demanding that Coolidge should tell him whether he, Coolidge, was or was not personally cognizant of the Teapot Dome deal. Coolidge remained, to all appearance, ignorant of Mr. Davis's daily demands; in fact, of Davis's existence and of the existence of any political campaign whatever; and this, though Coolidge's tranquillity so worked on Mr. Davis's feelings that in the later repetitions of his demands his voice seemed to rise from tenor to soprano and thence to falsetto.

About ten days before election Coolidge did speak—not in quotation marks and not even through that popular phantom, the Official Spokesman. He merely permitted the information to leak out that the President considered the election over and himself elected, and was paying no further attention to the campaign. The subsequent proceedings in the first week in November showed him to have been correct; he could, indeed, have let that information leak out at any time after the Cleveland Convention. Being a perfect judge of political futures, he knew it as well then as he did in October. There never was any campaign in the sense of a contest; Coolidge was elected at Cleveland and long before Cleveland.

It was demonstrated in 1924, and in 1926 and 1928, that Coolidge was stronger than his party, that he could get along without it—at the polls, if not in Congress—and that it could by no means get along without him. Thus did virtually all the Republican candidates in 1926 vociferously appeal for votes for themselves in his vote-getting name and try to make their people believe they were Coolidge men, often in the face of their own records to the contrary. Thus, in 1928, did the very Congressmen who were throwing down every recommendation he made as President try desperately to get him nominated for a third term in defiance of his repeated refusals, so that his name at the head of the ticket might pull them through in November.

The Intellectuals can't understand why such a commonplace, ordinary dumbbell should be so popular, though many of them account for it on the hypothesis that Mr. Mencken is right in his belief that Americans are mostly boobs. But they have to admit that he is popular, even though he ought not to be. This puzzling popularity of his is entirely apart from the popularity of his party, granting that it has any. It always has been. When he began to stir about in the politics of Northampton the bewildered Republicans in that city learned that there was a body of voters there whom they came to classify as "Coolidge Democrats." He first went to the Legislature from a Democratic district, and as he spread out locally the Coolidge Democrats spread out too—spread out all over Northampton.

Then he became a figure of State-wide importance. "That will settle his hash," said the political wiseacres; "the Coolidge Democrats of Northampton are a local phenomenon. Outside the city they don't know him, and the State Democrats won't do a thing to him." But behold, as Coolidge spread out over Massachusetts the Coolidge Democrats kept exact pace with him. As campaign succeeded campaign the existence of a body of Democrats who always voted for Coolidge, but not for any other Republican on the ticket, became a factor to be counted on as steadily as any other physical fact. Coolidge Democrats ranged from Cape Cod to the New York border.

At last he became a national figure; and now surely the

existence of the Coolidge Democrats would become an impossibility. He would spread out pretty thin when he had to spread himself all the way to the Pacific. So Congress chuckled, and trampled on him—until the Cleveland Convention and his unanimous nomination. Then came November. And behold, the Coolidge Democrats had spread out of Massachusetts all over the country.

On election day of 1924 the sidewalks of New York bristled with Democrats yelling for "Cal and Al." They voted Governor Smith's State ticket, but they cut the Presidential electors. This was made the basis of a false assumption that Tammany was selling Davis out for Smith votes. Those who assumed it were unable to explain why the same thing happened in every other Northern State which had a popular Democrat at the head of its local ticket. But as a matter of fact, it simply was not so. It wasn't by the treachery of local Democratic machines in New York, Ohio or anywhere else that Coolidge accumulated those majestic millions in his popular vote.

After the Intellectuals had assimilated the incredible fact that this uninspiring and mediocre man was, for some ungodly reason, popular, they began looking forward to the inevitable time when his popularity would ebb and vanish. It does not seem possible, but they really did; and they gave each other reasons; they took to studying the sky and figuring where the break in the cloud would come. Chiefly they pinned their hopes on the fickleness of the American public. These hopes were vain. Our political history demonstrates with tiresome persistence that the American people are not fickle once a public man has made them sure that he is studying their interests and not something else. After that he can very nearly get away with murder. That once fixed in the popular mind, it doesn't much matter what the "issue" is in any campaign where he is a candidate. As

Mr. Dooley said to the dubious Mr. Hennessy, this statement is not opinion; " 'tis histh'ry." The wonder is that it has not been tried oftener. This and this only is the explanation of Al Smith's ownership of the State of New York; it alone is the reason why "issues" avail nothing against him; why New York Republicans vote for a Democrat; why the body of Al Smith Republicans in that State corresponds to the body of Coolidge Democrats who always voted for one Republican in Massachusetts.

The wonder is that it hasn't been tried oftener. Clatter about one's devotion to the "people" or the "masses" never yet has won a Presidency for any politician. Simple words and straightforward acts are the components of the magic potion. The few who have hit upon this brew have given the voter medicines to make him love them.

This and nothing else is the secret of Calvin Coolidge. This is why Democrats and Republicans joined in sending him to the Legislature, why no voice was raised against him for Mayor of Northampton, why in the General Court he became successively leader and President of the Senate, why in years that were perilous to the Republicans he was successively elected Lieutenant-Governor and Governor. Those who think he is not an inspiring man to look at now may be interested to know that he was a good deal less impressive in appearance then. Finding that he had not the voice of an orator, he never wasted time trying to acquire it. He had the gift of phrase, but seldom employed it. He did find out that he could be a leader—of men if not always of Congress—and all through his life in Massachusetts he led; not because of his commanding appearance nor of any magic in his personality.

As for the Mystery of 1924—the mystery of his election by a tremendous majority when so many towering geniuses had demonstrated that he hadn't a chance—that, too, was psychological. He was elected on that day in 1923 when he sent his first message to Congress. The country had heard language for many years. The unceasing, all-embracing sea of it had swollen until it reached high tide under Wilson. Harding, however, did his best with his promises of "normalcy" and a government of "the best minds" and so forth. The country was apathetically resigned to a permanent government by language.

Therefore, the first official word it heard from Coolidge was sensational. Not only was there no purple in the message, but there was no ratiocination, no argument, no stock official phrases. He told Congress what he thought would be for the good of the country and told it as briefly as he could. One of the things it wanted was economy. The burning question of that day, the soldiers' bonus, he treated in a single sentence, merely saying he was opposed to it; this at a time when the conventional attitude for politicians on the bonus question was astride the fence.

The country rubbed its eyes. Here was a President of an entirely new kind. The country waited long enough to see if Coolidge meant what he said. He had just one session of Congress to prove it in. He did. Throughout that session he worked hard to get Congress to carry out the recommendations he had made.

Congress, with its historic political wisdom, banged him around the Capitol walls by the hair of his head. For a while the alert political scientists of the press continued to speculate on whether Hiram Johnson, Frank Lowden or William E. Borah would get the nomination. The big black head-lines on the news dispatches were all about the oil investigation. It was expected to settle the infamous Coolidge Administration for all time, despite the fact that whatever had happened had happened before Coolidge became President.

The people are largely inarticulate. Those who write letters to the editor are not a majority. Neither are those who do the yelling at mass-meetings. It sounds imposing to say that fourteen thousand enthusiasts cheered the candidate to the echo, but fourteen thousand are not a majority of the million or six million inhabitants of a city. Those who stayed away either because they didn't like the candidate or didn't care were more numerous than the fourteen thousand who cheered him to the echo. In this case the inarticulate had concluded in the preceding December that Coolidge was a man who concerned himself with their welfare, and the succeeding six months had hardened the conclusion into a certainty. But, being inarticulate, they didn't talk about it, and the Intellectuals did. Hence the Great Bewilderment of November.

Coolidge has above most men the ability to foresee political results. Just as he knew in October, in the midst of Mr. Davis's hopeful noises, that the election was over, so he knew he was going to be nominated long before the politicians and the newspaper experts did. At the Cleveland Convention everybody was busy proving that he had been for Coolidge all along and had only dissembled his love. They besought him to name his candidate for Vice-President. He said he guessed the Convention could do that. "It did in 1920," he remarked in the subtle Cooldgian manner, "and it picked a durned good man." It was all over, but then, it had been all over as far back as the preceding December.

There has been many a President who was a riddle to the country when he came to the White House. But it has been because the country didn't know him. Wilson was such a riddle; so was Lincoln, so was Cleveland. But a fierce white light beats on the White House, and the country soon came to know them all, except Lincoln, who was still a good deal of a mystery in 1864, even so near at hand as at "the other end of the Avenue." The only one whose character was still the subject of debate at the end of his term was Calvin Coolidge. The country liked him immensely; it did after he had been President only a year, as it proved in 1924; but it was still trying to make him out as late as 1928. It is yet.

"Only a year" is an understatement. It liked Coolidge in 1923; it even made up its mind definitely that he was the kind of President it wanted. His first message to Congress fixed his popularity, and it increased until, to the astonishment of the politicians, they had to nominate him in obedience to a popular demand they did not understand and could not account for. Throughout that campaign the Intellectuals were confident that even so stupid an electorate as the American one could not elect such a poor boob as Coolidge, and they never did account for the avalanche which swept him into office. Senator La Follette did emerge from under the avalanche long enough to offer a sort of explanation; he intimated that the sixteen millions who voted for Coolidge were bought up, and self-sacrificingly promised to go on working for the interest of these corrupted "masses"; but the Intellectuals didn't accept that explanation, and finally concluded that it was just another proof of the incorrigible wrong-headedness of the electorate, or, as Henry L. Mencken calls it, the "booberie."

There was exactly the same mystified feeling in 1864; among the Intellectuals, that is. Even in 1865 none of them had got over it except Charles Francis Adams, Jr., who, alone among the Intellectuals, was convinced that, since there must be something in Lincoln after all, he had better study him at the first opportunity; so he did. The first opportunity was at his second inauguration. Adams listened attentively to his speech and reported to his father his gratified surprise at finding what a sensible one it was. The other Intellectuals continued to regard the American people as a booberie. In 1865 there was, however, one teachable Intellectual, Adams; in 1928 there was not one; the record was impressively unanimous.

I am not saying that Coolidge was a Lincoln. I am only saying that the attitude of the Intellectuals toward both was the same. It ought not to be necessary to explain this; but many years of writing for publication have convinced me of the value of Quintilian's rule for writers; "Take care not merely that the reader may understand if he likes but that he can not misunderstand."

CHAPTER XXVII

COOLIDGE EMERGES

When I first looked Coolidge over, which was when he was Governor of Massachusetts, he did not strike me favorably. He did not suggest any of the celebrated men I had known. His voice was dry, his manner ordinary, his appearance not at all notable. He seemed to me just one of the usual ruck of politicians. But there was something I could not understand; I found that Massachusetts was rather fanatical about him. My years of political experience had taught me that this never happens unless there is a reason for it. I knew, therefore, that in Coolidge's case there was a reason. It interested me enough to make me try to find out what the reason was. But in those early months of 1919 I had to give it up; nothing occurred to give me a clue. I ticketed it, mentally, as an exception to the hitherto invariable rule; here was a State which obviously was somewhat daffy about a man, and still there was no reason for it. It was an aberration. Now, in political psychology there is no such thing as an aberration. I used to think differently, but I had been forced by experience to the conviction that aberrations in political psychology simply do not exist, in spite of a general belief to the contrary. Emerson says, "Of one will, the actions will be harmonious, however unlike they seem," and this is as true of the mass mind as of the individual. Here seemed to be an unaccountable deviation.

In saying that Massachusetts was dotty about Coolidge, I do not mean to imply that everybody was for him. But the opposition which I found to exist in the State puzzled me too, for it ran counter to another fact of experience. I thought him a colorless man, and I was staggered to find that the men who were not for him hated him bitterly. This almost never happens. You can despise a colorless politician, but you can not actively hate him. Yet I found old political friends of mine in Boston whose faces became purple and whose voices rose into a scream when I mentioned the Governor. These men were Republicans, and Republicans of importance and standing. When they pounded their fists on the table and got raucous over Coolidge, it was not with contempt but with that hate which is compounded partly out of fear.

I considered him, from what I saw of him, a jog-trot politician of a rather flabby sort. And though I could not account for these two things new in my experience, I dismissed him from my mind and considered more important personalities, such as Hiram Johnson, since it was my profession to study the important. Then the police of Boston struck, the country focused its startled attention on a city abandoned to the lawless, the head of the American Federation of Labor telegraphed the Governor urging him to uphold the rights of the strikers, and Coolidge wired back that pulverizing sentence, "There is no right to strike against the public safety, by anybody, anywhere, any time."

For the first time I got a clue to Coolidge. I decided that Hiram Johnson and the rest could wait; that it was necessary for me as a writer on political affairs to begin an examination of the Governor of Massachusetts. The clues were slow. He stayed busy at the day's work. He did nothing spectacular and said very little. But occasionally he would make a speech somewhere or write something, in those 1919 months, and he never said or wrote anything that did not have a certain peculiarity about it. That peculiarity was that there was always at least one sentence which made you say as you read idly through, "Hey, what's that? Let me read that again." It hit you between the eyes. When you read it again you stopped for a while to think about it. I perceived that I was beginning to find out about Calvin Coolidge.

A Presidential boom was started for him. He did not, as Governor Woodrow Wilson had done, help it along with timely political utterances. But in that Fall and Winter he did deliver addresses, not often, on non-political subjects. He made them, when he was asked, to such bodies as bar associations, chambers of commerce, and similar organizations. He did this without much regard to their strategic position politically. Instead of speaking in New York and Chicago he spoke—of all places in the world—in such strategically unimportant places as Oregon and the Mountain States. Each one of these non-political speeches had in it that quality of arrest; there was something in it, unpretentious as it was as a whole, that made you stop and think.

There was nothing spectacular about him yet, or ever; there was nothing very interesting. But wherever he went, in 1919 and 1920, he was remembered. The things he said were remembered, too. And on that fact hangs the history of the United States from Harding's death in 1923 to the Presidential election of 1928.

When Harding was nominated by the little coterie of Senators and ex-Senators in George Harvey's "smoke-filled room at two A. M.," they planned to make a clean job of it and run away with the Vice-Presidency as well as the Presidency. It was to be an all-Senate ticket; Senator Harding, of Ohio, for President with Senator Irvine L. Lenroot, of Wisconsin, for Vice-President. With the Presidency safe in the Senate's game-bag and the Presidential succession itself taken care of, the next four years would be years of peace and comfort for the "Senatorial Soviet." While Lodge, Brandegee and Smoot, together with ex-Senator Murray Crane, were the foremost figures in the Soviet at Chicago, the dominating figure was lying on a sick-bed in Philadelphia with a telephone in reach of his hand. He was Senator Boise Penrose, who was slowly dying, but whose will and intellect were as strong as ever, and who was steering the course of his Chicago accomplices as firmly over the telephone as if his cigar were contributing to the general volume in Harvey's room.

From the day the delegates began to drift in to Chicago the ruthlessness and audacity of the Senatorial Soviet had got on the nerves of the hundreds who were being ruled and driven by the little handful of manipulators. The day before the Convention met the National Chairman, Will Hays, coming out of his office and being confronted by a group of newspaper men of whom I was one, had a happy thought and smilingly introduced us to Governor Beeckman, of Rhode Island, who had just arrived in Chicago. To Hays's utter dismay the Governor made a speech to us in which he demanded to know whether this was going to be a Republican Convention or a Senatorial caucus. He wanted to find out whether mere Governors and members of the House were going to have anything to say or would just be allowed to vote as the Senators told them to. Hays's face was a study in distress. Beeckman ended by inviting us to ask questions, and we went to it with glee. He began answering in a manner even more truculent and threatening, when Hays, whose professional glad-hand smile had become fixed and ghastly, seized him by the arm and said imploringly, "Come, Governor, let me show you around the building so you can see what nice arrangments we have made!" He had set off a mine, but he did not intend it to wreck anything more, and he steered Beeckman away from us. When we printed his speech it reverberated through the incoming delegates and gave a head to the mutinous feeling that was rising.

However, the baker's dozen of rulers drove their program through relentlessly. They kept the delegates playing futilely at being a Convention—this was done by delaying every move that was made—until the ending of the week and the dismal prospect of another one in Chicago stared every flattened pocketbook in the face. Then came two o'clock and the smoke-filled room; the notification to Hiram Johnson and Governor Lowden that they would not be nominated; the notification to Harding that he would be named by the delegates the following afternoon.

When the delegates reconvened, the news that they were to vote for Harding and start for home that night slowly filtered through the sullen and resentful crowd. They did as they were told, with rapidly rising disgust. Then they waited to be told whom they were to make Vice-President; and with every moment the sullenness grew. Still, there was nothing they could do about it, and they growlingly waited to take their medicine and go home.

Senator Medill McCormick had been picked by his colleagues to finish the job by driving in this last nail. In pursuance of the agenda he started jauntily for the platform to notify the delegates who was to be the next Vice-President; it was to be Lenroot. But as he was proceeding with his speech, and before he had got to the point of revealing the candidate's name, a man from Oregon named Wallace McCamant called out in a clear, penetrating voice, "Coolidge! Coolidge!"

After a moment the cry was taken up by others. The apathetic delegates began to stir, to look around at one another. Those sunken faces began to take on expression. McCormick hurriedly brought Lenroot's name in, sooner than he had intended; but amid the scattering applause hisses rose from many parts of the hall. The moment McCormick finished and turned to leave the platform, McCamant sprang up in the Oregon delegation and shouted, "I nominate Governor Calvin Coolidge of Massachusetts!"

It was electric. In a second the smoldering animosity and self-contempt of the Convention blazed up. McCamant, of Portland, was unknown to the delegates and had no political alliance or influence in the Convention; but he had roused the angry crowd to a high pitch of excitement, and it followed him pell-mell and smashed the slate. Coolidge got six hundred seventy-four votes, Lenroot one hundred forty-six, with scattered votes for others, and the Senatorial Soviet was overwhelmed. The destinies of the Presidency had never been settled in so offhand a fashion before.

Watching this drama from the press seats, I was quite certain, and I have been certain ever since, that no name but Coolidge's could have united the Convention in its victory over a detested despotism; and I knew why then and afterward. The moment I saw McCamant rise in Oregon, all that I knew of Coolidge's ways and all my reading of those utterances of his the previous Winter rushed together and formed a coherent picture in my mind. McCamant was one of the men whom Coolidge had addressed in those nonpolitical speeches of his. I knew that men are so much alike that what will affect one mind will affect others in the same way, and that the impression produced on my mind by Coolidge's sayings would also be produced on others. I knew, too, that this dry-spoken, unimpressive-looking man had a way of impressing himself on other men, whether they could explain it or not; and I knew that what he said and did was remembered, not forgotten. As I saw Oregon lead the way and California, Washington, Idaho, Wyoming, Montana, fall over one another in the rush to follow her, the whole thing was clear to me. The thought in the minds of those delegates was the same the moment McCamant spoke, "Why, sure! We know! He's the very man!" Coolidge had planned no such dramatic finish when, in his usual way, he simply said what he thought; but he garnered then, as he garnered through life, the fruits of being himself and showing people what that self was; and this without any self-advertising, in an age of bluff, bunk and ballyhoo.

McCamant turned out to be an ex-Judge and a man of serious worth. When Coolidge became President he appointed him to a Federal office. But though years had passed and much water had gone over the dam, the Senatorial Soviet remembered that Chicago scene vindictively. Penrose was dead, Murray Crane was dead, Lodge was in his last days, Brandegee was soon to make his exit from this world through a self-inflicted revolver shot, and the Soviet was going or gone; but it still had life enough for one last revengeful kick. It refused to confirm the appointment.

One more glimpse of the Calvin Coolidge way:

The Hoover Convention of 1928 was in fact the second Coolidge Convention, counting 1924 as the first. In both his silent and absent figure dominated everything, informed and inspired everything. Felicitously *The New York Evening Post* said, when a shift in the Convention's sentiment on one point was recorded, "our dispatches report that Mr. Coolidge, by one of his strange methods of making himself understood without speaking," had caused it. The truth of the phrase had been observable throughout his Presidency; in the Kansas City Convention it was dramatized.

Ultimately, not soon, it will dawn on the country that a very remarkable man has been President since 1923, and that the peculiar quality of his remarkability is solitary in history. The politicians and Intellectuals have been puzzled still more by the fact that at the moment when he seems to have been delivered over to the Philistines bound and gagged the Philistines always have to rush to him and clutch his coat-tails, begging him to save them. This comedy of the coat-tails has been played to crowded houses ever since Harding's death. The public never tires of it. The performance of it at Kansas City broke, not exactly the box-office record, but the artistic record. Never did the star, Silent Cal, seem so at home in the center of the stage, where he was physically absent; never did the involuntary comedians play the parts forced on them with such hearty and unwilling fidelity to the rôle. These comedians, by the way, are not limited to Kansas City, nor to those Congressmen who, after flouting the President's recommendations for five years, always ended by sprinting frantically to him with the cry, "Help, Cassius, or we sink!" No; high on the list of comedians rank the Intellectuals all over the country; and no mean place in the cast is to be assigned to Mr. H. L. Mencken and Mr. Frank R. Kent.

The silences of Calvin Coolidge are powerful weapons. By his meaning silences he made impossible the nomination of Lowden or Dawes, brought about the collapse of the farm revolt at Kansas City, and nominated Hoover. The whole program was mapped out by him long before he said, "I do not choose to run." He was determined not to issue a formal refusal, as had been done with trouble-making results by Blaine in May, 1888, and by Roosevelt in November, 1904. The "draft Coolidge" movement persisted and gathered strength until he made another statement, saying even less than the first.

Aside from this one deviation into speech, the silent program cruised on to Kansas City. Once only did it become necessary to break the stillness, when the program seemed endangered. That was when he vetoed the McNary-Haugen bill. The severity of his language caused surprise; he is not usually severe. He chose it because, after that language, Congress must either sustain the veto or cut loose from him at Kansas City, which it could not do.

His main concerns were to have a Coolidge platform and a Coolidge candidate, that is, a candidate in sympathy with his five-year purposes. The only such candidate was Hoover, and his irresistible silences forced that nomination without involving him in the charge brought against Jackson and Roosevelt, that they imposed an unacceptable successor on the country. The impalpable weight of his unspoken disapproval crushed the booms of Lowden and Dawes, which logically—by politicians' logic, the best in the world on paper and the most foolish in fact—ought to have been potent. How potent they proved to be against the silent man was shown at Kansas City, when the Coolidge legatee got eight hundred thirty-seven votes on the first ballot, Lowden sixty-six, and Dawes three.

For months the wise men of the East and West had been cocking their eyes knowingly over that sentence, "I do not choose to run," and doping out Machiavellian meanings from it. After the Convention Charles Michelson revealed, in *The New York World,* that "the New York group," including "large, important figures in finance," were deeply aggrieved and held that the President "had double-crossed them, saying that he knew every move they were making on his behalf, and never said a word to discourage them." According to Mr. Michelson, "for the past six months" they had been "dropping in at the White House" and telling Coolidge how well the draft-Coolidge movement was progressing. "He listened," according to Mr. Michelson. "Nobody says he wished them godspeed in this mission, but he certainly did nothing to discourage them." So, Mr. Michelson reported, "they are pretty sore." Undoubtedly he told the exact truth; and any one knowing Calvin Coolidge, and what Michelson later called his "sense of mischievous drama," can picture these White House visits with a delighted grin, and even visualize with pleasure the pained faces of those "large, important figures in finance."

Summing up the results of the Hoover Convention, *The New York Times* concluded: "It is now definitely established that when Mr. Coolidge said 'I do not choose,' he meant that he did not choose." And *The New York World,* always hitherto ironically skeptical about Coolidge, published a cartoon by Rollin Kirby, showing the President clutching in his fist a card saying, "I do not choose to run." The artist depicted him as looking very grim, dour and Yankee-like; and the title of the picture was:

"Guess, By Thunder, They'll Understand Plain English Now!"

CHAPTER XXVIII

COOLIDGE THE STYLIST

"ONLY a handful of our Presidents have been writing men of great distinction. Lincoln deserves to head the list, with Woodrow Wilson next," observed Heywood Broun as late as 1928. "But Calvin Coolidge is one hundred per cent. wooden."

It represents, no doubt, the general view. "He seems to me," said Broun in the same essay, "the least gifted author the White House has known in many generations." However, it is not the fact. From standpoint of style alone, Coolidge is one of the two most gifted men who have lived in the White House for two generations. He is, in fact, one of the very few Presidents who can be thought of as literary men.

The difference between him and such a stylist as Woodrow Wilson is that he used his style only as a tool and not as an ornament; he only used it when there would be some advantage in using it. In this, as a literary man, he somewhat resembled Lincoln. To hear people talk you would think Lincoln never opened his mouth without uttering a Gettysburg Address. The truth is that nearly all Lincoln's public utterances are just as trite and commonplace as Coolidge's or Taft's or McKinley's or those of any other President. The White House is no nursery for style. The inconceivably great volume of things the President must be writing for publication every day of his life is fatal to it.

Not after he has entered the White House, and not until he leaves it, will he have any chance to show what he can do in the writing way, or pay any attention to artistry in composition.

Out of the great mass of Lincoln's writings in the White House only two are much quoted, the Gettysburg Address and the Second Inaugural, but people talk about him as if he had uttered Gettysburg Addresses by the ream. Most of the things he said that are memorable were said before he became President and when he had time to polish his style, such as the house-divided-against-itself speech. There are isolated fragments that are superb, such as one of his letters to Hooker, one of his letters to Greeley, his letter to Mrs. Bixby. But the million words he had to write are mainly just the hard-driven commonplaces of an overworked man. The same thing is so true of every President that I distinctly remember the gratified and surprised comment aroused in 1891, when Benjamin Harrison swung around the circle and made speeches that showed a command over the English language. It was remarked upon everywhere as something unprecedented in a President.

The astonishing thing about Wilson was that, unlike all other Presidents who had style, he did not have to put his style away when he started to carry the United States on his shoulders and resume it when he dropped his burden eight years later. He came talking remarkable English and kept it up. There was no diminution in his excellence. And he could talk as excellently over a small matter as over a weighty one. Wilson was sui generis; there never was anybody like him in this respect.

I have already described the circumstances which in 1919 led me to scrutinize Coolidge's writings very microscopically. I did it to find out why he had such an inexplicable grip on Massachusetts, and not with any interest in his diction. But in the course of my studies I could not help making certain collateral observations. By the time I finished them I came to the conclusion that if he became President he would be one of the most literary men who ever occupied the White House. He was the possessor of that rare quality, even among literary men, of style in addition to "a" style.

The Attic style is not popular at present and has no masters except Coolidge. However, a writer who has nothing but style to recommend him lacks something, and this is not the case with Coolidge. His weapon is the short sentence, but anybody who gives his mind to it can acquire, though with difficulty, the use of the short sentence. The difference is that each of Coolidge's short sentences, when he is producing a real composition and not merely giving commonplace voice to one of the perfunctory utterances his position calls for, is the distillation of a long process of thought. What another man might need a page to express can be set forth by Coolidge in a sentence of a dozen words and set forth completely, so that it does not need another syllable.

In 1889 Doctor Lyman Abbott, who was pastor of the church I then belonged to—Plymouth—said of sermon-making: "It requires a great deal of churning to get a pat of butter out of a pan of milk. The congregations of the present day want the pat of butter and not the pan of milk." He may have been mistaken about the tendencies of the times, but if there is any such demand as he thought there was, Coolidge satisfies it.

The Intelligentsia will be moved to hilarity on being informed that Coolidge is a master of the epigram, but he is. He uses it sparingly, because he has a dislike for startling effects, but for that very reason it is all the more stunning when it comes. As for the prevalent belief among the Intellectuals that Coolidge does not read, the evidences of his wide and thorough reading are abundant. He does not talk about it—"Why can't we be like that old bird?"—he only uses it. What misleads the Intellectuals is that he does not quote, if he can possibly avoid it. He prefers to give the essence of his author, or of many authors at once. His tenderness for the classics sticks out visibly from his speeches; but he would rather be shot at sunrise than say, "As Cicero tells us," or "In the language of the blind bard."

The way in which the public leaped up in fervent response to Coolidge's telegram to Gompers ("There is no right to strike," and the rest of it) was not merely in enthusiasm over the fact that arrogance had been met and crushed; it was also a response to the way the thing was said. That sentence compressed so much, and its fifteen words could neither be subtracted from nor increased. What many men had been verbosely thinking was said with a cosmic minuteness. The outpouring of grateful jubilation at that sentence of Coolidge's brought to mind what George Bernard Shaw wrote about John Bunyan's sentence: "My sword I give to him that shall succeed me in my pilgrimage, and my courage and skill to him that can get them." Shaw's comment was: "The heart vibrates like a bell to such an utterance as this." That just about describes the feeling all over the United States when the swelling impudences of organized labor got that smash in the face from a politician who did not truckle.

In Massachusetts they were used to such sentences from him, whether the country was or not. They did not get many of them; it is not the Yankee way to be always orating. But they quoted often, and still do, what he had said in his speech to the Massachusetts Senate when he was elected President of it. There are words in it which, in these days of pink thinking, ought to be in every American citizen's Bible, such as this paragraph:

"Do the day's work. If it be to protect the rights of the weak, whoever objects, do it. If it be to help a powerful corporation better to serve the people, whatever be the opposition, do that. Expect to be called a standpatter, but don't be a standpatter. Expect to be called a demagogue, but don't be a demagogue. Don't hesitate to be as revolutionary as science. Don't hesitate to be as reactionary as the multiplication table. Don't expect to build up the weak by pulling down the strong."

As for the things he said in this speech, aside from his way of putting them, they were novel-sounding in that year. Of late, those ideas have found voice, at first timidly and then increasingly. We must put ourselves back into the second decade of the twentieth century, when every man who had any political ambitions seemed to be for either stamping down the weak or pulling down the strong, when it was a matter of course that one must be either revolutionary or reactionary, a standpatter or a demagogue. To say such things in that decade was nothing short of intrepid.

Herbert Spencer, in his essay on *The Philosophy of Style,* says: "If it be an advantage to express an idea in the smallest number of words, then will it be an advantage to express it in the smallest number of syllables." Nevertheless, a continual procession of short and compact sentences would grow wearisome in time. Just at the point where it is about to grow wearisome, Coolidge relieves the pressure with a long sentence—that is, a long one for him. Take this, probably his best expression of an idea that he expresses in other places:

"No man was ever meanly born. About his cradle is the wondrous miracle of life. He may descend into the depths, he may live in infamy and perish miserably, but he is born great. Men build monuments above the graves of their heroes to mark the end of a great life, but women seek out the birthplace and build their shrine, not where a great life had its end but where it had its beginning, seeking with a truer instinct not the common source of things in that which is gone forever but in that which they know will again be manifest. Life may depart, but the source of life is constant."

It is characteristic of his severe style that he is not fond of rhetorical figures, but there is one he certainly fancies—that of antithesis. The following may not be a good example of the figure, but it is a good example of Coolidge's way of building up contrasts. It is from a speech on one of his favorite topics, classical education:

"There have been great men with little of what we call education. There have been small men with a great deal of learning. There has never been a great people who did not possess great learning."

Eloquence seems to be abhorrent to Coolidge. His style, to misapply a phrase of Jeremy Taylor, "moves with a still foot and a sober face." However, at times he can not help breaking forth for a moment out of the narrow bounds he has set himself, as in the last of the three sentences I now quote:

"We wanted peace, and rightfully; but it was the voice of Roosevelt that roused the nation to the meaning and the menace of the war to America. In this he was never so disinterested, so patriotic, so eager for the right for its own sake. He appealed from the things that seemed to be to the soul of the things that are."

That last sentence is actually poetry and can be scanned. His speeches are strewn with evidences that he could be rhetorical if he chose to be. It is usually assumed that the alternative to rhetoric is dryness, but Coolidge, when he is writing on anything that interests his well-stored and observant mind, is never dry. His passion for the pat of butter instead of the pan of milk comes to the surface almost amusingly in the startling suddenness with which some fugitive phrase reveals his intimate acquaintance with history. The same thing is true of his dislike for direct quotation. Where another writer would say, "As John Fiske says," Coolidge gives you the pat of butter:

"John Fiske has demonstrated very clearly that of necessity evil and good are coexistent possibilities. What virtue would there be in choosing the good unless thereby the evil was rejected?"

Nevertheless, he does quote. When he does, he does not get his copy out of Bartlett's *Familiar Quotations*. I open at random to his commencement address at Holy Cross College on June 25, 1919:

"Here is the hope of the future, brighter yet in the young men today sent forth,
'The unarmed youth of Heaven. But o'er their heads,
Celestial armory, shield, helm and spear,
Hung bright, with diamond flaming and with gold.' "

Here, as always when he permits himself to be driven to quotation, the quotation is not dragged in by the heels, but falls naturally into its place because it belongs there. These things are rare among politicians, whose poetical granary consists of Bryant's *Thanatopsis* for mortuary and eulogistic occasions, and Polonius's advice as constituting pretty much the whole of Shakespeare. If this appears to be a sarcasm on my part, let me assure the reader that it is the literal truth, and proof can be found in any issue of the Congressional Record after a session devoted to eulogies of departed members. I once had a delicious illustration of it. In commemoration of the three hundredth anniversary of Shakespeare's death I was getting up, among other things, a symposium on "What is your favorite passage from Shakespeare?" The question was sent to hundreds of prominent people in all walks of life, from inventors to musicians, from actors to professors, and of course included all the prominent politicians. The answers covered an incredibly wide range. Only one class turned in, invariably, the same quotation; it was the politicians, from William J. Bryan down or up. As the replies kept flowing in, the thing became such a stock joke in the office that as soon as my staff caught sight of a politician's letterhead on one of the replies, they would begin to chant, without looking at it:

"To thine own self be true,
And it must follow, as the night the day,
Thou canst not then be false to any man."

If Coolidge does not use the ordinary weapons of the literary man, it is not because he can not. For epigram he has as little use, in general, as he has for quotation. But when he does strike out in epigram it is with the same perfect, easy mastery that he displays in his sparing use of quotation or of rhetoric. At random I take from a volume of his collected speeches, *The Price of Freedom,* a handful of epigrams unrelated to one another and merely serving to prove my point:

"In its last analysis, what the workman sells is his intelligence. . . .

"Men are not so constituted that selfishness satisfies them. . . .

"The old saying that there are but three generations from shirt-sleeves to shirt-sleeves has had its counterpart in the history of nations. . . .

"Human progress must be paid for, but it can not be bought. . . .

"Innocence is not enough in government administration."

And this, an illustration both of epigram and antithesis. It is from his speech on the budget, delivered in Washington on June 11, 1928: "Prosperity is only an instrument to be used, not a deity to be worshipped."

He has the power, too, of condensing into one luminous sentence an entire political situation. After he had said, "I do not choose to run," the dismayed Republican politicians tried to compel him to run; the very Congressmen whose favorite pastime was the kicking around the Capitol of every recommendation he made were frantically asserting that Coolidge must be "drafted"; not that they loved Coolidge all of a sudden, but that they loved their jobs and needed his unaccountable popularity. Coolidge listened to the daily reverberations about how there was a "crisis," in which the despairing country appealed to him not to desert it. Then he compressed the whole disgusting humbug in one flashing sentence. He said, when some one asked him his opinion of the "crisis":

"I wonder who could beat Al Smith if I didn't run."

He retained that Yankee gravity which fooled so many of his countrymen so long because the Yankee is such an unknown species, but does not fool as many of them now. In 1928 his exploits as a fisherman on the Brule River were so remarkable that they became the theme of much newspaper comment. Finally the reporters asked Coolidge how many fish the Brule waters were estimated to contain. He said the number was given as forty-five thousand. "I haven't caught them all yet," he hastened to add, "but I've intimidated them."

In spite of Coolidge's wide reading he is not governed by it; he thinks for himself. No phrase, whether of applause or scorn, deludes him:

"Men said in derision that Roosevelt had discovered the Ten Commandments. What they said derisively let us state seriously. He had discovered the Ten Commandments, and he applied their doctrine with great vigor in places that had assumed they had the power to discard the Ten Commandments."

These "places" were the places where Big Business had become too arrogant. Coolidge's short history of what he felicitously called "private control of government" and its necessary fall is found in his address on Roosevelt in the volume already quoted. His story of Big Business from its innocent and laudable beginnings to the swaggering and plutocratic end leaves nothing unsaid and yet fills only two pages of large type.

Sometimes Coolidge uses the short sentence without any notable relief by the interspersion of a long one. He does this without making the rhythm wearisome, though it would be a dangerous experiment for most men. An example not only of this, but of the unerring felicity with which he seizes upon the central point in any theme and discards all the rest is from his analysis of the benefactions of Andrew Carnegie:

"He offered opportunity. He knew it was all his beneficiaries could profitably receive. If they were to have life more abundantly he knew it could come only through their own effort. He did not pauperize. He ennobled."

In this there is a reminiscence of the style of Robert G. Ingersoll at his best, despite the fact that Ingersoll was an eloquent orator and Coolidge lacked that grace.

On one subject Coolidge's steady reiteration makes it evident that it is close to his heart. It is the reverse side of freedom. The reverse side of freedom is obedience, and without it there can be no freedom. This he regards as the issue of the twentieth century, or at least of the first third of it. It appears over and over again, and once with this admirable clarity:

"Independence is exceedingly exacting, self-control is arduous, self-government is difficult. . . . This is the reason that to certain of our foreign-born, the American Republic proves a disappointment. They thought that self-government meant the absence of all restraint, that independence meant living without work, and that freedom was the privilege of doing what they wanted to do. It has been a hard lesson for them to learn that self-government is still government, that the rule of the people does not mean absence of authority, that independence means self-support, and that complete freedom means complete obedience to law. They are disappointed more than ever when they learn, as ever they do, that these are so, not because they have been decreed by some body of men, but that they are so by the very nature of things, and all the governments in the world are powerless to change them."

In that last sentence, and in many others in different speeches, Coolidge indicated his disbelief in the power of a statute to insure righteousness—or to secure anything else. Without "the intelligence and the motive," he says in another place, the enactment of a law is vain.

An odd thing happened after Coolidge became President. He found himself under a mountain of infinite details of which no one but a President can form any conception. A President not only has to deal with all the natural duties of his office, which are multitudinous beyond belief, each day's grist far too great to be coped with in a mere twenty-four hours; he has also to do enough unnecessary things to keep half a dozen men busy all day. They are things not related to the Presidential office but devolving on him because he is a President, such as holding receptions, going to public dinners, opening exhibitions, tossing out the first ball of the season, writing letters and, worst of all, making speeches.

In Edward Everett Hale's story, *My Double, and How He Undid Me,* a minister, similarly oversloughed by unnecessary but inescapable duties, hits on the scheme of hiring a doppelgänger to impersonate him. The double, who looks exactly like him, goes to the church teas, attends dinners, and all the rest of it, giving the minister leisure to write his sermons, keep abreast of current theological changes, and otherwise handle the real duties of his profession. Unfortunately the double finally blunders at a public meeting, breaks into his natural Irish brogue, and creates a deplorable scene; and the minister, unable to refute the injurious suspicions about his personal habits that are thus excited, has to resign his pastorate.

It was not from this story that Coolidge got his idea, but from the practise of other statesmen. He was not the first President to use a "ghost writer" to get up public papers for him, not by a jugful. Washington's Farewell Address was written by Alexander Hamilton, though Washington was almost the only President who ever had his "ghost writer" draw up a document of such immense importance. Not quite the only one; Andrew Jackson's famous proclamation on nullification, when South Carolina threatened to secede, was written by Edward Livingston. As a rule, however, Presidents have employed "ghost writers" only on the endless list of routine speeches their hard lot forced them to make; and letters, too, of course. The speeches of real importance they have gotten up themselves.

No President ever used this device to such a great extent as Coolidge. It left him free to give his mind to the important and necessary part of his work; or as free as the rest of his catalogue of senseless routine would let him. During the five years of his Presidency the Government ran so smoothly under his hand that people did not conceive the immense amount of work he did. As a matter of fact, he was working every second of his waking hours. Compared with him Wilson was an indolent sluggard. It was Coolidge's nature to tackle every job thoroughly and leave no loose edges; his own nature, and Yankee nature as well. So, to give himself all the room possible for the performance of his real tasks, he threw the ornamental tasks on the shoulders of his "ghost."

He was not much luckier with this than he was with his creation of the "Official Spokesman." He was not the first President to employ that fiction. Presidents see reporters constantly, but there is a rule that the President must not be quoted; so the Washington correspondents used to get around that rule by saying, "It was learned from a source close to the White House," or "A high official in the President's confidence is authority for the statement." It never attracted any notice, probably because the phrases did not fit the President too closely, and also because the correspondents varied them, bringing out the "high official" to-day, the "source close to the White House" to-morrow, the "Administration circles" the day after. But Coolidge's Official Spokesman was instantly recognized; and when the Spokesman was observed to be talking every day, the nation's risibles were roused.

The Spokesman was cartooned, paragraphed and versified. It was taken for granted that Coolidge had invented the idea of talking through a veil, which he had not. Inevitably the Earnest Souls who comprise so large a part of American thought became alarmed. Those whom Jay House happily describes as "the sad, fierce thinkers" saw something sinister in the Spokesman, something portending, perhaps, the downfall of the Republic. Coolidge must be contemplating something devilish; he had created the Official Spokesman so that he could stealthily infiltrate the unsuspecting American mind with the felonious schemes he contemplated and, with that mind thus heinously prepared for it, could venture finally to bring them out to the light of day and, most likely, drug the public into drowsing supinely while he administered another biff to the cause of virtue.

So Coolidge had to kill the Official Spokesman. He did not suffer so much from the "ghost writer," but he suffered considerably; for Coolidge, being careless and contemptuous of his reputation as a literary man, took no pains to employ an Alexander Hamilton or an Edward Livingston; or, for that matter, a Dan Lamont. The result was that the public read, with growing distaste, a long procession of speeches something like this:

"You are gathered here to-day to observe the anniversary of Silas Pipkin's birth. He was a great man. He was born in Middlebury, Kentaska, October 7, 1837. Educated in the public schools, he was elected to the Assembly of his native State at the early age of twenty-two. At the age of twenty-four he wrote his celebrated treatise on——"

A little reflection would have shown anybody that a President who was forced, by our absurd conventions, to deliver several such speeches every week would have to devote himself entirely to getting them up and have no time left for the mere administration of the American Government, if he really wrote them himself. But the criticism was, as always, unintelligent. If a single writer of the many who condemned Coolidge's wooden style ever surmised the real state of the case, the fact escaped me. One and all they sighed for the good old days—which never existed—when Abraham Lincoln used to write a Gettysburg Address every day in the week.

The result was that when, on May 24, 1928, he sent to Congress his smashing message vetoing the McNary-Haugen farm relief bill, he dazed Washington. He did not seek for any graces of diction, but he hit straight from the shoulder in a state paper that sounded like the crunch of a fist on the point of a jaw. The Washington correspondents reported it in words which show how startling it seemed. For instance, the correspondent of the *New York Times* said Coolidge's language was "so vigorous as to produce amazement," and proceeded: "The whole tone of the message suggested the reverse of the traditional Coolidgesque calmness and caution. Its vigor recalled the vetoes of Grover Cleveland. It fairly bristled with hard-hitting adjectives aimed at the bill's provisions."

However, it was not "the reverse of the traditional Coolidgesque calmness and caution." It was right in line with the "traditional" message to Samuel Gompers: "There is no right to strike against the public safety by anybody, anywhere, any time." The "tradition" that Governor Coolidge set so many times in Massachusetts was the tradition followed by President Coolidge when he returned the McNary-Haugen bill to Congress saying, "This is bureaucracy gone mad. . . . This plague of petty officialdom would set up an intolerable tyranny. . . . The bill runs counter to an economic law as well settled as the law of gravitation. . . . The futile sophistries of such a system of wholesale commercial doles for special groups."

Yes, it was "traditional." Only it was so long since they had heard the Coolidgesque trumpet that the Washington correspondents—and the Senators and Representatives—had forgotten what the tradition was. They were so imbued with the idea of a colorless Coolidge that it never occurred to them to revise their estimate; instead, they began casting about for an explanation of why he didn't seem, in this instance, to fit the clothes they had made for him. It was obvious that they could not be mistaken in him. Yet how could the dull, passionless, uninspired, heavy-witted man they knew him to be rise to such heights of indignation and fire such deadly bullets with such accuracy into the bull's-eye? Ah, they had it; and within a few hours this interesting head-line appeared over a Washington dispatch to *The New York Evening World:* "Hoover Blamed by Corn Belt for Farm Bill Veto."

Hoover!

Hoover was the masterful man who had guided the dull pen of the ventriloquial dummy in the White House.

Hoover!

Well, it was not Hoover. It was the same man who, in a day when everybody was pretending to be a friend of the down-trod, had said to the legislative body over which he presided, "Expect to be called a standpatter, but don't be a standpatter. . . . Don't expect to build up the weak by pulling down the strong." Coolidge had not changed; but there had grown up a false Coolidge, not in the popular mind—which has always, through our history, been very good at sizing up public men—but in that totally different and indeed opposite thing, the Washington mind. Early in Coolidge's Presidency Frank R. Kent, disgusted by the refusal of the crass public to see what a dub Coolidge was, enlightened them by an article in *The American Mercury* showing them that their idea of the President was all wrong. He called their delusion "The Coolidge Myth." There was, indeed, a Coolidge myth, but it was not the myth Kent thought it was. The Coolidge myth was the one he and men like him created; the myth of a boob in the White House. And whenever, as in the McNary-Haugen veto, he did something out of character for a boob, they concluded, not that they had created a myth, but that the man they understood so perfectly had an unaccountable habit of refusing to stay put.

Coolidge does not agree with me about his style. A year after he became President, growing somewhat wroth with the thickness of the Intelligentsia, who were blatting in their Olympic way about his boobishness, I published in *The New York Times* an article analyzing his diction. What he himself thinks on the subject is shown in the following letter:

"THE WHITE HOUSE
"WASHINGTON
"December 29, 1924.

"My dear Mr. Thompson:

"Your article in the *Times* of December 28th has been called to my attention and I want to thank you for the interest it displays in some of the things I have said.

"I am not conscious of having any particular style about my writings. If I have any, it is undoubtedly due to my training in the construction of legal papers, where it is necessary in the framing of a contract, or the drawing of a pleading, to say what you mean and mean what you say in terms sufficiently clear and concise so that your adversary will not be able to misinterpret them, or to divert the trial into a discussion of unimportant matters. The rule is to state the case with as little diffusion as possible.

"Another influence on my writings has been the fact that most of that which is published was composed when I was Lieutenant Governor and Vice-President. Quite naturally, I left to the Governor and to the President, during those times, comment on current political problems, and dealt myself in more general and fundamental principles. While this did not create so much interest at the moment, it has, perhaps, lent a more permanent value to some of the addresses which I have made.

"But, I merely wish to express to you my appreciation, and to express, also, the hope that if you are in Washington I may have an opportunity to thank you in person.

"Very truly yours,
"CALVIN COOLIDGE.

"Mr. Charles Willis Thompson,
"C/o New York *Times Magazine,*
"New York, N. Y."

He was modest, being a Yankee. Nevertheless, wherever he got his use of words from, whether from the law or somewhere else, the point was that he had it. There are plenty of lawyers with as much experience as he who have not his power of statement, and so I told him in disagreeing with his theory about it. It is necessary to say what you mean as clearly as possible, just as he said, but there is also the danger of trying to get everything in, which is a necessity of legal documents and is fatal to style. I suppose he remained of the same opinion. But if he is right, then all lawyers ought to be masters of style, and hardly any of them are.

Somebody may inquire why Coolidge's verbal mastery has been so little noticed. There is nothing new about that. In 1863 Edward Everett delivered an oration at the dedication of the battle-field of Gettysburg. It was reported in full in the newspapers, and commented on as a magnificent specimen of literary eloquence. When he got through Abraham Lincoln anti-climaxed the proceedings by uttering a few sentences in his high-pitched voice and Kentucky brogue. The newspapers ended their accounts by two paragraphs in small type, saying that when the great oration was ended "President Lincoln then rose and spoke as follows." You can read it in the files to-day.

Do you remember Everett's great oration? The few unadorned words that Lincoln spoke, and that passed unnoticed, were the Gettysburg Address. Coolidge is no Lincoln. Besides, he has a nasal voice and a Yankee brogue. Lincoln died and left no successors; but the purblind crowd at Gettysburg did. That crowd we shall have with us as long as the world lasts. In 1863, however, they did not call themselves Intellectuals.

THE END